DAY CARE

*Dedicated to the children and staff
of the Castle Square and Hawthorne House
Day Care Centers*

DAY CARE

how to plan, develop, and operate a day care center
by E. Belle Evans, Beth Shub,
Marlene Weinstein

Beacon Press

Library of Congress catalog card number: 76-156448
International Standard Book Number: 0-8070-3178-X

Beacon Press books are published under the auspices of the Unitarian
Universalist Association

Published simultaneously in Canada by Saunders of Toronto, Ltd.

Printed in the United States of America
Third printing, April 1972

Grateful acknowledgment is extended to Peter Bernett for all photographs
in this book, and to two of our teachers, Greg Tobias and Richard Fisher,
as well as other teachers, for their time and effort in designing and
building the classrooms.

CONTENTS

Part IV

FOREWORD

Under the administration of the Division of Family Health Services of the Massachusetts Department of Public Health, a small, storefront demonstration nursery school was established for training preschool teachers in Boston. The school was created because of the enthusiasm and concern of the Division Director, Dr. Dorothy Worth, who, long before the current interest, recognized the need for quality day care. Due to her support we were able, in only two years, to develop the original school into a flourishing program with two day care centers of nine classrooms and a college-accredited training program for preschool teachers. Our book is based in large part on the knowledge and experience gained in the day care centers and training program, and we would like to express our thanks and appreciation to Dr. Worth, who made it possible.

Our thanks also go to George Saia, who convinced us that such a book was needed and encouraged us to write it.

INTRODUCTION

People throughout the country are becoming acutely aware of the need for day care and increasingly interested in setting up their own day care centers. Unfortunately, to date there are few resources to which people can turn for help in starting day care programs. To fill this need, we have written a practical guide to setting up day care centers. Whether the impetus for your program comes from small parent, neighborhood, or community service groups; or from large public or private organizations, this book will answer your questions and provide alternative solutions to problems you will encounter. Even if you are not starting a center but simply want to know how to evaluate your child's day care programs or to understand the current day care phenomenon, you will find the information you need here.

While there is no question that day care is a pressing need in this country, we would like to make clear at the outset that we do not endorse just any day care program. Rather, we emphasize the need for high-quality programs which address the needs of children's social, psychological, intellectual, and physical growth and development. Day care programs which function solely to provide baby-sitting services for working parents are unacceptable. We consider good day care to be an effective, positive, educational experience which we recommend for children of parents who do not "need it" as well as for children of parents who do.

Historically, day care has not been primarily from the educational perspective. The overriding rationale for day care has been as a necessary evil for working mothers. While day care has a long history in this country, the first center having opened in 1838, only during wars have we had a substantial number of day care programs because women had to join the work force. When the wars were over, the men went back to their jobs, the women went back to their homes, and day care went back to its low, prewar priority. For example, the period following World War II was characterized by the glorification of the family and the home. It was thought that women could find complete fulfillment through child-rearing.

This idealized view of homemaking has received a serious if not fatal blow in the past few years from the women's liberation movement. Now it is acknowledged that many women must look outside the home for complete fulfillment. We can expect that with increased acceptance of women seeking outside interests, there will be more and more families needing day care.

In fact, there have been millions of women with preschool children working all along. It has only been since the recent change in attitudes toward women that the need for day care has been seriously considered on a national scale. Unfortunately, the recognition of mothers' need for day care hasn't altered the view of day care as a necessary evil. Whether women are working in order to supplement the family income, to get off welfare rolls, or to seek fulfillment, attitudes towards day care are still ambivalent. No matter how justified women feel in making the decision to work and put their children in day care, they are still carrying a burden of guilt because they fear they are depriving their children of an essential mother-child relationship.

Although women have felt guilty about putting their children in day care, they have viewed nursery school and kindergarten programs as enriching, educational experiences for their children. The nursery school-kindergarten movement has always been seen as a positive supplement to the mother-child relationship. While nursery school is a two-to three-hour program for the middle class, day care has been an all-day program for the working poor. The Head Start program was the first major effort to bridge the two movements. It brought the nursery school model of pre-school education to the poor on a half-day basis. Its purpose was to overcome educational deprivation by providing an enriching, comprehensive intervention program. Although it maintained a focus on disadvantaged children, it did stimulate general interest in early childhood education and the positive effects of high-quality group care for very young children.

In addition to the nursery school tradition and the success of Head Start, research in cognitive development has provoked new thoughts about the potential benefits of day care. It has become clear that the first five years of life are crucial for an individual's intellectual as well as emotional development. Although the controversy rages on, there is now a considerable body of research to support the view that a child does not suffer deprivation as a result of experiencing high-quality group care in addition to good mothering during those early years. It is the quality of those experiences that is important. And there are some who feel that it is imperative to expose children to other significant adults. This eases the enormous burden of responsibility society imposes on parents to single-handedly raise their children and at the same time relieves children of their total dependence on one or two adults. And early peer-group experiences have long been considered valuable for children.

In our view, day care is not a necessary evil; it can be a positive supplement to family relationships. Any day care center has a responsibility to provide a program which facilitates children's optimal growth and development. Day care can be terrible. It risks realizing all the negative stereotypes of institutional care unless adults prevent that from happening. This book shows you how to develop only high-quality, child-centered programs which consider the needs of children as well as parents.

We discuss primarily the programs operating five days a

week during a daytime schedule of eight to twelve hours for children two to five years old. We touch only briefly on such variations as infant care, weekend care, and twenty-four hour care. We have limited ourselves to this model for the sake of expedience, not out of any sense of disapproval of these kinds of programs. Weekend and twenty-four hour care do not differ significantly from the program we present. Infant care, on the other hand, is not simply an extension of our model but has unique program implications. We feel it would require another book to cover infant care adequately.

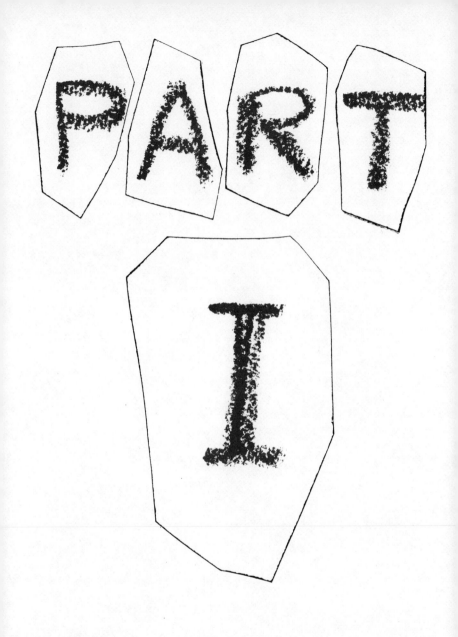

PART

I

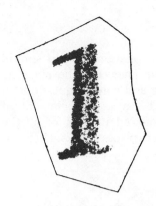

STARTING YOUR CENTER

When people decide to start a day care center, the first questions they ask are "How do I start?" "What should I do first?" There is no universal point of departure. When we're asked these questions the advice we give is to become aware of the many variables in developing a day care center: the needs you must meet, the resources you have, the kinds of problems likely to arise. This book is useful for developing that initial understanding. We suggest as a good first step that you skim the entire book for a complete overview of what is involved in setting up a day care center.

As a result of skimming for an overview of day care, you will have a checklist of both the things already taken care of and those left to do. For example, you may already have a specific population of children to serve; you may have a site already picked out; or you may have a definite theory of day care you want to execute. Or, you may discover that all you have is interest and everything else is yet to come.

You will soon realize there is no linear progression of planning steps; rather, all things should be considered more or less simultaneously. So many variables are operating and influencing one another in the process of developing a day care center that you can begin to define and plan your program only after many hours of brainstorming and research. It is not necessary to have specific answers to all your questions before actually getting the program started, but minimally all members of the planning group should agree about the range of acceptable answers. The planning process is one of repeatedly posing and solving questions in increasing complexity and detail. Because each element of the planning process must be considered in light of all the others over and over again, it is perhaps best to visualize this process as a circle.

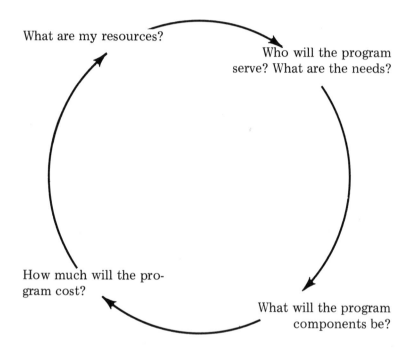

What are my resources?

Who will the program serve? What are the needs?

How much will the program cost?

What will the program components be?

No matter how well you anticipate and resolve problems, how much you learn, how many preventive measures you take in planning stages, you will inevitably find as you begin your program that you have made mistakes and will continue to discover better ways of doing things. In a sense, you never reach the end of the planning process; you just have to make the decision to begin at some point while you continue to learn.

You might find the following anecdotes about our early experiences reassuring. One of our first efforts in using free materials was the construction of a large wall of cardboard tubes in floor to ceiling layers. We didn't realize just how precarious our bright, attractive wall was until it collapsed around the startled representatives of our funding agency. Now we know enough about homemade materials to consider practicality as well as cost and beauty.

On the other hand, we have sometimes been bamboozled by expensive and glamorous equipment which catalogs hailed as a "lifetime investment for highly effective learning experiences." Our several hundred dollars' worth of imported geographic puzzles are one such case. Not only did it take three adults three hours to put one puzzle together, but within five weeks, most of the pieces were warped or broken, and after two years, we found that no teacher ever used them in the classroom.

We were right in anticipating that parents would show active concern about their children, but we were wrong about the kind of concern and in many cases did not anticipate the misunderstandings to come. One parent, for example, went to the trouble of buying a special belt which we were specifically instructed to use when his child misbehaved. Another took the trouble to spend an hour explaining why children in general, and her child in particular, should not be comforted when they fall and hurt themselves. Still another parent expected that her concern would be rewarded with a telephoned progress report of her child's behavior every hour. We've learned that at some point the line between parent involvement and program policy has to be drawn. Now our staff chiefly see parents at evening meetings and home visits, and our social worker spends more time talking about the program and philosophy of our center with parents.

On the other hand, we didn't realize the extent to which parents would be willing and able to contribute to our program. One Chinese mother did more for her little boy's adjustment in class than the combined efforts of his teachers by preparing a Chinese meal for the whole class and sharing it with them. Other parents have volunteered time in renovating our classrooms, and still others have kept a careful watch for free materials we could use. One mother even managed to have two televisions donated to us.

These are just a few of the many, many ways we've found that trial and error, and just plain experience, have been the best teachers in making our center better. We're still making mistakes and still learning, but after two years, our center is still successful and flourishing. Don't be over-whelmed by your apparent lack of knowledge or the seemingly endless obstacles to setting up your program. The important point is to be aware of the inevitability of mistakes and the opportunities to learn.

After your preliminary skimming, you can use the handbook for more detailed planning and development. The chapters are organized around fairly discrete sets of activities. For example, the chapter on site selection and development is separate from the chapter on curriculum areas (developing the classrooms), even though both are concerned with the physical facility. The planning and decision-making processes for the total site are different from those for setting up a classroom, and we did not want them to be confused.

For similar reasons, we do not discuss staff in one place. Rather, we discuss teaching staff, administrative staff, and auxiliary service staff in separate chapters. Planning and decision making for each staff category are then related to the program component they serve.

In each chapter we present a full range of alternatives so you will not be limited to preconceived notions about the range of possibilities and can apply the information to your own circumstances.

The book does not assume any professional knowledge or skills. It is designed to assist anyone — and we believe we have included enough information to mean literally any-one — in setting up a day care center. On the other hand, there are limitations to the breadth of information we could include. We can tell you what must be done in order to have a good program, but in most cases we cannot tell you exactly how to do it. For example, we talk about what good teaching is, what good supervision is, and what good equipment and supplies are, but we don't explain exactly how to teach, how to supervise, or how to use equipment and supplies. While we could not provide a how-to guide for everything, we do specify when it is essential to have someone who does know "how-to" and, if you cannot hire someone who is knowledgeable, the bibliography of relevant readings includes several books you can use to teach yourself.

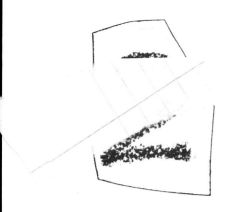

RULES AND REGULATIONS

State Rules and Regulations
One of the first things to do when planning a day care center is to contact the licensing agency in your state and request a copy of the rules and regulations for day care centers. All states license day care facilities, and licensing is mandatory except in Louisiana, North Carolina, and Mississippi. You must, then, have a copy of the rules in order to plan intelligently.

In most states, the Department of Welfare is the principal licensing agency. But in Arizona, Connecticut, the District of Columbia, Kansas, Maryland, Massachusetts, and New Mexico it is the Department of Public Health, and in New Jersey, the Department of Education.

A day care center, or a "group day care" program is generally defined as the care of X number of children away from their homes for all or part of the day. The number of children who must be in care before the program falls under the rules and regulations for day care centers varies among the states. Below this number, the program is generally called "family day care" and is subject to different rules and regulations. Some states exempt certain kinds of programs from their jurisdiction. These might include programs run by religious organizations (Sunday schools) or educational organizations (public schools). Check the exact definition in your state to be sure that the rules and regulations apply to you.

The intent of rules and regulations is to exercise public responsibility for the group care of children outside their homes by enforcing minimum standards for their protection.

Specific regulations vary widely from state to state, so it is difficult to make any kind of summary statement that can be useful throughout the country. In general, they focus on the "hard" data of health and safety and have little or nothing to say about educational standards for a day care program. They are, with few exceptions, oriented toward a "caretaking" approach to day care, rather than an educational or enrichment approach. What this means in practice is that you will in many cases have to meet a large number of rules and regulations relating to the facility's health and safety; but once you have met these criteria, you are given little or no guidance, and fewer formal requirements, about the quality or kind of program you must have. Because each state has detailed health and safety requirements, we have not dwelt on the custodial aspects of day care in this book.

The heavy if not exclusive emphasis on environmental safety and basic custodial care of children is beginning to change. Many states are revising rules and regulations in order to upgrade program standards in terms of staff qualifications, teacher-child ratios, and program content.

It is really not necessary for us to say more than *get the rules and regulations of your state and read them;* but we would like to touch on a few major points concerning educational aspects of day care which rules and regulations do cover.

1) Square Footage per Child. The great majority of states require a minimum of thirty-five square feet of classroom space per child, and seventy-five square feet of outdoor space. We feel that the thirty-five figure is rock bottom for a good classroom program and strongly suggest forty-five or fifty (*See chapters on Site Selection and Development and Curriculum Areas*).

2) Adult-Child Ratio. Most states demand ratios of one teacher to ten children or more, and this is true for two-year-olds as well as for four's and five's. For three-year-olds, the average ratio is one to ten; for five-year-olds, it is about one to fifteen. In our opinion, these ratios provide for a minimal quality custodial program — enough adults around to make sure children are safe, fed, and supervised. These ratios are oriented toward a baby-sitting program, not an educational one. Additional staff are, of course, expensive; for this reason centers (especially profit-making ones) strongly oppose lowering ratios. The ratios we suggest in this book are substantially lower, since we take as our starting point child-centered, enrichment-oriented programs. We suggest ratios of one to five — one to eight for three-year-olds and one to eight — one to ten for four- and five-year-olds with the range depending on the teachers' skill. (*See chapters on Teachers, Child Development, and Budget.*)

3) Director and Teacher Qualifications. The great majority of states do not require any education beyond high school for directors, head teachers, or teachers; nor do they require previous experience for the two supervisory positions. The few states that do usually provide an equivalency formula so that, for example, a director will need a college degree in early childhood education *or* two years of college plus experience *or* high school education plus more experience. Other states are setting standards for a future date so that, for example, by 1975 a teacher will need X number of courses in early-childhood education or a related field. At present, however, you can meet the legal requirements in most places with a staff that is inexperienced and uneducated, as long as they are of "good character."

4) Program Content and Quality. Almost all states limit program requirements to general statements about providing for the needs of the children in care. Some states make some minimal equipment requirements, such as requiring large muscle items, items which encourage manipulative skills, and indoor and outdoor equipment. But the standards are generally vague to the point of being meaningless. Just as the teachers must be "suitable," the program must be "adequate."

In summary, do not consider minimum state standards a guide to a good day care program. The program standards are so general they cannot serve as a guide: they don't tell you what to do or what you need; and rules and regulations in general do not set standards for good day care programs in our sense of the term — they set standards for child custody programs — but you are, of course, within the law if you meet only government requirements.

Federal Interagency Day Care Requirements
Federal requirements apply only to centers receiving funds under specific federal programs. These requirements are now being revised by the Federal Panel on Early Childhood, an interdepartmental group representing Health, Education and Welfare; Labor; the Office of Economic Opportunity; Agriculture; Housing and Urban Development. The Panel, and the day care requirements, represent an attempt by the federal government to coordinate federal programs having to do with day care and to impose general standards that apply to all of them.

The federal requirements apply to day care centers receiving any funding under the following programs:

— Title IV of the Social Security Act
    Part A — Aid to Families With Dependent Children
    Part B — Child Welfare Services
    Part C — Work Incentive Program
— Title I of the Economic Opportunity Act — Youth Programs
— Title II of the Economic Opportunity Act — Urban and Rural Community Action Programs
— Title III of the Economic Opportunity Act
    Part B — Assistance for Migrant, and other Seasonally Employed, Farmworkers and Their Families

— Title V of the Economic Opportunity Act
  Part B — Day Care Projects
— Manpower Development and Training Act
— Title I of the Elementary and Secondary Education Act
  (Programs funded under this title may be subject to
  these Requirements at the discretion of the State and
  local education agencies administering these funds.)

As they now stand, federal interagency day care requirements call for a comprehensive and high-quality program. If they apply to your program, you must meet them, and even if they don't apply, we urge you to read them as a therapeutic antidote to the minimal state rules and regulations. You can obtain copies from your state welfare department, or your regional HEW office. We will touch on only those aspects of the regulations that are especially relevant to program aspects discussed in this book.

Federal regulations require:

1. comprehensive social, health, and nutrition services.

2. extensive parent participation on a program and policy level.

3. teacher/child ratios of 1:5 for three-year-olds, 1:7 for four- and five-year-olds and 1:10 for children over six.

4. group sizes of no more than fifteen for three-year-olds, twenty for four- and five-year-olds and twenty-five for children over six.

5. educational activities under the direction and supervision of a person with preschool teaching experience or training in child growth and development.

6. continuous in-service training for all staff.

7. no specific educational or experience requirements are included for teaching staff, and volunteers may be used.

This book is oriented toward the kind of high quality program which federal requirements seek to implement. We do not agree with all of them, and we discuss program aspects they do not cover. They do, however, provide a reasonable "skeleton model" for day care centers.

SMALL COOPERATIVE DAY CARE CENTERS

A cooperative day care center is one that is planned and controlled by parents. Theoretically, such a center could have sixty or more children, offer a full range of services, and be staffed by paid professionals. In this chapter, however, we are concerned with a single-classroom program of up to twenty children — a program controlled and operated by parents staffing the center on a rotating basis. Many parents are coming together to plan and begin day care for their children, and we are convinced that the small cooperative center will prove a viable and popular alternative to larger, more professional operations.

If you want to start a small cooperative day care center, you can read this book in terms of your own needs. No matter what the size and scope of your program, the definitions of good teaching, good equipment, preschool curriculum, and exciting environment for children remain the same. However, in some ways the needs and goals of such a program will be very different from those of the larger center we use as our example throughout the book.

We will assume you are planning to operate on a shoestring budget, and it is therefore important that you not be intimidated by the budget for a larger, more comprehensive program. It is possible to have a very good center on a shoestring budget.

While cooperative parent groups typically lack knowledge as well as money, their genuine interest in the quality of the program can go a long way toward counterbalancing their liabilities, and the resulting program can be quite effective.

You can be thoroughly self-centered in creating your program, making your own wishes for your children the priorities of the center. For example, while larger centers often exclude infants or children who go to school half days, your center, because of its flexibility and because you control it, can simply expand to include infants and kindergarteners. Since you will be an integral part of the program's operation, you will not become removed from what happens to your children and will have the right and the responsibility to tailor the program continuously to your children's needs.

Program Components

Because you will not be taking responsibility for other people's children, and because your small size enables you to be more flexible, you can limit the scope to a good classroom program.

Health and social services which we discuss later will not be necessary, except for minimal record keeping and health checks on the children and adults in the center. (Read the sections on minimal provision of services in the chapter on Auxiliary Services.) Parents will be responsible for the health care of their own children. The program will be small enough so that parents will be constantly aware of how their children are adjusting to the center and of any problems that arise. Moreover, parents will be in constant communication with each other so that no special social service staff will be needed to facilitate this communication.

If the center is not within easy walking distance for the families, transportation can be handled on an informal basis by a parent car pool.

For meals, the small size of the center allows you to choose several alternatives. You could, for example, limit the food program to snacks and lunch only, or have children bring lunch from home. In this case, you would need only a small refrigerator for juices, milk, and snacks, and perhaps a small hot plate. On the other hand, if possible, we would suggest that you do have a hot lunch program in addition to providing snacks. This would require a fully equipped kitchen, but it would be a small "home-sized" working kitchen. For twenty or fewer children, you would not need a special cook; teachers could prepare food, or perhaps other parents could come in to prepare lunch and breakfast too, if you serve two hot meals.

A small kitchen can be a real program advantage. The teachers or other parents prepare the food, and the kitchen looks like the one at home so that meal preparation can be immediate and real to the children. The huge kitchens with oversized equipment which larger centers must have make this aspect of the day care program foreign and removed from the children's everyday world.

The Classroom

Parents and volunteers will staff the center, usually on a part-time and rotating basis. If parent-teachers do not have the experience or educational background for teaching young children in groups, you will probably find a 1:5 teacher-child ratio is best. A center for twenty children open ten hours a day and maintaining a 1:5 teacher-child ratio will require the equivalent of six and two thirds full-time teachers (see the chapter on Teachers) who work six hours in the classroom. However, the actual staffing arrangement permits many variations including part-time work, and can be arranged to suit the needs of parents. If not enough parents are available because of their work schedules, another source of staff is volunteers — students and others who have free time during the day.

In addition to being flexible about teaching schedules, your smallness will enable you to be somewhat flexible about hours. Larger centers usually must have rigid opening and closing times, and must stay open at the beginning and end of the day, though only few children are present. But you could easily arrange to have one parent look after a few children in her/his home at the tail ends of days if some parents' work schedules make this necessary.

In arranging the staffing schedule, there are some limits to your flexibility. Each person should work a substantial block of time, such as a morning or afternoon, rather than just one or two hours. Having different teachers coming and going every hour or so creates an unstable situation, prevents continuity and planning, and results in a baby-sitting program. For the same reason, once you have set a schedule, make it fixed, the same each week. With a fixed schedule children can learn to be prepared for changes in teaching staff at certain hours and will not be faced with a chaotic turnover of adults.

Make a concerted effort to have one person serve as the program's supervisor-head teacher. The head teacher will work full-time and be in the classroom for a good part of every day, providing continuity and reassurance to the children as other adults come and go. The head teacher can also provide continuity by planning activities for the day or week by sensing the general mood and format of each day and planning later activities with this in mind, and by evaluating the progress of each child during successive weeks and months. It would be ideal if this person were a professional with a theoretical and practical background in early-childhood education. This would enable her/him to supervise parents and volunteers — teach them to improve their skills in working with the children — and to evaluate and improve the program. If a professional is not available as supervisor-head teacher, then the group can find professional people to act as consultants on a regular basis, advising and instructing the staff on ways to improve the program. Even if you do hire a full-time professional, it is a good idea to engage additional consultants from time to time to give you new ideas. (See the chapter on Training.) In a less ideal situation with no outside resources, you can form a study group among yourselves, and through reading and mutual help, learn together how to improve the program.

While each parent should be expected to contribute equal time to the program, it need not necessarily be teaching time. Some parents may be working full-time and find teaching during the day impossible; others may just not want to teach. Here is a partial list of other important jobs parents can do to fulfill their time committments:

1. Cleanup and janitorial work.
2. Repairs: plumbing, electrical, mechanical, etc.
3. Build and design equipment.
4. Solicit donations and/or materials.
5. Keep books and pay bills.
6. Recruit volunteers, consultants.
7. Type and telephone.
8. Care for those few children who must arrive before the center opens or stay after the center closes (this could be done at her/his home).
9. Provide transportation for children to and from the center.
10. Organize a training program for parent-teachers.
11. Research program ideas and curriculum for pre-school children.
12. Pick up and deliver materials, supplies and equipment.
13. Teach during an evening or weekend program.
14. Prepare meals for the children.

The Budget

Costs for a small cooperative day care program can be quite minimal. At the end of the budget chapter (page 227), we have included a separate sample budget for such a center. It allows for one full-time professional teacher, for consultants, and a hot lunch program. Other costs include space rental, equipment, and supplies. Even assuming that all these items will have to be paid for, costs would be entirely covered if parents contributed an average of fifteen dollars a week on a sliding scale according to income. But the small size of the program will probably help you cut costs even further. It is easier to find a small space free or at nominal cost than to find a large one; easier to round up donated equipment for twenty children than for sixty; and easier to persuade consultants to donate time when you are small and struggling.

In addition to donations, fund raising is another way to lower costs, and here again your small size will help. For a small program fund-raising efforts are ideal since a little will go a comparatively long way. We know of one school in Cambridge, Massachusetts, which survived for over two years solely on money raised through flower sales and benefits, without charging parents any fees at all. And don't overlook the possibility of getting grants from foundations and local business. (See the chapter on Funding.)

Rules and Regulations
Since day care is defined by the states as the care away from home of just a few children, your small cooperative program will still be covered by the state's rules and regulations, and you will be subject to them. Therefore, be sure to obtain a copy of these standards and make sure that you meet the necessary requirements.

In conclusion, you can, without money or expertise, plan and operate a successful small cooperative center for your children. All the chapters in this book can be useful to you and relevant to your program. But keep in mind that the costs will not necessarily reflect the actual costs of your small program.

WHO WILL THE CENTER SERVE?

Number of Children

The number of children must, of course, reflect both your budget and the needs of the community you serve. Usually there is a greater demand for day care than any single center can accommodate, or the demand will be skewed heavily in the direction of one age group (usually under three) while you are unable to take so many children of that age. It often helps to canvass neighborhoods you will serve to get an idea of the potential number and the ages of children who will apply.

Unless you intend to have a small single-room operation for ten to twenty children, we have found that the optimal number of children is forty-five to sixty children divided into three classrooms of fifteen to twenty children. This size allows teachers to feel close to one another while still being a large enough group to allow for sharing of materials, cooperative program development, and substitution in case of absence. In addition, it is the most efficient grouping in which a single supervisor can be effective. Fewer children and classrooms will not make full use of a supervisor's time, and more will dilute the benefits derived from a good supervisor.

Similarly, classrooms of fewer than twenty children will require considerably more money in the way of basic furnishings, staff salaries, and space needs while more than twenty children becomes unwieldy with respect to both ease of supervision and the kind of individual attention teachers can offer. Since you will rarely have full attendance every day, the lower range of the optimal classroom size in practice is even lower.

At any rate, we urge you not to have a center for more than one hundred children. The institutional effects combined with other problems mentioned above will destroy both the efficiency and the sense of warmth which should characterize your program.

Age Range of Children to be Served

Although preschool is generally defined as three years old through five years, there is no reason to feel limited by that definition. Often, the three to five range is not sufficient to meet the needs of parents involved. The children under three for whom there is no available care and the children over five who may be in half-day kindergarten programs at public school are equally in need of care, especially when both parents work or for some reason are unable to stay home with their children. If neither legal requirements nor the special curriculum and program demands of the younger and older age groups is prohibitive, the full age range of children not yet in school for the full day is appropriate for a day care center.

The most efficient age range for any program is no range at all, but rather a single age grouping. Generally this is a reasonable option for very small centers only. Other options are most efficient as they approach the no range condition and avoid large gaps in ages. For example, a program for three-, four-, and five-year-olds is more efficient than one for two- and five-year-olds or infants and three-year-olds.

By "age," we really mean a combination of chronological age and developmental level. However, we refer to different ages in years as a shorthand for the more complex definition.

There have been many debates about the best combination of ages for a classroom. Some people feel that only one age per class is acceptable; others feel that "family groups" of children two to four years apart and therefore similar to the ages of siblings in a family is best. Still others feel that family groups of only a limited range for older children is workable.

At our own center we experimented with several age combinations both because of need and because we wanted to find an optimal combination. We found that the following groupings work well:

— Infants up to one year
— Toddlers one year to twenty or twenty-two months
— Two-year-olds
— Three-year-olds
— Four- and five-year-olds

Infants may also be together with toddlers, but the space needs for children who walk is greater than for those who don't yet walk. If there are enough children between eighteen months and twenty-two or twenty-three months, that too is an effective age group for a single classroom. The activity range of two-year-olds and toddlers is often too great to be satisfactorily accommodated in one classroom.

Three-, four-, and five-year-olds are the typical age groups for a family group, but careful screening of three-year-olds is important. Some may be too immature even for this wide a range. Two's and three's generally are at vastly different developmental levels, but there are always some three-year-olds who are more appropriately placed with younger children, especially if there is more than just one such child to place with the two's. It is important to consider emotional and other developmental factors when actually placing each child. Sometimes such considerations as the need to separate twins, to keep friends together, and other practical points will be as important as simple age considerations.

It may also be that you will want to have one classroom per age group along with one for a family group, provided there are enough children of each age to do so. However you ultimately arrange the groupings, it will have to reflect the theory you have adopted tempered by the reality of the specific children you serve.

Days and Hours of Operation

Often, parents are in need of weekend or evening care which most day care centers do not or cannot provide. If a sizable number of your group needs that kind of service, you can thumb your nose at precedent and tradition and give it a try. In both instances, to offer coverage during those new hours, the only real additional need is manpower. The materials, space, and program should remain virtually the same. In fact, evening care should be less difficult because it cannot help but be baby-sitting for sleeping children and can even take place in someone's home on a rotating basis.

Regardless of when you operate, it is important that all parents and personnel agree to and respect the hours set for the day care center. If any program is to run for maximum educational benefit, it cannot be subject to the whim of parents bringing and retrieving children throughout the day. Rather, a time after which children will not be accepted and special times after which children can leave must be established. These times should be set with parents' needs in mind, of course, but the needs of your program should be considered, too. The schedule we have found to be most useful in a 7 A.M. - 6 P.M. program does not accept children after ten o'clock and allows children to leave up to one-half hour after lunch, up to one-half hour after nap, and any time after four o'clock.

The range of hours should be such that the needs of all participating families are met. If yours is a small cooperative venture, more options will be available for meeting those needs. Public or agency centers simply open early enough to accommodate the earliest need and close late enough for parents to return from work and pick up their children. You need not be so limited. The earliest and latest hours of a program rarely involve more than two to five children, and yet the whole center must operate for them. In a parent-run program, there can be rotating shifts of parents whose homes will be available to early and/or late children.

In order to give staff preparation and cleanup time, most day care centers find it is best to have the first teacher arrive about a half hour before the children arrive and the last teacher leave about a half hour after the children leave. This often encourages parents to consider the center open to them when teachers are there, but they will learn to be respectful of the difference between your hours and their hours if you are firm and insistent about their keeping to the formal schedule.

Parent Participation

A major consideration in developing program plans is the question of parent participation. To what extent and for what purpose you involve parents in your program should be determined both before you start and while your program progresses. Some centers simply offer an invitation to parents to observe their children either by appointment or on an open invitation basis. Others elaborate further by including periodic parent-teacher conferences in their program.

At the beginning of the year especially, and throughout the year generally, teachers can make home visits to parents in order to learn as much as possible about children who will be in their classrooms. This often is more helpful to teachers than parents, but it does serve a valuable purpose and should not be excluded from your program if teachers are willing and able to devote time to home visits.

On the other end of the parent-participation continuum is a program of formal involvement in the ongoing planning and development of your program. Often, there is no choice as to whether or not parents are involved to this extent because the federal day care requirements include an advisory board of which at least half must be parents of attending children for day care centers accommodating forty or more children. The role of such a parent body, whether it is legally required or not, is to meet regularly with your administrative and possibly your teaching staff in order to evaluate the program and to make decisions relevant to major program policy.

Some staffs choose to omit parents from policy-decision making and include them only in the individual classroom evaluation and planning. This is generally accomplished through periodic evening meetings at which teachers present a summary of their program to date, introduce topics for discussion, and make announcements. The meeting is then opened up for questions and general discussion. Many teachers have also found that parents are anxious to participate in workshops relevant to things they can do with their children at home and to child-rearing practices.

Regardless of the degree to which parents are involved in the planning, evaluation, or decision-making procedures, there is another aspect of parent participation which is always rewarding for parents, children, and teachers. That is actual classroom participation. It need not be elaborate to be effective. Some possibilities for this kind of participation include inviting parents who speak foreign languages to sing songs, tell folktales, or teach some new words from their native language or culture. Other parents may want to cook a meal of food from their native country or just a favorite dish for the children. If you find parents who are either too shy to make such contributions or who feel they have nothing to contribute, you can invite them to have lunch with their child's class, or to help in the supervision of a field trip, or to join in some special event. Many parents regret not having time to take from work to participate in their children's classroom program, but they too can often be included by offering their place of work as a field-trip site. In fact, if you really want to include parents and they too are anxious to feel they are part of their child's preschool education, there is always some way to include everybody.

The pride children and parents feel in such participation, as well as the increased understanding parents derive from all of the activities we discussed, make them well worth the effort to have parent involvement as a permanent, frequent part of your program.

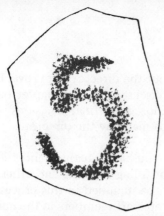

WHO WILL DIRECT THE PROGRAM?

Regardless of the kind of program you ultimately choose, it is best to have the administrative staff involved in the initial planning stages. They, more than anyone, must function well within the context of the final program.

While there are several methods of taking care of administrative functions, depending on the size and scope of your program, we suggest a model based on the hypothetical center of three classrooms for twenty children each that we use throughout the book. Whether the actual division of responsibilities we outline is appropriate for your center or not, all the functions we define must be served.

The most efficient administrative staff for our hypothetical center consists of two people: a director and a secretary-administrative assistant. Their job descriptions are as follows:

Director

Program Development Responsibilities

Policy-Making Decisions.   When the director is hired, he or she must be included in all policy-making decisions, and should have at least a significant voice if not final authority in making those early decisions.

Site Location.   If the director is hired before a site is located and developed, then this too is his or her responsibility. No site should be accepted without the director's approval based on all of the considerations discussed in the chapter on site selection and development. Moreover, final decisions about necessary renovation should be made by the director.

Hiring and Firing.   Whether you have a team of interviewers or just a single interviewer for filling teaching and other staff positions, the director should be included in this process. He or she will have to work with all staff members in the context of the policies and philosophy of the center and should feel that all applicants hired will be able to fulfill expectations, at least at the start. Similarly, the decision to terminate and the task of terminating any staff member is the director's responsibility.

Funding and Budget.   The director must procure sufficient funds for at least one day care season. Generally, this requires skill in writing proposals for government and private foundation grants, but it may also include determining a schedule of fees for parents to pay, overseeing fund raising activities, or seeking donations from local business. In addition, the director must devise a workable budget based on both the anticipated funds and the financial needs of your program. The budget, like the actual funds, should reflect the cost of operating the center for at least one season.

Recruiting.   The task of recruiting children belongs to the director. If you have a social worker or other staff member responsible for recruitment, the director must nevertheless work out acceptance policies and recruitment procedures with that person and continue to keep abreast of the actual recruiting.

Ongoing Responsibilities

Supervision and Training.   In a center of sixty children, there shouldn't be any need for a separate child care supervisor. Rather the director should be expected to assume that function (discussed in the supervision section of the chapter on training). Similarly, there should not be an additional training supervisor unless you plan to have an extensive on-the-job training program. Generally, however, the director should be responsible for planning, coordinating, and overseeing any training programs.

Authority. Unless you have a special board with formal voting power, the director has all final authority over matters relating to the day care center which are not legally under the jurisdiction of another agency. It is important that the director keep tabs on all elements of the program and be available to solve problems, make periodic evaluations, and hold regular meetings with all people in the program. Because this kind of authority is a daily concern, the director must be physically present at the day care center just about every day. Outside meetings and responsibilities must therefore be kept to a minimum.

Staff Meetings. The director should preside over all general staff meetings and as many special-purpose staff meetings as possible. It may be that other people will be more appropriate chairmen of the special-purpose meetings, but the director should nevertheless try to attend them.

Public Relations Responsibilities. The director is responsible for maintaining community understanding of and good will towards the day care center.

Many other kinds of public relations activities are the responsibility of the director. These include advertising, attending conferences, speaking before interest groups, and helping other people set up day care centers.

Secretary-Administrative Assistant

Secretarial Duties. All general secretarial duties like typing, filing, answering phones, receiving visitors, and keeping a calendar of meetings and appointments are the responsibility of the secretary-administrative assistant.

Fiscal Responsibilities.   The secretary-administrative assistant will also be the bookkeeper-accountant for the center. As such, he or she is in charge of all money matters including overseeing the budget, paying bills, receiving funds, and, most important, making out the payroll each pay period. The latter requires both an accurate record of staff and child attendance, and responsibility for dispensing and recording fringe benefits.

Program Responsibilities.   The secretary-administrative assistant is responsible for assisting the director as needed, for ordering and dispensing all equipment and supplies, and for accepting various forms required from teachers and parents.

You will notice in the budget chapter that the director and the secretary-administrative assistant have high salary allotments. Those figures are based on our anticipated qualifications for both of them. We feel the success and efficiency of your program depends to a large extent on the quality of your administrative staff and therefore urge you to hire only highly qualified people. Ideally, the director will be both educated and experienced in early childhood education and day care administration, and the secretary-administrative assistant will have both bookkeeping and secretarial skills of the highest quality.

A very small center may find that many of the responsibilities we list for the director are either not necessary or not time-consuming enough for a full-time job. In that case, the director can also teach, reducing the budget allotment for teachers.

A prospective director may be unable to fill certain of the required functions but nevertheless should be hired as the best person for the job. For example, some directors find the task of training staff in any but the most basic training programs too difficult to undertake and therefore delegate that responsibility to consultants or well-qualified teachers; The director may not be able to write proposals well or supervise teachers well, and as a result he or she has to find teachers or consultants to take those responsibilities. In those instances, you may adjust the salary for the director to reflect his or her abilities and job description.

If your center is very large, you will probably need a full-time administrative director who will not have the time, regardless of ability, to fulfill many of the functions outlined above. You will probably need additional administrative personnel with more specialized responsibilities. However, it is only when such additional staff are hired on a part-time basis or when they have fewer qualifications that you can expect any salary reductions for administrative staff. Even if an administrative director chooses not to hire additional staff, the functions outlined above must be served; and, it may be that the director will have to delegate them to teachers. Again, this does not call for a salary reduction. Whether administrative functions are delegated or not, the director must at all times be aware of what is going on and continue to have ultimate authority and responsibility for the daily and long range operation of your day care center.

However you ultimately delegate administrative responsibilities, we want to emphasize again that in order to benefit your program you should determine very early who the director will be. Once the director is chosen, you can be sure of continuity and understanding as you begin to develop your center.

PART II

FINDING AND DEVELOPING A SITE

Perhaps the most unalterable decision you make in setting up your day care center will be the selection of a site. For, unlike your staff, your equipment, or your program, the site cannot be changed with ease. You must anticipate that once a site has been selected, it is going to be *the* site for at least one full day care season and probably for quite a bit longer.

Legal Requirements

Before beginning your search for an appropriate site, be sure to consult the legal requirements regarding licensing Day Care Centers in your community. Attempting to meet licensing requirements for a building can be a difficult and complex task. Do not become discouraged by the required inspections and the seemingly endless rules and regulations with which you must conform. Most states provide consultation assistance for all phases of program development, and inspectors are generally helpful both in advising you of ways to meet requirements and in agreeing to waive requirements.

Although one public agency usually is responsible for the establishment of regulations, the issuance of licenses, and the on-going supervision of programs, the approval of other state and local agencies of your prospective site may be required. For example:

Building Inspector.   Local and/or state building department approval may be required. Inspections usually cover electrical safety, plumbing, health and safety, and general building construction.

Department of Sanitation.   In many states, sanitarians are required to approve and to inspect periodically toilet and kitchen facilities.

Fire and Safety Marshalls.   Fire Department approval may be required to insure that fire and safety regulations are maintained. General requirements may include ground level space, fire alarm systems, adequate sprinkler systems and/or fire extinguishers, heavy insulation, and at least two exits from all rooms used by children. Moreover, some communities will not allow day care programs to operate in wood frame buildings.

Zoning Commission.   Housing for the day care center must conform to state and local zoning regulations. Sometimes a special exception, called a variance, may be obtained by vote of a council or board of appeals after a public hearing.

Summary
Once you have discovered who licenses day care in your area, you must ascertain what is actually regulated by this agency (agencies). The specific environmental standards required for the operation of day care centers vary from state to state as does the enforcement of such rules.

With the increased pressure for day care services, rules and regulations in many states are currently under revision. The old regulations were based on hospital and restaurant licensing requirements and have demonstrated little transfer value for standards regulating day care services. Therefore, do not become too overwhelmed by the seemingly endless list of present environmental requirements. Many of these rulings are being changed and are often overlooked or "waived." In addition, most inspectors fully recognize the difficulty in complying with all regulations in all respects.

Criteria for Selecting a Site

The design of your site is extremely important as it will determine the amount and kind of space available for activities. However, your program will determine how you use and modify the existing facility.

In order to make the best decision about which site is most appropriate, try to keep foremost in your mind, *before* looking for a site, both the legal requirements set by your state and the criteria you have for site selection, and their relative priority. This may sound like an obvious suggestion, but typically, inexperienced site seekers err in their translation of program need to site requirements, and in spite of cautious investigation, they wind up with a "lemon" of a site. Since it will be a rare stroke of good fortune to find a site which is tailor-made to suit your needs, it is even more imperative that you think in terms of the potential any given site offers rather than in terms of a one-to-one correspondence between your needs and the site's assets.

Let us begin to define criteria for site selection with a brief statement of the ideal and then consider how to appraise the possibilities of approximating that ideal according to the categories of site requirements. The ideal site will conform to the following requirements:

1. It will be a spacious, single-purpose building with from forty-five to fifty square feet of classroom space per child.
2. It will be appropriately subdivided into the right number of classrooms, meeting rooms, offices, and/or multi-purpose rooms as your needs require; and all classrooms will be on the ground floor for easy accessibility and quick evacuation during emergencies.
3. It will have a fully equipped kitchen and the appropriate number and quality of toilets, sinks, entrances, and windows.
4. It will be in excellent general repair and have heating, lighting, and electrical accommodations

which are adequate in terms of both your state's requirements and the needs of your program.

5. It will have an extensive outdoor area of at least seventy-five square feet per child at play, and preferably one-hundred square feet, in a combination of concrete or tar and grassy surfaces which are fenced for protection from street traffic.
6. It will be conveniently located to the community it serves and to public transportation.
7. It will have adequate parking facilities.
8. It will be within the limitations of your budget.

Unless you have a site specially designed and built for you, we can guarantee that this ideal will not be found. Rather, a site with more or less potential to satisfy the ideal will be found, and you will be responsible for renovating it.

Renovation, in fact, is the key word for site selection. Almost any site can be remodeled to suit your needs, but the cost of doing so is prohibitive. Therefore, you must learn to judge a site not by its most visible appearance, but in terms of the kind and scope of the renovations required.

Indoor Space

The first four items in the list of requirements for an ideal site concern the indoor facility. Let us review them now in order to focus on renovations.

The major error of judgment people make in selecting a site is to be repelled by the shabby conditions of a building and reject it immediately without looking into it further. In fact, shabbiness is the least expensive, least time-consuming evil to overcome. Generally, the most immediately visible characteristics of a site are the most easily renovated or repaired. The hidden elements, on the other hand, are the most costly to renovate. Following is a reorganization of the variables relevant to the interior of a site mentioned above which reflects the relative expense involved in their renovation:

— Least Expensive
  Adding room dividers
  Appliance repair
  Changing door locks
  Minor floor repair
  Painting
  Plastering
  Window repairs

— More Expensive
  Adding doors or sealing up doors
  Adding vestibules for coatrooms or for protection from
    the outdoors
  Minor plumbing or electrical renovations
  Tearing down and/or relocating one wall

— Most Expensive
  Kitchen renovation and installation
  Major plumbing: toilets, sinks
  Renovating heating system
  Major electric renovations
  Tearing down and/or relocating many walls
  Ventilation renovations: air conditioning and adding
    windows

In other words, a place that looks as if it is falling apart but which also is equipped with the appropriate room divisions, heating, lighting, and plumbing is far superior to one which needs nothing in the way of general repairs but does require plumbing, heating, lighting, or room construction changes.

There is nothing you can do about the requirement for a ground-level site. In many states it is required for younger age groups, so a site must be rejected if it is not on the ground level or if at least the space for young children is not available on the ground level. If you are not limited to a ground-level facility by law, you can be much less concerned about it than you are about other variables. Story level should not significantly interfere with any major program priorities. Similarly, if you prefer a site with many windows and can find one with only the minimum required amount of window space, it should not be a major concern as it will have only nominal ramifications for your program.

Square footage of available classroom space, on the other hand, is crucial. Most states require a minimum of thirty-five square feet of classroom space per child, but we suggest forty-five to fifty square feet. This will not apply to those centers in geographic locations which allow for very extensive use of outdoor space on a daily basis. Thus, a space which offers only the minimum number of square feet of classroom space per child but which is otherwise excellent should be very carefully considered in terms of your program and the anticipated portability and storability of your materials and equipment. If you can neither store and move equipment frequently nor willingly eliminate a sufficient number of activities from your program, this kind of space should be rejected. (*See page 53 for some ideas on maximizing a limited space classroom.*)

Subdividing a large space is less expensive than tearing down an inappropriately divided space and relocating the walls and rooms; but both endeavors can be very expensive. Unless you can use prefabricated or homemade room dividers and/or can make do with tearing down or putting up just one wall, beware of the poorly subdivided space. It can lead you to many projects which are too expensive for the demands of your budget.

Finally, consider the kitchen. If you do not plan to offer hot meals or if you have arranged to have food delivered, your kitchen needs will be reduced to a refrigerator, a sink, a few counters and cabinets, and a small stove if a hot plate is insufficient. On the other hand, if you plan to have meals cooked on site, you will need a much more elaborate, up-to-standard kitchen which is fully equipped for such large-scale cooking. A site which lacks a kitchen or which has a poorly equipped kitchen may seem useless at first glance; however, do not overlook renovation possibilities entirely. If there is sufficient space to install a good kitchen, and if basic electric, plumbing, and ventilation renovations are not too costly, you should check to see whether you are eligible for the seventy-five percent reimbursement of the cost for installing and equipping your kitchen available through the National School Lunch Act. (*See page 114 of Health and Social Services.*)

If you are not eligible and cannot find funds to enable you to install a kitchen, you will have to choose between rejecting a site because of inappropriate kitchen facilities and changing your program plans so that you will need only the kitchen facilities available at the site.

Outdoor Space

Unfortunately, the sad fact of our more and more urban society is that good, grassy, safe outdoor space is very difficult to find. Rural and relatively high income suburban areas will offer some hope of finding a site with a good outdoor area, but urban and more densely populated suburban areas will generally offer very little in the way of outdoor space accompanying potential sites. While we feel that a good outdoor area is extremely important, our own center functioned very well with no more outdoor space than a cement courtyard in an urban housing project, with no protection from the heavily trafficked main street on which it borders. We accomplished this by including both the money and the transportation for numerous field trips to places where children could play outdoors.

In other words, if you are forced to accept a site with little or no functional outdoor space, you must be aware of the effect it will have on your original program plans. Generally it will have the following kinds of effects:

— Space and equipment for robust play must be made available indoors.
— Money and transportation for an elaborate schedule of field trips must be available.

— Teachers must be able to provide very careful supervision to local outdoor play and may have to limit the number of children who can be outside at any given time.

If any of these effects appears to be prohibitive, you must simply wait until a site with a good outdoor area materializes; if they do not seem prohibitive, sites without outdoor space need not be rejected.

Location

As the sixth requirement indicates, the location of a site is an extremely important variable. We feel strongly that your center should serve the community in which it is located. If you locate your center within a subcommunity like a hospital, university, or factory, you may feel that by serving the needs of that subcommunity you are fulfilling your community responsibility. To some extent, you *are* fulfilling your responsibility, but we would urge you to give as much consideration to the needs of the larger community as possible. Community residents will become justifiably angry if they have pressing day care or employment needs and you arrive on the scene in order to serve children and hire staff from other locations.

If you do not provide transportation and many parents do not have cars, you must also be careful to locate your center within easy access to public transportation. Accessibility to public transportation becomes an even more important factor in areas where seasonal weather changes cause severe travel difficulty. It is not unusual to find enrollment dropping from sixty to twenty children during winter months simply because parents are unwilling or unable to walk a few blocks in snow, rain, or very cold temperature with their children.

Parking

The parking facilities listed as the seventh requirement for an ideal day care site are perhaps the least important variable. Unless there are absolutely no parking possibilities and both parents and staff will be driving to the center, you should not feel overly concerned about considering a site which has no parking facilities. Parking problems somehow manage to work themselves out, so if everything else at a potential site is acceptable, grab it.

Cost
Finally, but by no means least important, you must consider the cost of a potential site. The major cost factor is the rental or purchase price. Beyond that, however, there are many costs which must be considered for an accurate appraisal of whether or not you can afford to accept a given site. These costs include renovation expenses, of course. Other, less obvious expenses for which you should determine whether you or the landlord are responsible are as follows:

> Extermination
> Garbage disposal
> General repairs, including periodic painting and plumb-
>   ing and electrical repairs
> Heat
> Improvements which raise the market value of the
>   property
> Janitorial services for general maintenance including
>   periodic window washings
> Landscape and other outdoor maintenance including
>   shoveling snow
> Lights and electricity
> Telephone installation and maintenance
> Vandalism, fire, and theft insurance
> Water

If you rent your facility, be sure the lease or other contract includes a statement of landlord and tenant responsibilities. It is never safe to assume anything regardless of your previous experiences. Nor should you feel that you can rely on a verbal agreement. If your landlord is unwilling to put his promises in writing, you can anticipate that he will also be unwilling to follow through on those promises.

Where to Look

Once you are familiar with the licensing requirements in your area, have determined the amount of money you have to spend, and have decided upon your space and program needs, you are ready to begin searching for a site.

A housing or building authority exists in each city, town, or region. This agency is responsible for maintaining building listings and can give you an idea of existing or soon-to-be-vacated sites in the area you wish to serve. Real estate agents also have listings of apartment or building vacancies. If you explain your needs to them, they can be of tremendous assistance.

Another approach is to drive or walk through the area in which you wish to locate your day care center. When you discover a potential site, check back with the housing authority to find out if it is or might be available shortly.

The ideal location for a day care center is in a one-story building especially designed for children which adjoins an outdoor play area. If you have money to build your own center, then you can design your site to fit your program needs. There are numerous examples of such buildings designed around programs including: American Child Centers, Inc., of Nashville, Tennessee; the primary division of Casady School, Oklahoma City; The Early Learning Center in Stamford, Connecticut; The Harold E. Jones Early Education Center in Berkeley, California; The Lamplighter School in Dallas, Texas; and The Phoebe Hearst Pre-School Learning Center in San Francisco.

While land and construction costs depend upon location, materials, and center size, most new buildings range from a low of $14 per square foot to well over $25 per square foot.

Since most of you will be unable to build your own center, we will explore alternatives. One of the best locations for a day care center is in a one-family house. Such homes have existing toilet and kitchen facilities and usually an outdoor play area. With minor renovations, many private residences can be converted into warm, comfortable day care centers which provide a homelike atmosphere for the children attending. Examples of day care centers now operating in former homes can be found at the Central Plaza Day School in St. Petersburg, Florida; the Child Minders School in Greenwich, Connecticut; and the New Nursery in Greeley, Colorado.

Private residences are not the only single buildings possible for conversion to day care centers. Our first day care center at Castle Square opened in a simple storefront in Boston. Fortunately, renovation costs were minimal since heating, lighting, and plumbing facilities were in good condition. Further examples of the successful conversion of a store into a day care center can be seen at the Hilltop Center in Dorchester, Massachusetts, and at the Sea Pines Montessori School on Hilton Head Island, South Carolina.

Sometimes space for a day care center can be found in an old school building no longer in use. While such buildings may appear shabby on first inspection, these facilities are usually structurally sound since they were constructed originally with the safety of children in mind. Unless the heating, wiring, and plumbing systems need complete redoing, old schools can be developed fairly inexpensively. The Kemper School and Strawberry Cottage in Arlington, Virginia, are two examples of old school buildings remodeled for day care.

Barns, former nursing homes, and other miscellaneous single buildings are further possibilities. While renovation costs are sometimes prohibitive, the possibilities of such locations should not be overlooked.

If single-unit locations are out of the question because of lack of available sites or financial circumstances, separate quarters or shared quarters in another building unit can often be found. However, separate quarters with separate entrances are preferable to a room which must be shared with other groups. A ground-floor location is desirable for easy accessibility and quick evacuation in case of fire.

Day care centers located within larger building units, such as churches, public schools, apartment buildings, community centers, are often more economical to maintain and often have the added advantage of being within walking distance of the children's homes. A possible drawback to such locations may be high renovation costs necessary to prepare such sites for use as a day care center. It is anticipated that many community day care centers will be attached to such larger building units.

Sometimes adequate space can be secured from local churches. Our second day care center at Hawthorne House in Roxbury, Massachusetts, is located in a former convent. The area we use for day care was the orphanage, and thus plumbing, lighting, and heating facilities are adequate for children. When we first viewed the site, it was run-down — shabby, windows broken, walls in need of paint. However, it was structurally sound, and renovation costs have been minimal.

Sometimes churches can offer space in classrooms used for Sunday school or in their basements. Many states will not license basement locations for day care, so be sure before accepting such a site there are no legal restrictions. Also, be sure the basement has windows which allow adequate natural light, a good heating and ventilating system to prevent dampness, and a minimum of two means of exit. If church Sunday school classrooms are available, be sure there is adequate space to store your program materials and equipment, unless they are to be shared freely with the church group.

Occasionally, public schools are able to offer space for day care use. Such space is often, again, the basement or a shared activity area, such as a seldom-used auditorium. However, some schools may be able to provide at least one classroom which can be utilized exclusively for day care on a long-term basis.

Sometimes empty apartments can be found within a housing complex. While plumbing and kitchen facilities will be available, usually renovation is required to remove a wall in order to make a workable classroom area. When locating a day care center in such a complex, attempt to secure a ground-level apartment situated at an end of the building and near an outside entrance. Such a location will provide the easiest accessibility for children.

Additional site possibilities can be found within settlement houses, community centers, and local Y's. Again, separate quarters are preferable in these locations, but sharing space with other groups at such sites is not uncommon. Having the child-care space utilized by several groups at different times often presents problems. It is very difficult to maintain high standards of cleanliness and hygiene so important for safeguarding the health of young children when the room is used by large numbers of different individuals. The continual setting up and storage of materials and equipment not only is a bother, but wastes precious time which could be better spent in program planning and curriculum development. Finally, the noise of happy, exuberant young children may disturb the functioning of other groups in the building, causing ill feelings, and, what is worse, other noisy groups may distract and cause disruptive confusion to the young day care group of children.

However, do not rule out completely the use of shared community space. Such sites do have advantages. Except for donated space, this type of location is often the least expensive to operate since there is multiple sharing of costs. In addition, such sites often promote community involvement and produce interested volunteers of all ages who wish to help out at the day care center.

Possible site locations can sometimes be found outside the children's immediate neighborhood. For example, one such location is to have the day care center at the mother or father's place of work. If this is in a hospital, factory, or large industrial complex, additional benefits may be realized. One such benefit might be that parents could share their lunch hour with their child. Another advantage of such locations is the possibility of utilizing available medical personnel and associated auxilliary services. Often such services are donated to the day care center by the larger organization or can be purchased at nominal cost. In addition, such organizations are sometimes willing to donate space for day care or charge only minimal rent.

Since World War II, industries, mills, and factories intermittently have been receptive to day care. We feel strongly that day care enrollment at such centers should contain not only employees' children but also the children of community residents. This combination has proved successful at the KLH Child Development in Cambridge, Massachusetts, and at the AVCO Corporation Day Care Center in Dorchester, Massachusetts.

Many hospitals are now interested in providing day care services as a means of attracting employees to work. The Lemmuel Shattuck Hospital, in Jamaica Plain, Massachusetts, now has such a center which enrolls both employee and community children.

Recently, colleges and universities have become interested in day care and have provided space on campus for such centers. Brandeis University, in Waltham, Massachusetts, and Tufts University, in Medford, Massachusetts, are two such examples.

Therefore, when seeking site locations in the area you wish to serve, do not ignore the possibility of stimulating an interest in day care at any nearby industry, hospital, college or university, shopping center, or other large business complex.

The previously mentioned locations have all been fairly standard suggestions, but do not stop with just the known. Try to think of new possibilities afforded by your area because of climate, location, or special circumstance. While it is impossible for us to know and thus be able to recommend the specific options available to you in your community, you should be constantly on the lookout for unexplored possibilities.

For example, if you happen to live in the West or Southwest, your climate may enable you to locate a day care center partially out of doors. Such centers can be housed in tents and partial shelters at camping areas, tenting and fair grounds, and many other outdoor locations. Your choice of site will be limited only by your imagination and the rules and regulations governing day care in your area, so let your imagination run wild!

Site Development
Once you have selected a site, the real task of actually developing your day care center begins. Taking an empty space and creating an effective environment for children and teachers in day care requires planning with an acute awareness of the objectives of your program, the components of your program, and the needs of children and teachers.

This section of chapter 6 is designed to focus on those elements of the curriculum areas and child development chapters which are directly relevant to classroom environment and to elaborate them so that basic objectives and principles are defined. We begin with the assumption that your site is renovated to the point where all you have left to do in the way of developing it is to design the interior of the classrooms. Because each site will be unique in terms of the variables it provides, we cannot offer a single blueprint for development. Rather, we can suggest the kinds of considerations and requirements there are in developing the classroom environment and can encourage you to visit as many other centers as possible for ideas and to play around with ideas for your own design until you find one which best suits your program and budget.

Objectives
It is not enough to say that you want an environment which is "good," or which "works well." There must be some careful thought given to what you want your classroom environment to accomplish. There are generally six major categories of such objectives, as follows:

Security.   Children will be unable to make effective use of the program offered if they do not have a sense of security. The environment helps to create this simply by being safe, secure, and comfortable. Among the means of creating this kind of environment are providing furniture which is designed for children; offering consistency in the accessibility of materials (which should also be designed for children); providing places where children can rest, relax, and be alone when they want to; maintaining stability in the classroom enrollment and teaching staff; carefully arranging equipment for minimum hazard or distraction; and offering adequate supervision at all times, while avoiding materials which might lead to mishap.

Independence.   One important program objective is to encourage children to use the inventory of skills they have rather than always relying on adult direction or skills. A good day care program will help each child develop skills at his or her own rate of need and ability. The essence of independence in this respect is that children will want to rely on their own abilities and will learn to feel confidence rather than frustration in facing obstacles. Often, such confidence is easily accomplished with patience and an appropriate environment. For example, by offering materials on shelves or other storage facilities marked by signs children can read with ease, in shapes and sizes which children can readily manipulate, and in an orderly, uncluttered display, you are indicating that you want children to succeed at being independent and are confident that they will. Further, environmental encouragement would include installing child-sized, child-height toilets and sinks, supplying children with cleanup materials they can use, and offering enough environmental stimulation so that children can involve themselves in interesting activities without requiring assistance, suggestions, or approval from adults.

Cooperation.   Of course teachers must necessarily explain to children the rules and regulations operating in their classrooms if they are to expect children to cooperate in maintaining those rules, but the environment can go a long way to support the teacher and to encourage children to cooperate without teachers having to take, or threaten to take, disciplinary measures. Some more common techniques for accomplishing this are to keep out of children's reach (and sight if possible) those materials which they are not allowed to use. In some instances it will be impossible to do so, as when certain activity areas are off limits. Effective barriers which clearly imply *Do Not Use* must then be incorporated into your classroom design. Sometimes, all it takes is a large sign saying, for example, *The Carpentry Table is Closed*. While most children cannot read it, they will get the message from a single explanation and will recognize it elsewhere. You can also arrange equipment so that it cannot be used. For example, by pushing easels and art tables into one tight group, you are saying that they should not be used. Covering blocks with a cloth, the sandbox with cardboard or plywood, and the access to puzzles and table games with a plant or additional storage shelf will also serve this function. If you want to limit running and boisterous play in some parts of the room, you should arrange your space so that there is no long extension of the room which literally begs to be run through and do not overcrowd areas where very active, boisterous play is expected.

Similarly, you should avoid using elevated structures that permit climbing and jumping from over three feet off the ground where climbing and jumping is inappropriate. Solid-sided platforms and other elevations are impossible to climb on, and elevations five or six feet high will not be hazardous if there is a sizable railing (about two feet high) which is narrow enough to avoid children's climbing onto it.

Finally, provide a place for all children's materials to be stored with ease. In that way they will be reasonably able to adhere to rules about cleanup without frustration.

If your teachers are firm and consistent about the meaning of such environmental cues, there will be less need for teacher-directed cooperation and a greater use of self-directed cooperation from the children.

Supervision.   While supervision is a variable which affects each of the other objectives, it is presented here as an environmental objective from the teachers' perspective, that is, in terms of the teachers' needs. If teachers are to do the best job they can, they too must find that all of the other objectives are met, but in addition to those objectives, they should feel confident that the classroom environment is designed to allow for effective supervision. Perhaps the single most important variable in this respect is the need to plan carefully for elevated structures.

While on one hand we encourage use of different levels or platforms in developing your site, we must also warn against designing platforms which significantly block teachers' view of other parts of the classroom. When teachers cannot see what is happening throughout the room, they cannot feel relaxed and usually communicate their tension to the children. While children feel more able to concentrate on a given activity if all other activity stimulation is blocked, adults are less able to concentrate because they cannot feel certain of children's safety and well-being. Thus, it is important that elevations and other similar boundary delineators be constructed to allow full visibility of the classroom for teachers, while at the same time separating one activity area from another for children.

Supervision is further facilitated through the environment when activity areas are planned to accommodate enough children without chaos. How much is enough depends, of course, on the number of children in the room and on the children's preferences; but it also depends on the teacher's plans and expectations. It is important to include as many teachers as possible in the planning of their classroom's design so that you can be sure the teachers you hire will be able to function well in the classrooms you provide.

Observation.   Any day care center can expect to have a constant flow of visitors who are anxious to see what you are doing. It is important that you define a workable visitors' policy which you are prepared to enforce; otherwise, visitors will become a source of chaos and frustration which will affect both the children and your staff.

There are many possibilities with respect to the means of accommodating visitors. Some centers limit the number of people who may come at any given time by requiring an appointment to visit. In that way, anyone who is responsible for showing visitors around and explaining the program will always know who is coming and how many people are expected. In addition, limiting the number of people who may visit allows for the possibility of having visitors actually enter the classrooms and participate actively with the children. Not all people are comfortable with that policy, but many find that it is the most effective means of allowing people to learn about their program and that their activity is not disrupted by it.

If you do not want visitors to participate in the classroom activity, or if you want to allow parents to observe their children anonymously, you will have to provide some kind of observation facility.

Simple provisions for observation can be provided by cutting a window in the door or wall of the classrooms and covering it with double screening or a two-way mirror. Observers stand in the hallway or sit in a space adjacent to the classroom. This observation "space" is best when it is a separate room used solely for observation purposes so that there need not be any lights on or any distraction from other noise. However, it is sometimes necessary to utilize office space for an observation area when no other room adjacent to the classrooms is available.

If neither office space nor specific observation space is available, then more elaborate booths must be constructed inside the classroom. The most effective design for such a booth that we have seen is one which elevates the booth from the main floor so that the floor of the booth begins four feet or so off the ground. It is not necessary to make the booth wider than four feet in order to accommodate chairs and the need to walk from the door to a chair. If possible, the stairway leading to the booth should be in another adjacent room, but it can be in the classroom itself so long as it is near the entrance and precludes having to traipse through the classroom to observe anonymously.

Such an elevated observation booth is effective for several reasons. First, it places observers above the children's usual line of vision and thereby makes the children less aware of being observed. Secondly, it provides the observers with greater visibility of the room; and finally, the space under the booth can be used for storage and/or for a private place that children can crawl into when they want to.

Any observation booth can be made with either the double screening or the two-way mirror mentioned earlier, but the latter significantly muffles sound so that if observers are to hear what is happening in the classroom, as well as see it, an expensive system of microphones must be installed. In our experience, the microphones and the mirror are unnecessary. Children become aware of the function of the mirror in their classrooms very quickly, and therefore the purpose it serves — that is — to keep visitors hidden, is not effective. Screening, on the other hand, allows for more visibility for the children, but they are rarely so self-conscious about it that they will act differently with visitors than they do without visitors. The difference in cost for the two methods does not represent an index of the difference in their effectiveness, so we recommend double screening.

Stimulation.   The final objective for the classroom environment is somewhat different from the others in that it is the function of the teacher's efforts more than of the basic classroom design. This last objective is stimulation. By stimulation we mean those variables of the classroom environment which create activity areas which are maximally educational and interesting to children. A stimulating environment is one which not only provides activities for children, but also encourages full participation in those activities.

The kinds of stimulation which are appropriate for the preschool classroom can be divided into three major categories: sensory stimulation, activity stimulation, and cognitive stimulation. Sensory stimulation, as the label implies, excites the senses. Rooms should be decorated in bright, warm colors; children's art and literature should be displayed at the children's eye level and changed periodically so it will be noticed. Within each activity area there should be appropriate pictures, again, displayed at children's eye level. Pictures should be a variety of photographs, paintings, magazine cutouts, hand drawings, and posters. They can be in collages as well as separately displayed; and they can be about specific activities, or just generally relevant to the area. Pictures are not only nice to look at, they are also a catalyst to conversation, exploration, and inquiry. They might suggest activity possibilities, offer information, evoke laughter, or simply provide pleasant decoration.

Sensory stimulation comes through offering a variety of floor levels and textures; object shapes and textures; and the opportunity to touch, smell, listen to, and even taste a variety of materials. It distinguishes purely functional materials from exciting, educational materials.

Activity stimulation comes from a room arrangement which both encourages children to participate in activities and defines the scope and limitations of the activities. One example of this is an art area which has been prepared so that a table with six chairs is set up with all the materials necessary for a particular activity, in a manner which offers immediate visibility and access to the materials. Such environmental preparation will be a significantly more effective technique for stimulating participation in that activity (while at the same time encouraging only six children to participate) than a teacher's verbal statement that anyone who wants to make collages can go to the table and she will get out the materials for them.

Just the basic arrangement of your room figures significantly in the kind of activity which is stimulated. For example, you will not find children throwing their jackets and sweaters into the water-play table or sandbox if they are not located near the front door. Similarly, you may find that dramatic play will treble by the simple addition of a homemade stage or puppet theater near the housekeeping area.

In other words, the task of involving children in

activities which are both interesting and productive does not stop with developing activity ideas. Rather, a good teacher will provide visual stimulation which fairly compels children to participate.

Finally, cognitive stimulation refers to the teacher's utilization of the environment to encourage children to work in areas and at levels that will promote their cognitive development. For example, if a child is beginning to learn to read and a teacher is aware of the words that the child already reads, she/he can both reinforce the lexicon of known words and introduce new words through the classroom environment. The teacher can include signs, labeled pictures, flannel-board letters, pictures representing those words, and homemade books based on those words in the classroom. The child need not feel that he is practicing reading when he shouts with glee the word he reads from the wall, but the sense of pride in that small success is an invaluable asset in promoting his eagerness to learn even more words. If the words he knows are presented in conjunction with new words which either use the same letters or are deemed simple enough for him to learn quickly, an effective impromptu reading lesson can be stimulated. Whatever it is that teachers feel children are ready to learn and develop, the environment of the classroom can be a significantly effective catalyst to that learning.

There are, of course, other objectives which a well-designed classroom can serve, especially if you are very familiar with both the children and the teachers who will be working there. However, regardless of what kind of room, program, or staff you have, the objectives just discussed must be taken into account.

Special Space Problems

The ideal classroom for twenty preschool children measures approximately 25 by 40 feet. Not all programs will have this ideal space available; therefore we must explore what one can do with a room that is too small or too short, too large or too long.

Small Room. A small room which barely meets the minimum space per child requirements can be expanded through use of raised platform areas. Such platforms provide visual variety and utilize two levels for activity. While platforms have been referred to throughout the book as a means of adding variety to any room, nowhere is the use of platforms so critical as in a room which is too small. For in a small room it is essential to make optimum use of not only the linear space available, but the vertical space as well.

Carefully planned use of platforms can perform many functions in a small room and help create the effect of a larger area. One such use of platforms is to decrease the need for large numbers of multiple storage units. By storing materials and equipment under platforms, you double your use of vertical space. In addition, platforms can maximize your use of space by creating boundaries for activities and thereby limit the need for area dividers. The platforms may partially serve the additional function of large muscle exerciser, in that they afford children an opportunity to climb and jump on the "steps" they provide. Since a small room will probably include only the five basic curriculum areas on a permanent basis (see chapter on Five Basic Curriculum Areas), you will not have much more in the way of indoor large-muscle activity facilities. Therefore, such activity must be reserved for outdoor play.

Similarly, the activities associated with the other desirable but nonbasic curriculum areas can be included by bringing in the necessary materials on a temporary, rotating basis (e.g., those for music or water play) or by reserving them for outdoor play (e.g., carpentry, water play, sand play).

Short Room. A classroom which is almost square in shape will appear longer if one wall is painted a darker color than the rest. In addition, the placement of activity areas on only three sides of the room will help to make the area seem less boxlike. Finally, the construction of one long raised platform along a side wall will expand the visual as well as the actual space within such a room.

Large Room.   Large classrooms can present as many problems as small ones. Children feel lost in such areas and the barnlike quality often encourages undirected, wandering activity.

If money permits, the best solution to an overly large area is to divide it into two rooms, one of average classroom size and the other a smaller room. The smaller room could be used for such activities as special projects, nap area for children who have difficulty sleeping with the larger group, cubby area, isolation room, office space, storage, and so forth. If a wall cannot be constructed, the large space can still be divided into two areas through use of large storage units, packing cases, and partial partitions.

Every attempt should be made to define curriculum areas and produce an atmosphere of cohesiveness. Such areas can be defined physically through use of storage units and book cases, and visually through the suspension from the ceiling of large pieces of canvas, painted cardboard, or floor to ceiling ropes secured tightly at both ends.

Long Room.   A long room is apt to create a tunnel feeling and encourage running. Therefore, special care should be taken to suggest traffic patterns in the classroom. Curriculum areas should be staggered so one does not run into another in trainlike fashion.

Placing permanent areas, such as housekeeping or sand at each end of the long walls helps to create a more manageable central area. Activities can then radiate from this core outward. As in the large room, well-defined curriculum areas are essential in a long room.

Summary.   One does not necessarily have to be limited by a less than ideal classroom area. With careful planning and minimal remodeling, many of the problems inherent in such spaces can be corrected or compensated for. The resulting classroom will be well worth the extra effort in the pleasure it brings to children and teachers alike.

THE TEACHING STAFF

Teachers

An excellent teaching staff can go a long way toward overcoming scanty supplies, less than adequate equipment, or a somewhat cramped building. It can make the difference between a thoroughly effective program and a merely adequate one. But what is an excellent teaching staff? What are they supposed to do? What kinds of backgrounds should they have? Where do you find them? How many teachers do you need?

Functions of a teacher

Everyone knows who works in a nursery school — a nursery school *teacher*. But who works in a day care center? A "teacher"? An "attendant"? A "child care worker"? An "adult"? These terms which different states have used in their rules and regulations reflect the confusion about what a day care center is and therefore about what a staff member does. Our view is that a good day care center must not only keep children safe and healthy but must be a learning environment.

The teacher, then, must be able to create a learning environment; evaluate the needs and capabilities of each child; plan and execute daily activities appropriate for each child; coordinate the myriad activities and interests of the children; and work with other teachers as part of an organic unit. Caretaking, in the sense of assuring the children's health and safety, is just one of a teacher's many functions.

What does a teacher of preschool children do? If you take a look at our day care center in the middle of a morning, you might see one head teacher with a group of children at the water-play table. She is answering questions and chatting with the children as they splash, pour, measure, test, color, bubble, and channel the water through tubes and jars. She encourages them to learn about power systems (on their own level) or sinking and floating through their own discoveries, their own native curiosity. In another corner, an assistant teacher has a few children help him set out materials for an interesting art project. Another teacher is reading a story to several children. In another classroom, one of the teachers is taking a child to the toilet, another is watching gerbils with a group of children. They are chatting about what they see the gerbils doing and about what they know about or do with other animals. Another teacher is outdoors with children who are playing on a climbing structure. And so on ad infinitum.

Composition of the Teaching Staff

We feel strongly that the traditional conception of a preschool teacher as female is not only inappropriate, it is damaging. The benefits derived from having at least one male and one female teacher for each classroom cannot be exaggerated. And we are talking about all classrooms, not just those for older children. It is a myth that all men will refuse to change diapers or perform other caretaking tasks traditionally relegated to women. Although our experience is that younger men (twenty to twenty-five) are generally more willing to teach young children, it is not impossible to find older men as well, especially now, when the role expectations of men and women are changing and the status of such educational occupations as teaching young children is rising.

In addition to including both sexes, we urge you to have teachers from a variety of racial and ethnic backgrounds. The preschool classroom is the earliest introduction to the world at large for the child, and is at least partially responsible for the attitudes he will develop toward the people in that world. Children stand a better chance of growing up without prejudice and fear if they have been given the chance to grow up with, and have important relationships with, people of different races and ethnic origin.

a) Staff Positions.   Most centers assign one teacher in each classroom the major responsibility for that classroom program. This person is known as the "head teacher." The head teacher is responsible for supervising and directing other teachers working in the classroom; for planning the program with the other teachers, and for evaluating the program and the progress of the children.

The amount of control and direction the head teacher exercises over the other teachers' activities can vary from giving specific assignments and direction to simply being available for advice and support. Whether the head teacher functions more as a classroom director or more as an available resource, it is important that there be one person who can give direction to the classroom program.

b) Volunteers.   The teaching staff working under the direction of a head teacher can be volunteer as well as paid staff. Volunteer resources abound in local college and high school communities. Often, college students receive course credit for teaching at a center. Departments of Early Childhood Education, Education, Psychology, Sociology, Home Economics, Urban Studies, and Speech Therapy are all likely sources for student volunteers. Other students will simply volunteer just to learn more about children and day care. With the growing interest in and need for day care, many high schools are developing programs of study in early-childhood education. Most students in these courses are desperate for practical experience, and there is no reason why the more responsible and mature students cannot be part of your teaching staff.

The elderly are generally overlooked or ignored as a

source of day care teachers. To be sure, many elderly people will not be able to handle the physical demands of preschool teaching, and your screening must be rigorous, but the greater the heterogeneity of your staff, the more effective it is likely to be.

Finally, many parents and other adults will be willing to volunteer time if you make your needs known.

Teacher Qualifications

a) State rules and regulations.   These will not prove very useful as a guide in deciding what kind of background teachers should have. Only about one quarter of the states have any requirements for formal education of child care staff. Many states require you to hire teachers with the "appropriate" education training or experience for taking care of children, but will require no particular background, leaving you to decide what is "appropriate." The emphasis in most rules and regulations is on the personal qualities of teachers.

b) The "natural" teacher.   A quick survey of state rules and regulations can give you an idea of the personal qualities a teacher should have. Examples of qualifications required by various states produce the following composite picture of the "natural" teacher: "interested in children, has the capacity to enjoy them, to understand their problems, to respect their individual personalities and cultural differences, to discern their feelings and needs, to be sympathetic, sensitive, flexible, dependable, objective, consistent, mature, willing to learn, able to learn, resourceful, creative, non-punitive but firm, pleasant and cooperative with other adults, capable of handling emergencies, able to accept violently expressed feelings, of good physical and mental health, warm and spontaneous."

There *are* natural teachers who seem to be able to combine all of the above qualities, and who cannot be categorized by their backgrounds. Some people who have had a great deal of experience caring for young children and who have been more or less self-taught will be excellent teachers. So will some people who have had very little experience but are especially creative in particularly appropriate subjects such as art or language development. Others just seem to "click" with children in the day care center context. We've seen them. They are often the superlative teachers that parents and children dream about in spite of their lack of training and experience. There is no formal way of finding such people, but consider this a word to the wise about degree snobbery.

All your teachers — from the completely inexperienced to the M.A. degree holder — should not only like children, but should be enthusiastic about helping children follow their naturally curious, questioning, exploring, creative natures. We call this their "teaching approach," the basis for the more specific elements of their teaching.

c) Education and Experience. While having the right approach toward teaching and the innate characteristics that make a good teacher are very important, the emphasis on the personal characteristics of preschool teachers tends to obscure the fact that a great deal of knowledge is also necessary in order to be a good teacher. The crucial areas of knowledge are:

1. A theoretical knowledge of child growth and development: an understanding of the needs and capabilities of children, and of how children grow, develop, and learn. It is extremely helpful for example, to have a working knowledge of Piaget, the noted Swiss developmental psychologist, so that children's stages of development can be a positive guide in developing appropriate curricula.

2. Curriculum: a practical knowledge of how different games, objects, and activities can meet the children's needs and capabilities.

3. Teaching techniques: an understanding of how to work with children; a sensitivity to their needs, their moods; an ability to direct a group.

All of these can be learned through experience to some extent, but a theoretical background in child growth and development and curriculum can only help a teacher. Many aspects of good teaching which seem to be intuitive, such as sensitivity to the needs of individual children or spontaneous and creative approaches to using materials with children, can be developed and improved through education and experience.

The ideal teacher would have an intuitive sensitivity and enthusiasm for working with children; experience in a classroom which has given her/him confidence and poise, a personal knowledge of how to introduce and work with materials; an understanding of what children can learn at various ages and how they can be encouraged and helped to do so; and a formal educational background in child growth and development which provides the insight to interpret and learn from practical experience.

d) Classroom staffing patterns.   An optimal staffing pattern for a classroom would have a head teacher with a master's degree in child growth and development and several years of teaching experience. The other teachers would have college degrees in a variety of fields relevant to preschool teaching ranging from child growth and development to art, or they would have a great deal of experience in working in group programs for preschool children.

A less than optimal staffing pattern can take a great variety of forms, but there are some limits. When supervision of other teaching staff is involved, it is necessary rather than helpful that the supervisor have a working knowledge of early childhood education, and the procedures and techniques of putting that knowledge to work in an effective program. Therefore, the head teacher should have a good educational background, preferably an M.A. or A.B. in child growth and development, and substantial experience so that she/he can supervise less experienced assistant teachers and improve their skills. The teachers may have no formal credentials or experience, their major qualification being an interest in preschool teaching and your sense that they have the potential to become good teachers. With good head teachers and a good training program *(See the chapter on Training)* this pattern can work well.

The Hiring Process

Hiring will be very subjective, based on your expectations about both teaching approach and personal background. Nevertheless, we can give you suggestions about how to structure the hiring process and about what to do during the interview.

The interviewers should be people with the most responsibility for the program and with the most knowledge about preschool education. The Director should certainly be part of this procedure. Head teachers should be hired first so that they can participate in hiring the rest of the teaching staff.

Ideally, more than one person should interview each applicant. Since the personality of the prospective teacher will be important, it is risky for one person to make a judgment alone (a bad mood, for example, or a bad start to the interview could erroneously color one's opinion).

For the same reason, it is a good idea for applicants to make repeated visits (at least two).

1. If applicants are "performing" for you, it will be difficult to keep up the false front during repeated visits.

2. You can reinforce your positive feelings if they remain unaltered after several visits.

3. Generally an applicant will feel more comfortable and therefore articulate ideas and present a natural self more readily after the first visit.

4. Important ideas overlooked in the first interview will be remembered and handled later.

5. The applicant can benefit too by having more than one chance to assess your program and decide if that is what he or she is looking for.

Interview as many applicants as you can. The first applicant may seem perfect or awful, but after several interviews with other people, he or she may very well take on an entirely new complexion.

If the Director is in the position of having to hire a head teacher but has no background in preschool education herself, it is wise to do a little homework first. A good method is to spend some days or weeks observing existing day care centers or nursery schools and talking to the teachers. This is the best way to be aware of the variety of classrooms and teachers and to help define the kind of program and teaching approaches your program will have.

If many program decisions are going to be left to the teachers once they are hired, the Director must be clear about what the center's program will be. For example, the kind of curriculum each classroom has is a potential source of stress and conflict among staff unless there is careful consideration before staff is hired so that hiring can be done with an eye towards harmony (not necessarily homogeneity) of ideas. Questions the Director might ask before hiring a teaching staff would include:

1. How autonomous do I want my head teachers to be?
2. How strongly do I feel about any given approach to teaching and curriculum?
3. How much do I want the head teachers to think as I do?
4. Which curriculum approach do I feel can be within our financial means?
5. Is there any teaching approach I cannot accept?

The more you limit the finances and program, the more carefully you must select teachers. It is worthwhile to spend a long time to be sure of your answers to these questions and of your staff's ability to fulfill the needs you have. Frustration, in-house bickering, and disappointment can easily result from a staff with contradictory expectations of one another. Moreover, the task of solving difficulties as they arise will be infinitely more pleasant if there is harmony with respect to the expectations of all staff members towards one another.

One good interview technique is to pose hypothetical problems to a prospective teacher. For example, the questions "What would you do about a boy who is very shy and tends to just sit in the corner?" or, "What would you do about a little boy who receives a good deal of abuse at home and acts out his violent feelings in the classroom by throwing toys?" would elicit the applicant's feelings about discipline, the objectives of a preschool program, and his or her attitudes toward children in general.

The subject of discipline (what methods would you use, when is it warranted, what is its object) should be raised as a way of learning an applicant's general philosophy along a curve of authoritarianism and permissiveness. Ask applicants to discuss their views explicitly, taking as much time as necessary to be sure you understand each other and to make your expectations clear.

Ask the applicant to plan a typical day for you. This would immediately tell you how structured the classroom would be, and how the teacher perceives his or her relationship to the children (is the day full of group activities which he or she supervises, or is it less planned, with the teacher interacting with individuals or spontaneous groups). It would also tell you something about the applicant's theory and knowledge of curriculum. Ask the applicant why he or she has included specific activities. (But remember it is often easier for someone to articulate a philosophy than to put it into practice.) Always make every effort to see the applicant teach. If necessary, ask teachers elsewhere if you may use their class as an interview laboratory.

If the applicant has had formal education in child growth and development, ask what or who influenced her/him the most. Why? Ask the same question about experiences working with preschool children. The answers should help you understand the applicant's philosophy and approach.

If the applicant feels as you do about various questions, but is observed to teach below expectations, at least you will know that self-improvement goals will complement your expectations.

Finally, make the interview as relaxing, pleasant, and free of threat and tension as you can.

How Many Teachers Do you Need?
In order to decide how many teachers you need to hire, you must decide what your teacher-child ratio will be and how many hours teachers will work in the classroom.

Teacher-child ratio: how many teachers will you have for how many children? As indicated in the chapter on Rules and Regulations, we find that a high-quality program requires considerably lower teacher-child ratios than most states demand, although we think the federal interagency ratios can be raised if some professional staff are used. When ratios are too high the quality of the relationships between children and teachers suffers. Teachers are unable to spend time with children individually or in small groups because supervisory demands prohibit it. Similarly the quality of the educational and developmental benefits suffers because personal interaction between teacher and children for instruction, attention, or just conversation is reduced to times of necessity only.

The actual program cannot help but suffer, too. Teachers have less time to observe their children or to be aware of changing environmental needs, to say nothing of responding to those needs, when such difficult demands are made on their time.

The ratios we have found best and which we suggest, are as follows:

children age 22 months to 3 years: 1:5 teacher-child ratio

children age 3 years: 1:5 — 1:8

children age 4 and 5 years: 1:8 — 1:10

with the range depending upon the skill and experience of the teachers.

While we emphasize that state rules and regulations generally require too few teachers in the classroom, we also want to point out that too many teachers are also a hazard. Not only do such circumstances make a classroom too adult centered, they also dilute the coordination possibilities in planning, the extent to which independence can be effectively encouraged among children, and the development of peer relationships. With the exception of very young children, a teacher-child ratio lower than 1:5 leads to these disadvantages.

How Many Hours Will the Teachers Work in the Classroom? There is not much precedent, since practically all preschool programs have been half-day or school day (9 to 3) programs. There is some consensus that six hours in the classroom is a good limit. Working with young children demands so much energy and so much attention that in the seventh hour the teacher is often exhausted and irritable. And teachers need time to plan for the next day, to do research on curriculum or particular subjects that interest the children, to meet with other staff, attend workshops and other kinds of training sessions, order new supplies, and to think and evaluate. Most jobs have built into them some thinking time. But the preschool teacher doesn't have a moment to step out of complete involvement within the classroom unless that time is deliberately built into the schedule. Therefore, we suggest a seven-hour work day, with six hours in the classroom and one hour devoted to planning.

Of course, you are not limited to hiring full-time teachers, and can arrange for part-time schedules. But in order to know how many teachers you must hire, you need to determine the maximum time any one teacher will be in the classroom.

To calculate how many teachers you will need to hire use the following formula:

$$\frac{(\text{No. hours center is open}) \ (\text{No. teachers in class at one time})}{\text{Maximum no. hours each teacher can work in the classroom}}$$

equals the number of teachers you need.

In other words, you calculate the total number of teaching hours required, and divide by the number of hours one teacher can work. For a center which is open for ten hours each day and has one classroom of two-year-olds, one classroom of three's, and one classroom of four- and five-year-olds, with twenty children in each, the number of teachers required would be as follows:

1. two's: staff ratio is 1:5

$$\text{No. teachers} = \frac{(10)\,(4)}{6} = \frac{40}{6} = 6\frac{2}{3}$$

2. Three's: staff ratio is 1:8

$$\text{No. teachers} = \frac{(10)\,(2.5)}{6} = \frac{25}{6} = 4 \text{ (the extra hour can be ignored)}$$

3. Four's and five's: staff ratio is 1:10

$$\text{No. teachers} = \frac{(10)\,(2)}{6} = \frac{20}{6} = 3\frac{1}{3}$$

The center would need to hire the equivalent of 14 full-time teachers.

TEACHER TRAINING

Introduction
In the United States today there is a severe lack of trained personnel qualified to staff day care programs. The problem is becoming more and more acute as the need for child care services increases.

In other countries where child care services have been well established for many years, only those with professional qualifications are allowed to care for young children in day care programs. In Denmark, the day nursery system has been operative for eighty years. *Vuggestue* is the name of centers caring for children three months to three years in age.

A head teacher is in charge of each classroom. All head teachers are educators who have completed a special college program for preschool teachers. Their training program is as follows:

- 3 months: college classes (child growth and development, child psychology, educational curriculum, etc.)
- 6 months: apprenticeship in a nursery school
- 6 months: hospital pediatric aide
- 3 months: college classes
- 6 months: "au pair" (home care of children)
- 6 months: apprenticeship in kindergarten class
- 3 months: college classes
- Comprehensive examination

Children age three to seven are cared for in *Bornhaven* centers where a head teacher is in charge of each classroom. All head teachers are educators who have completed three years of a special college program for kindergarten teachers and have served an apprenticeship of six months in a child care center. Assistant teachers are educators who have completed their college work and are serving their apprenticeship.

In Sweden, *Barnstuga* is the name given to day care centers. There are two classifications for teachers who work with children in the *Barnstuga*. The child care nurses have taken a six-to-eight-month training program which prepares them to care for very young children. The primary school teachers go to college for two years, then spend a four-year internship before they are qualified teachers. The child care nurses mainly work with children under the age of three, while the primary teachers work mainly with children over the age of three.

Day care services have been available to children in France for almost a hundred years. As in Sweden, France has two classifications for personnel working with children. Child nurses care for children under the age of three. They are called auxiliary puericulturist and have taken a two-year vocational training program. At three, children receive instruction from regular primary school teachers who have been specially educated at college for this purpose.

Finally, in Yugoslavia, preschool teachers are in charge of all classrooms for children in day care centers. These teachers have completed four years of secondary school plus two years of college. In the creches (for children between two months and three years in age), a child care nurse assists the teacher. Child care nurses have completed three years of secondary professional school.

Thus, in many other countries preschool teachers have professional status and extensive training and are available to staff new programs. In the United States, however, trained personnel are scarce. Therefore, you will have to create your own program to train your teaching staff.

Teacher Training Techniques

Since the traditional four-year college program for educating preschool teachers will be unable to fill the demand for day care personnel (and there is some question as to whether this is the most appropriate education for child care), college early-childhood education programs will not be discussed in this chapter on training. A list of such programs can be found in the Appendices, pages 283-287, and inquiries regarding the teacher education program offered can be made directly to the college or university.

While a few states require directors and head teachers in day care to be professionals with early-childhood education backgrounds, most have minimal requirements for preschool teachers. Thus, it will be mainly up to you to provide the appropriate training experience necessary to suit your partic-ular needs and the needs of your staff.

We will describe several different training techniques and then discuss how they may be combined into training programs. For purposes of simplification, we have divided teaching staff into two categories. Professionals are defined as those teachers with a college degree, whether it be an associate in arts (2 years), bachelor's (4 years), or master's degree (1 or 2 years of graduate study). Nonprofessionals are categorized as those having less than degree status. (*See Appendices, page 292, Training Program Models.*)

Since teaching staff will have a wide range of skills and varying backgrounds, it is impossible to describe one appro-priate training program for all the various categories, person-nel variables, and program components you may want to meet. Thus it is up to you to take a look at your program needs, staff, and budget and decide for whom training is necessary and for what purpose.

Regardless of the qualifications or expertise of your teaching staff, there are three basic training techniques which should be part of any program which cares for young children. These three basic components are staff meetings, supervision, and workshops.

Staff Meetings

Staff meetings are fundamental to the successful operation of
your day care center. It is through such meetings that good
communications are established. The real strength of your
center, the harmony, the atmosphere, can be developed
through working cooperatively at staff meetings and solving
problems together.

All staff, whether professional or nonprofessional need
to be involved in staff meetings. If well planned, such
meetings are perhaps the most efficient and effective method
of in-service training.

Objectives of staff meetings
1. To provide a definite time for sharing and communi-
   cating relevant information
2. To discuss current problems and difficulties regarding
   the program and its administration
3. To formulate plans for solving such problems
4. To increase the staff's understanding of individual
   children
5. To create an interdisciplinary approach to problem
   solving
6. To develop an atmosphere of cooperation and harmony

Program Format Weekly staff meetings are essential for
accomplishing the above objectives. It is important that such
meetings be scheduled and well planned. Meetings should
start and end on time; long, drawn-out meetings should
definitely be avoided. Such meetings usually indicate a lack
of organization and planning, and are destructive to staff
morale because they waste time. It is better to have a one- to
two-hour meeting each week than to attempt to accomplish a
month's work in one long session.

We suggest you devote about one third to one half of
the staff meeting to discussion of current difficulties or
problems having to do with the program and its administration. All staff meetings should be recorded in summary form,
and problems, recommendations, procedures, and suggestions
recorded and followed up.

The rest of the meeting should be centered around a discussion of individual children, their needs, and staff suggestions for understanding and handling such children.

Meetings should be conducted in quiet, informal surroundings so staff can feel relaxed and comfortable. If meetings are scheduled to last over an hour, it is wise to take a short break midway and relax over a cup of coffee or tea. Such a break is well worth the time and money if it refreshes and helps the staff to contribute to the remaining discussion.

A suggested format for staff meetings is as follows:

1. Review of last meeting
2. Follow-up reports
3. Notices, announcements
4. Discussion of current problems, difficulties
5. Suggestions and recommendations
                    Break
6. Teacher presentation of one child for discussion or general discussion of several children
7. Suggestions for handling problems
8. Summary review of meeting and reminder of next session

Personnel Involved.   Attendance at weekly sessions depends upon the hour of the meeting, number of staff available, and whether or not auxiliary service personnel are part of the day care program. Minimally, attendance is required of all head teachers and supervisor or director if she/he is responsible for daily ongoing program operation. If the meeting is held during the day, as many assistant teachers should attend as possible and still have children adequately supervised. There should be a rotating schedule so every assistant teacher has the opportunity to attend staff meetings as often as the rotation makes feasible.

If auxiliary personnel (nurse, doctor, social worker, psychiatrist, etc.) are attached to the program, they should be scheduled to attend when individual children are presented for case discussion. Often they will be the ones to present such cases and the knowledge gained from discussion with other members of the multi-disciplined team (teachers, other auxiliary personnel, etc.) can prove most valuable for all.

Supervision
The ongoing supportive relationship between the supervisor and each teacher is important for personal growth and the development of increasing skills as a teacher. Objective evaluation and constructive criticism are essential elements in learning. Thus, if teachers are to grow in their abilities to work with young children, they need guidance and assistance.

Both nonprofessionals and professionals alike need supportive supervision, for one never reaches the point of knowing all. A skilled supervisor can do much to increase one's self-awareness and understanding. Therefore, supervision is essential for all staff caring for young children.

Objectives of Supervision
1. To periodically observe and evaluate teachers' working with children in the classroom
2. To discuss observations with teacher, offering support and constructive criticism
3. To help teacher work more effectively with young children through developing a better understanding of self
4. To develop a cooperative plan with teacher for strengthening weak areas
5. To note improvement in areas needing work

Supervision Format. In order for supervision to be truly helpful, it must be perceived by the teachers as a learning tool rather than as a means of passing judgment on performance. A supervisor gains an impression of a teacher during the brief daily attendance rounds necessary to insure adequate staffing. However, such spot impressions should never be used for evaluation purposes without the support of sustained periodic observations.

If the supervisor acts in a supportive rather than a punitive manner in the daily contacts with staff, teachers will see her/him as a helpful person to whom one can turn when there is a question to be answered or a problem to be solved.

The supervisor should try to arrange to observe each classroom at least once a week for no less than one hour. Observation notes should be discussed with the teaching staff that day, if possible, or as soon afterwards as is feasible.

Written evaluations based upon brief daily and extensive weekly observations and discussions should be submitted periodically. For new teaching staff we suggest written evaluations should be done once during the first three months, again at six months, and periodically every six months thereafter. All staff should receive biannual evaluations. *(See Appendices, pages 288-9, Teacher Evaluation Form, for suggested areas to be included in a teacher evaluation.)*

Personnel Involved. The supervisor or program director is responsible for all ongoing supervision of program operation and evaluation of all day care teaching staff. Through brief daily and longer scheduled observations of teaching performance, the supervisor offers constructive criticism and assists staff in drawing up plans for improvement.

Head teachers may be asked to evaluate their assistant teachers and work with the supervisor in developing plans for increasing teaching skills.

Workshops
Workshops provide an opportunity for teachers to broaden their practical skills and teaching techniques by giving them firsthand experience with a wide range of curriculum materials and teaching styles. Teachers then can create a more varied and stimulating environment for the children.

Workshops will vary in content, focus, and design depending upon the interests and expertise of your staff, and the variety of consultants used. We are defining workshops at this point as mainly one-shot sessions geared to dispersing information to all staff regardless of professional qualifications. In addition, while workshops may cover many areas and topics, we will discuss only those which deal directly with curriculum.

Objectives of Workshops
1.   To provide teaching staff with firsthand experience with a wide range of teaching techniques and a variety of different materials
2.   To help teachers develop an understanding and appreciation of the creative arts so they can provide creative experiences for young children in their classrooms
3.   To assist teachers in developing specific teaching skills in basic curriculum areas

Format for Workshops.   It is difficult to find a time when all staff are available to meet. During the day, children must be supervised and too many night meetings are unwelcome no matter how interesting and informative they might be. One solution to this problem is to have the same workshop given twice. Morning staff could then participate in afternoon sessions and vice versa. However, this can become very expensive if paid consultants are used for such workshops.

Another   solution is to alternate paid consultant workshops and staff workshop presentations. Still another might be to have the paid consultant come to a night meeting for all staff once a month but have center staff prepare workshops for double presentation during the day.

The workshop sessions will therefore depend upon the needs and interests of your particular center. You need to decide: What time is scheduling possible? What kinds of workshops do your staff want? What workshops do you feel would be most beneficial? How much money can you spend on consultant services?

We   suggest you have one consultant workshop and one staff workshop presentation per month. Under the general heading, "Preparing the Teacher: Equipment and Material as Tools for Learning," the following topics might be covered:

1.   Art experiences
2.   Blocks
3.   Carpentry
4.   Childrens' literature
5.   Creative movement and dance
6.   Language skills
7.   Math
8.   Music and singing
9.   Nature
10.   Science
11.   Social studies

Personnel Involved.   Workshops are helpful to teaching staff as they often stimulate new ideas and give practical advice and experience in specific curriculum areas. In addition, such sessions may help teachers gain self-awareness as well as additional insight into children and their feelings and behavior. Hopefully, the combination of added understanding and concrete teaching skills will make staff better teachers of young children.

If your staff is mainly professional, many workshops could be conducted by them, drawing on their special knowledge and skills. In this instance, consultants would only be needed for those areas which could not be handled by available staff expertise.

However, if your staff is mainly nonprofessional and/or inexperienced, staff presentations will come mainly from the supervisor and/or director, any auxiliary personnel attached to the day care center, and outside consultants. Therefore, one can see that the more nonprofessional and inexperienced the staff at your center, the higher the costs of training that staff will be.

The preceding basic training techniques of staff meetings, supervision, and workshops, while the most important, are not the only methods for training preschool teachers. There are several additional optional techniques you may wish to employ in your particular program.

Group Discussion

The group discussion method is one of the most effective ways of teaching theoretical subject matter. This method allows for ease in discussion, question, and translation of theoretical content to applied, relevant examples. Therefore, group discussions should help to establish the theoretical framework for understanding children and the particular role teachers play in developing children's learning.

Objectives of Group Discussion
1. To interrelate theoretical-content material and direct, practical experience
2. To assist teachers in learning to understand children's feelings and how they affect behavior
3. To discover methods for helping children:
   a. Adjust to new experiences
   b. Learn through problem-solving
   c. Build feelings of security and competence.
4. To help teachers learn how to define and maintain limits and deal with behavior problems
5. To help teachers understand the importance of involving parents and the means for working cooperatively with them

Format for Group Discussion.   The actual content of group discussions will depend upon the interests, needs, experience, and background knowledge of your particular teaching staff. Group discussions are most meaningful when they are held regularly for a period of one to two hours once a week.

While there is no set format for such discussion-group sessions, we have found it helpful to begin with a brief history of child care and then delve into a discussion of the particular concerns regarding children voiced by your group. You then can begin to provide theoretical background knowledge in those areas of concern and link some of the most important theories of early childhood growth and development to actual examples provided by the group.

In addition, the group may wish to have various

consultants come and speak with them further on specific areas. For example:

1. Understanding children's feelings and behavior: (teacher, social worker, nurse, psychologist, psychiatrist, pediatrician)
   a. Relationship of self-understanding to understanding children
   b. Development of self-awareness, self-image, and self-concept in children
   c. Understanding behavior problems in children and how to handle them
   d. Principles of child development: the whole child — his physical, emotional, intellectual, and social needs
   e. Learning how to observe and interpret behavior in children
   f. Mental health aspects of child care

2. Other Topics:
   a. Medical care needs of children and basic first aid procedures (doctor, nurse)
   b. Parent-teacher relations (teacher, social worker)
   c. Means of promoting good oral hygiene and preventive dental care in day care centers (dentist, hygienist)
   d. Cognitive development: theory and research (teacher, psychologist)
   e. Comparing and contrasting educational philosophies (teacher)
   f. How to provide for individual differences in the classroom (teacher)
   g. Community relations (teacher, social worker, parent)
   h. Nutritional needs of children (nutritionist, dietitian, nurse)

Thus you can see some of the topics which could be

explored in group discussion. The actual content of the discussion is up to you and should be based on your particular staff needs and the kind of training program you wish to develop.

Personnel Involved. The discussion group includes the supervisor or director and those staff interested in learning more about children. While professional staff may attend, usually the group consists of the more inexperienced staff members, who are often anxious to learn more about child growth and development in order to apply such knowledge to practical experience in the classroom. Sometimes additional consultation may be sought for specific content areas.

Individual Conferences
It is important for there to be an ongoing, consistent relationship between the teacher and her/his supervisor, as this relationship provides an opportunity for true personalization of the program. Individual conferences provide the occasion to discuss with a trusted person any problems the teacher may be having and to integrate her/his past experiences as a child, adult, and perhaps as a parent into the present situation. Such an opportunity to explore problems develops self-awareness and understanding so cruicial for understanding children and interpreting their behavior.

Objectives of Individual Conferences
1. To help teacher gain awareness and understanding of self
2. To understand how one's feelings affect relationships with others
3. To receive support for maximal personal development
4. To help the teacher become aware of her/his strengths and weaknesses
5. To help the individual teacher evaluate her/his progress
6. To help inexperienced teachers develop their own natural teaching style and approach to young children

Format for Individual Conferences.   In order to establish a truly supportive relationship, individual conferences must be regularly scheduled. We suggest weekly conferences of one-half to one hour in length as the optimal period necessary to sustain a relationship of this sort. If too much time elapses between conferences, too many problems will have come and gone without the opportunity to work them out together.

Personnel Involved. The very personalized nature of this method naturally limits the personnel involved. The teacher and either her/his advisor, supervisor, or director are the only two persons participating in the individual conference.

Observation

Observing and recording techniques are important skills for teachers to learn as they provide one means of assessing individual children. Teachers who learn to be good observers of children are usually in the position to better understand children's behavior and to handle such behavior appropriately.

Objectives of Observation
1. To develop the technical skills necessary for observing and recording the behavior of young children
2. To learn how to interpret such observations of behavior
3. To gain better understanding of children and their needs.

Format for Observation. It is important for teachers to take time to observe children. Often in the effort to keep activities going in the classroom, teachers forget to set aside time to watch just what is happening. All too often one hears the complaint: "What an awful day! I just don't know what went wrong!" It is important for the well-being of the children, as well as the teachers, to be able to decide what it is that makes a day or a child "go bad," and equally important, "go well."

Only by setting time aside for regular observations of children can a teacher begin to gain insight and true understanding of their needs.

We have found that both numerous, short observations and longer, sustained observations are important. Each teacher should keep a logbook of observations on each child. While it is not necessary to record something about each child every day, there should be at least a weekly summary statement with specific illustrative examples. Not only is such a logbook helpful when it comes time to complete the periodic child evaluation form, but more importantly, it helps teachers be aware of the needs of individual children. For only through understanding how an individual child sees his world and responds to it can a teacher begin to provide for individual needs.

Personnel Involved.   Teachers, supervisors, directors, are all interested in young children at their center. However, since teachers are mainly responsible for daily child care, observation is an especially important technique for them to learn. As part of their education, most professional teachers learn how to observe young children. Therefore, it will be mainly inexperienced, nonprofessional teaching staff who need to learn observation skills and how to interpret behavior.

Field Trips

Field trips are an important means of discovering differences in teaching techniques and use of classroom space and materials. In addition, they enable teachers to see how children function in a variety of settings, and often stimulate ideas and promote needed program improvement.

Objectives of Field Trips
1.   To observe a variety of child care settings which stress varying goals for young children
2.   To contrast and evaluate these different settings for child care
3.   To gain new ideas for program improvement

Format for Field Trips.   If possible, teachers should observe other centers once a month. By staggering the scheduling for such visits, each teacher will have the opportunity to see the same setting, and your center will not be short of personnel.

Personnel Involved. It is important for all day care personnel, and especially for teachers, to have the opportunity to take field trips to other centers. Teachers need new ideas for their classroom, and field trips often provide the needed stimulation for exciting program change.

Inexperienced teaching staff need to view a variety of child care programs so they can see there is no one "right way" of teaching. Teaching style is dependent upon individual personality characteristics, values, and program focus.

Programs
We have presented a variety of different training techniques, three which we feel are basic for any good training program, and the rest optional. Now it is up to you to put these various training techniques into a program which best suits your particular needs.

There are two training models you ought to consider for this purpose. First is an in-service program which serves as general enrichment for all staff regardless of their experience or education. The second is a far more specific program of on-the-job training for inexperienced, nonprofessional staff to prepare them to be teachers.

In-Service Training Program
The main objective for in-service training is enrichment. The particular in-service program you develop at your center will depend upon the length of time you wish to allot for enrichment, the range of qualifications of your staff, the level of expertise within your training staff, and the amount of money you can spend on this program.

In-service training programs involve two possible components: theory and practical application. For purposes of discussion, we have separated these components into two areas with suggested time allotments for each. However, both are interrelated, and it is impossible to explore one area without drawing on the other. Therefore, it will be up to you to put these two components into the most meaningful program for you and your staff.

We suggest you spend approximately one-quarter of whatever time you have allotted for in-service training on theoretical subject matter. Such content material provides the formal background for understanding children and how they learn. We feel such content material can best be presented through the use of group discussions. In this way all staff can share information and learn from each other.

The ability to put ideas into practice and to use materials constructively with children is extremely important. Therefore, we suggest you allot three quarters of your program to practical application. Through field trips and workshops in various curriculum areas, theory can be related and applied to daily classroom activities. A general series of field trips to other day care centers, as well as observation of your own center, and exposure to curriculum and program ideas and materials, should be the major components in these training sessions.

The personnel involved in your particular in-service training program will depend upon your staff, their needs and particular qualifications, as well as the availability of outside resources and the money you have to pay for such consultation.

If your staff is mostly inexperienced, you will need a competent, well-qualified supervisor to direct and carry out the program. Your supervisor needs to be especially well qualified if there are no outside consultation services available or resources, if available, are too expensive for your center to afford. Some professionals are willing to donate their time, but this is a very individual matter. Often it will be necessary for the director, and/or supervisor to design and teach as many of the component areas as possible with assistance from any auxiliary service personnel attached to the day care program. Professionals from a variety of disciplines — child study, dentistry, pediatrics, nursing, psychology, psychiatry, and social work — should be asked to conduct seminars and workshop sessions whenever possible. Helpful suggestions can also be obtained through the use of pertinent books.

On-The-Job Training Program

On-the-job training programs offer a possible solution to the shortage of trained personnel available for child care today. Through this model, every day care center could be a potential source of training inexperienced personnel to be preschool teachers.

If you decide you would like to and are able to provide on-the-job training at your center, we have included some suggestions you may find helpful. However, your program will depend upon your particular needs and resources.

The objectives of on-the-job training are twofold: to provide staff development and increased promotional opportunities to nonprofessional teaching personnel; and to increase the teaching manpower qualified to work with young children. Thus, on-the-job training will help your center provide a higher quality of care for children through upgrading skills of inexperienced teaching staff.

To be truly effective, an on-the-job training program must be well planned and competently administered, for on-the-job training is more than a series of enrichment experiences for staff. It is a planned program of instruction aimed at preparing untrained personnel for teaching. As such, it must have a basic organization of learning experiences and regularly scheduled sessions to provide instruction.

In order to help staff develop into truly successful teachers, there must be a warm, supportive training atmosphere which encourages self-awareness and understanding in personal development. Through the use of supervision and individual conferences, such understanding can be accomplished. Teacher-trainees should be encouraged to develop their own natural style and approach in teaching young children. Ultimately each teacher must decide which teaching concepts, methods, and attitudes are most meaningful to her/him. Thus, while actual teaching skills and the mastery of subject matter are important, the most essential aspect of good on-the-job training for teaching involves the personal growth of the individual teacher. It is only when teachers feel comfortable with themselves, and are sensitive and understanding, that they can become good teachers. Therefore, we suggest that a good on-the-job training program will provide for weekly teacher-trainee supervision and individual conferences with the supervisor.

It is also important to provide trainees with the theoretical framework necessary for understanding child growth and development. We feel that group discussions are the best means of relating formal theory to practical situations. Not only should such discussions be scheduled routinely, at least once a week, but the actual content should be organized in some meaningful fashion. One area of learning should be relevant to and proceed logically on to the next.

There are many ways of accomplishing this task. One is to start with the newborn child, or even prenatally, and follow him/her through the preschool years. This direction can be reversed by starting with the preschool child and working back over the years to see how he got to that point. Whatever seems to be the most logical starting point for you and your teacher-trainees is where you should begin.

Teacher-trainees also need to have experience using equipment and materials as tools for learning. Workshop sessions best serve this function and should be conducted weekly. Additional information and curriculum ideas may be obtained through observation of other classrooms and visits to other child care centers. If at all possible, there should be either one observation or one field trip assignment per week.

If you wish to provide a quality on-the-job training program to ten or more teacher-trainees, you will need to hire a competent educational supervisor specifically for that purpose. However, if your program has only a few trainees, perhaps a skillful director or supervisor can organize her/his time to include such a training component. The less the expertise of your trainees and training staff (director, supervisor, other teachers, etc.), the more you will have to draw upon consultative services, and the more expensive your training program will be.

Another personnel variable to consider is the kind of staff coverage you will provide when trainees are given release time for training sessions. Do you have volunteers, parents, student teachers, who might be available to care for children during these times, or will you have to hire part-time staff to arrange such coverage?

Training Program with College Credit and/or Release Time for Courses

The most comprehensive and expensive training program you can offer is one which provides a college-accredited training program and specific steps for trainees to attain degree status while employed at your center. This program involves an extremely well-qualified training staff, as such staff must have college faculty appointments in order for the courses they teach to be accredited. In addition, your center must be located near a college or university which offers a program in early-childhood education, and the college must be willing to give credit to courses taught at your center and agree to allow your trainees to be part-time students in their program while employed there.

Finally, there must be a long-term commitment for such training on the part of the individual trainee, the affiliated college or university, and your particular center so that teacher-trainees can follow through for at least several years in order to attain a degree status.

Since we have developed such a training program in conjunction with Wheelock College at our Career Development Laboratory in Boston, we will explain how our program works. We hope this explanation will give you some ideas of how you might develop this kind of training program at your own center.

The objectives of our training program are: to institute a "new careers" program that would enable men and women with no formal training, education, or experience in the field of child care to become competent preschool teachers; to begin to meet the need for high-quality day care staff in a period of unprecedented need for day care; to provide a ladder of career advancement for trainees who are interested in pursuing higher education; to provide college credit for training courses taught by staff at our center; and to make provisions for continuing education at Wheelock College for trainees who have successfully completed our training program.

The Career Development Laboratory provides a ten-month training program for preschool teachers in day care. The program is divided into two semesters, and follows the Boston public school calendar for holidays and vacation schedules. Thus trainees can be home with their school-age children during vacation times. All preschool children of trainees are enrolled in our day care center if they need such a service, thus eliminating many problems surrounding child care.

Our training program runs approximately eight hours a day, five days a week, for ten months, minus school vacations. Trainees are expected to attend daily, and records of attendance are kept. We feel regular attendance is vital for the successful completion of our program, and it is required for college course credit from Wheelock. *(See Appendices, pages 290-291, for Training Schedule.)*

From our experience we have formulated three basic courses which can best be taught at a child care center. The first major area, student teaching, provides a supervised learning experience for each trainee, working in our class-rooms with groups of children ranging in age from infancy to six years old. The importance of such practical experience with children cannot be overemphasized, for it is in the actual working with children that all supplementary skills are developed. We have found that daily teaching in the classroom is important for sustaining relationships with children. Students, therefore, are in the classrooms teaching two to four hours every day.

The second major area is child growth and development,

which provides theoretical background for the actual work experience. In Part One, Formative Years, the growth and development of a child is explored from the earliest prenatal influences through various preschool experiences. Part Two explores the behavior and learning problems of childhood. Through teaching the child growth and development course at our day care center, the practical experience derived in the classroom during student teaching can be directly related to theory. *(See Appendices, pages 293-303, for attached course outlines.)*

The third major component we feel especially relevant for on-site teaching in day care is that of curriculum workshops. These provide practice opportunities for trainees to experiment with materials under the supervision of expert consultants and staff members. All basic areas of preschool programs are discussed, and techniques for teaching each area are explored. *(See Appendices, pages 304-306, for attached schedule of Curriculum Workshops.)*

We have found these three areas — student teaching, child growth and development, and curriculum workshops — to be the essential components of a good preschool teacher training program at a day care center. You may wish to include additional courses in your training program, such as creative movement, art, mathematics, and children's literature, but these should supplement rather than replace the basic training program elements.

After graduation from our program, trainees have been offered assistant teaching positions within our day care centers and are encouraged, while employed, to pursue six credits a semester in the Supplementary Training Program at Wheelock College. We give release time for such career development and supplement staffing in the classrooms with student teachers from other universities, parents, volunteers, and part-time teaching staff.

The steps leading to the 60 Point Certificate at Wheelock College include:

First year: 30 credits, Career Development Laboratory

Second year: 18 credits while employed, Wheelock College
Third year: 12 credits while employed, Wheelock College

In this way, we have maximized the opportunity for our trainees to become head teachers and to complete at least the certificate/degree requirements at Wheelock College.

At this time, trainees pay for all courses they take at Wheelock College. However, we are hoping to secure either scholarships or long-term funding for trainees interested in obtaining their degree. The first year of training at our center is funded by the Division of Employment Security, Work Incentive Program. *(See funding chapter on page 272, for details.)*

As we have a large training program (twenty-four new W.I.N. (Work Incentive) trainees a year) we have a number of full-time and part-time training staff, several of whom are classroom teachers as well. All training staff have Wheelock College faculty appointments.

If you decide to undertake such a training program, you will have to decide what existing center personnel you may be able to use for training staff and what personnel you will have to hire full- or part-time for this program. Depending upon the number of trainees in your program and the expertise of existing center staff, we feel a training program of such quality and complexity requires at least one additional full-time staff member, the training supervisor. She/he would be mainly responsible for coordinating all ongoing aspects of the training program and would be specifically assigned to supervise trainees' student teaching experience.

If you feel you are not able to undertake such an extensive training program at your center but still wish to provide a ladder of career advancement for staff who are interested in pursuing higher education, you should schedule release time for staff to pursue such courses on their own. The problem of classroom coverage during such release can be partially handled by careful scheduling so only one or two teachers are released for course studies at the same time. The other classroom teachers might be aided at such times by volunteers, parents, student teachers, or substitute part-time staff.

Funding remains a problem to staff taking college courses. If you are able, you might consider payment for educational courses to be part of employee fringe benefits. This, however, is very expensive, and unless you have a lot of money, probably not feasible. Another method is to accept student teachers from colleges and universities in the area. "Vouchers," which exchange one college course for placement of one student teacher, are usually given to the participating center by the college or university. Therefore, by accepting a number of student teachers, you are helping to train additional manpower for teaching, supplementing your teaching staff, and gaining free courses for your teachers desiring further education. Scholarships, fund-raising drives, and teachers' own payments of tuition are additional means of financing educational courses.

Summary

While the training models discussed in this chapter may not exactly fit your program needs, we hope they have provided at least some guidelines for developing your own training program. It is up to you to decide which model is most appropriate for your needs and to devise a program for training based on those needs and on the availability of resources.

Again we stress the importance for all centers to have some type of training program, not only to increase manpower for themselves, but also, indirectly, to increase the quality of care for children enrolled in day care centers throughout the country.

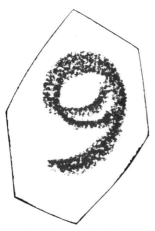

HEALTH AND SOCIAL SERVICES

Introduction

In addition to teaching functions provided by the day care center, there are certain special associated services which must be considered in order to protect the whole child and provide for his mental, social, emotional and physical well-being. These include: medical, dental, social, psychological, and nutritional care services. In each of these areas, the center can provide: (1) a minimal amount of service and leave most of the responsibility for care to the child's parents; (2) a maximum number of comprehensive services; or (3) some mode of service between these two extremes.

The choice of which model to follow will depend upon many factors: budget, availability of service staff, and the needs of the children and their parents. As the child center assumes the care of children for many hours each day, we believe it must help to take responsibility for the total well-being of each child. Therefore, in each area of service we will describe minimal, maximal, and modal provision models.

Rules and Regulations

Health standards in the United States are unevenly distributed. In some locations the Department of Public Health licenses day care centers. In others, the Department of Public Safety or the Department of Public Welfare may work separately or jointly with the Health Department regarding such licensing. Official inspection exists in some states; and a number of localities have written sanitary and building code regulations for centers providing day care to young children.

As rules and regulations governing health differ according to state, you must check your own state rules and regulations for minimum requirements of auxilary services.

Health and Medical Care Services

Minimal Provision Model
The Minimal Provision Model for medical care assumes that the health of the child in day care is the responsibility of the parents. Parents are expected to use their family doctor for health supervision and medical treatment of their child or else utilize such community resources as are available (well-child conference, hospital outpatient clinic, etc.). The major responsibility of the center is to maintain a healthy environment.

The minimal model for provision of health services is adequate where parents are willing and able to assume this responsibility, and where health care services are readily available. However, the minimal model provides a marginal health program where such services are either in short supply or not adequately utilized.

Responsibility of Parent
1. To secure for the child a complete preadmission examination from a private physician or public service agency. The record of this examination is filed at the center and should include:
    a. Complete health history
    b. Complete physical examination
    c. Record of immunizations given
    d. Formula or special dietary requirements when necessary
    e. Evaluative statement

2. To arrange for periodic medical examinations and insure that reports are forwarded to the center. Frequency of examinations depends on age of child and other special health considerations (rheumatic heart condition, etc.)

   a. Infants under one year, exam every three months
   b. One-to-five-year-olds, semi-annual check-ups
   c. Over five years, annual examination
   d. Special health conditions as determined by attending physician

3. To be sure all immunizations are up to date. This means the child must not only have received the original courses of injections, but also boosters at appropriate intervals. Most states require immunizations for the following, and some also require immunization against measles

   a. Smallpox
   b. Diphtheria
   c. Whooping cough
   d. Tetanus
   e. Poliomyelitis

4. To secure prompt medical attention for a sick child and to keep the child at home until he is entirely free from disease. This is for the protection of the sick child, as well as the other children in day care. Some states require a doctor's permission for readmission after recovery from certain communicable diseases. Check your rules and regulations regarding readmission requirements. Since the following symptoms are signs of possible impending infection or disease, or are contagious to other children, parents should exercise good judgment by seeking prompt medical attention for their child, keeping him home while he is ill, and not bringing him to the center to expose others

   a. Signs of a new cold: fever, cough, running nose, watery eyes, sore throat, etc.
   b. Diarrhea

    c.   Inflammation of the eyes (conjunctivitis)

    d.   Abscess

    e.   Draining sores or burns

    f.   Rash (until cause is diagnosed and determined noncontagious)

    g.   Headache or head pain

    h.   Vomiting

    i.   Loss of appetite

    j.   Excessive irritability or unusual passivity

5.   To secure a person whom the center may call in case of an emergency after attempts to locate parents are unsuccessful

Responsibility of Center

1.   To review all medical examinations and keep on file the name of each child's physician or health clinic used for continuing care. *(See Appendices, pages 307-314, Health Records.)*

2.   To observe each child when he arrives for symptoms of possible illness or contagious disease and send child home immediately with parent. However, if transportation is provided by the center, notify the parent and keep child in isolation until he can be taken home. *(See list of symptoms, No. 4 above)*

3.   To provide an isolation room for the child who presents symptoms of illness during the day. The child should remain excluded from the group until he can be taken home by his parents or until other arrangements can be made for his care.

4.   To arrange for emergency care of child as per agreement with parents. All centers should have a written plan for handling emergencies and injuries, and slips for emergency care of each child signed by his parents. Such a form should outline the procedure to be followed and include:

    a.   Name, home and business address of the parents and phone number where they can be reached

b. Name, address, and phone number of person to be notified in case of emergency when parents cannot be reached

c. Name, address and phone number of child's physician or clinic

d. Signed permission to bring child to a specified hospital in case of serious acute emergencies

5. To provide simple first aid treatment of injuries. During the hours of program operation, there should be at least one staff member familiar with basic first aid procedures. All injuries must be recorded and parents informed of the injury that same day *(See Appendix, Health Records)*

6. To secure all first aid materials in a locked cabinet. Suggested first aid supplies and equipment; amount depends on size of center:

a. Ointments: Rhulicream, Vaseline

b. Surgical supplies: bandage scissors, sterilizing basin with cover, pickup forceps

c. Dressings: sterile cotton, Ace bandage, gauze squares, assorted widths of roller gauze, cotton-tipped applicators, assorted widths adhesive tape, assorted-sized Band-Aids

d. Solutions: calamine lotion (USP), pHisoHex, alchohol 70%, hydrogen peroxide, aqueous Zephiran

e. miscellaneous: scale, ice bag, thermometers, etc.

7. To give medications to a child when necessary (diabetic or epileptic child, for example) only on written order from a physician. Such medications must be labeled with the child's name, name of the drug, and directions for its administration. All medications should be stored in the locked first aid cabinet and discarded or returned to parents when no longer needed

8. To ensure all staff personnel are in good health.

   a.   Before beginning employment, and every year thereafter, each staff member should receive a physical examination and secure a health certificate signed by his physician. This certificate should state that the individual has been examined and that there is no apparent illness present which might adversely affect the children in care at the center. These certificates should be kept up to date and on file at the center

   b.   Before beginning work all staff personnel should submit an authorized report of negative intradermal tuberculin test. Chest X rays are contraindicated because of radiation buildup from periodic testing. Tests should be repeated every three years unless shorter intervals are medically indicated to determine freedom from tuberculosis in a communicable form

   c.   No staff member should work with children if he or she has an upper-respiratory infection, gastrointestinal illness, or other contagious disease

9. To ensure all staff follow sanitary procedures regarding the care of young children at the center

   a.   Available handwashing facilities should be well supplied with soap and disposable hand towels. Hands must be washed before handling each child under six months of age, and after and between such activities as changing a child and feeding him

   b.   There should be individual towels and washcloths for each child. Infants require two washcloths, one for face and one for bottom, unless disposable cloths are used and discarded after each use. All cloths and towels should be washed and dried daily.

      c.   Bed linens should be kept clean and changed regularly, and when soiled. Each child should use only his own bedding

      d.   Toys and equipment used by infants should be washed daily

      e.   All items used by sick children must be cleaned and disinfected before reuse

10.   To arrange for a physician to speak at the parents' meeting to explain some concepts of child growth and development and answer questions

Maximal Provision Model

The Maximal Provision Model provides total medical care to the children within the day care center and sometimes to the parents as well.

Various programs using this model have been established in the past and can be found in America today where day care centers are run in connection with factories, community health centers, or hospital clinics. At a tobacco factory in Jacksonville, Florida, a day care center for 154 children ranging in age from fourteen months to six years has been established for the children of employees. The center has an infirmary staffed by a doctor and two nurses, who are responsible for the medical needs of children enrolled at the center. All the children receive preadmission physicals, routine examinations and immunizations, and are cared for in the infirmary when they are sick.

In New York City, the Brightside Day Care Center is part of a community health clinic. The children are given preadmission physicals, monthly routine checkups, and are cared for in the infirmary when they are sick. In addition, the physician-in-charge is responsible for supervising health and sanitary matters, and also gives medical examinations to the parents of children enrolled in the center.

Responsibility of Parent

    To provide the center with the name, address, and telephone number of the person to be contacted in case of emergency when parents cannot be reached

Responsibility of Center.
1. To provide a comprehensive medical program for children at the center which includes preventive health care, direct medical services, and treatment for sick children
2. To provide the services of a licensed physician who is responsible for:
    a. Administering preadmission physicals
    b. Giving routine medical examinations
    c. Administering immunizations
    d. Prescribing formulas and special diets as necessary
    e. Attending to emergencies
    f. Prescribing all sanitary precautions to be taken at the center
3. To provide the services of a registered nurse who is responsible for:
    a. Conducting a morning health inspection of all children
    b. Reviewing all medical records of children and staff to be sure all examinations and immunizations are kept up to date
    c. Treating minor injuries
    d. Giving medications to a child when necessary only on written order from the physician. Such medications must be labeled with the child's name, name of the drug, and directions for its administration. All medications should be stored in a locked first aid cabinet and discarded or returned to parents when no longer needed.
    e. Caring for sick children in infirmary when necessary
    f. Supervising prescribed sanitary precautions
    g. Training homemakers to care for sick child at home when it is contraindicated for him to be brought out of doors to the infirmary
(See Minimal Provision Model, Responsibility of Center, Nos. 5 and 6)

4. To provide an infirmary where children can be cared for when they are sick
5. To provide screening programs for vision, hearing, and tuberculosis
6. To provide emergency care of child as per agreement with parents. Center should make arrangements with a nearby hospital to handle serious acute emergencies which cannot be treated at the center. Permission for such emergency care must be secured prior to child's entrance into the program *(See Minimal Provision Model, Responsibility of Center, No. 4.)*
7. To ensure all staff personnel are in good health. *(See Minimal Provision Model, Responsibility of Center, No. 8.)*
8. To ensure all staff follow prescribed sanitary procedures regarding the care of young children at the center. *(See Minimal Provision Model, Responsibility of Center, No. 9.)*
9. To arrange for the physician to speak at parent's meetings to explain some concepts of child growth and development and answer questions.

Modal Provision Model

The range of possibilities within the Modal Provision Model for health and medical care is large indeed, for such a model encompasses all programs between the two extremes: parents assume all responsibility for child's medical care; center provides all medical care necessary with parents' permission. In this model, there is a shared responsibility between the parent and the center for the health needs of the child in day care. The center provides as many direct services to the children as possible, and parents are asked to supplement this care through private physician or public health agencies.

Examples

The medical component of day care in other countries provides many examples of differing Modal Provision Models. In Denmark a medical doctor visits each center once a month and refers all problems in need of treatment to the child's own doctor. He examines all infants under one year of age every three months and toddlers twelve to thirty-six months, twice a year. In addition, he gives all immunizations to children at the various child centers in his district. The doctor is also responsible for referrals to other associated services, such as dental, social, and psychological agencies. An isolation room is available for examinations and immunizations when not being used for sick children.

In France, a physician visits each center twice a week to give immunizations and routine physical examinations. He also takes emergency calls and makes additional visits if there is an epidemic or other illness at the center. The physician is responsible for prescribing the diet of the youngest infants. Each center has an isolation room for sick children.

In Sweden, a doctor visits each center every two weeks and refers children to their family physician for treatment as necessary. Immunizations are given at the center by the visiting physician. In addition, he refers all social and psychological problems to appropriate agencies as they occur.

In Yugoslavia, a school physician visits the crèche three times a week to examine infants and toddlers. He gives yearly examinations to children over three and is available for all emergency calls from the center. In addition to giving children at the center periodic examinations and immunizations, the school physician is responsible for the inspection and maintenance of sanitary and health conditions.

Depending on the extent of health services available at the center, the following responsibilities will be shared with the parents.

Responsibility of Parent
1. To arrange for continuing care and medical treatment for his child and for examinations and immunizations if the center does not provide such direct services. *(See Minimal Provision Model, Responsibility of Parent, Nos. 1, 2, 3.)*

2. To protect his own child and prevent the spread of infection to other children at the center by seeking prompt medical attention for the sick child and keeping him at home until he has recovered from illness or is free from disease *(See Minimal Provision Model, Responsibility of Parent, No. 4.)*

3. To provide the center with the name, address, and telephone numbers of physician or clinic, and person to be contacted in case of emergency when parents cannot be reached

Responsibility of Center:

1. To provide a doctor who visits the center periodically to give examinations, immunizations, prescribe formulas, and be available for emergency calls at the center. The physician refers children to their family doctor or health clinic for treatment as necessary

2. To provide the services of a nurse part- or full-time, or as a consultant depending on the resources available, the needs of the community, and the size of the center. If employed full-time, the nurse should be responsible for the morning health assessment of children, supervision and prescription of sanitary precautions, treatment of minor injuries, and care of sick children in the isolation room until parents come to take him home. She, moreover, reviews health records of children and staff to be sure all examinations and immunizations are up-to-date. If the nurse is employed part-time or as a consultant, she should prepare other staff members to carry out the described functions in her absence *(See Minimal Provision Model, Responsibility of Center Nos. 5. and 6.)*

3. To provide screening programs for vision, hearing, and tuberculosis

4. To provide an isolation room where sick children can stay until they are taken home by their parents. This room can also be used by the physician and nurse for

examinations, immunizations, etc., when there are no ill children

5. To arrange for emergency care of child as per agreement with parents. Even if the center has a doctor on emergency call, a plan for handling injuries and emergencies is necessary

6. To give medications to a child when necessary, only on written order from a physician. Such medications must be labeled with the child's name, name of the drug, and directions for its administration. All medications should be stored in the locked first aid cabinet and discarded or returned to the parents when no longer needed

7. To ensure all staff personnel are in good health *(See Minimal Provision Model, Responsibility of Center, No. 8)*

8. To ensure all staff follow prescribed sanitary procedures regarding the care of young children at the center *(See Minimal Provision Model, Responsibility of Center, No. 9)*

9. To arrange for the physician to speak at the parents' meeting in order to explain some concepts of child growth and development and answer questions

Dental Care Services

Minimal Provision Model
The Minimal Provision Model for dental care assumes that the dental needs of the child in day care is the parent's responsibility. The role of the center is to maintain an environment which fosters good dental health.

Dental care should begin in the early preschool years. By the time a child is two years old he should have routine dental examinations and cleanings. A preschool child can become familiar with the dentist and learn not to fear him. In addition, cavities or other problems which may be found in the first teeth can be corrected before they affect the child's permanent teeth.

Responsibility of Parent
1. To arrange for a dental evaluation and continuing dental care for his child either from a private dentist or health clinic
2. To instill habits of good oral hygiene and mouth care by encouraging the brushing of teeth after meals at home

Responsibility of Center
1. To review all dental examinations and keep on file the name of each child's dentist or health clinic used for continuing care *(See Appendix Health Forms)*
2. To provide each child with a toothbrush at the center and instruct him in its use so he can brush his teeth after meals
3. To arrange for a dentist to speak at a parents' meeting to explain the importance of providing early examinations and dental care to young children

Maximal Provision Model

The Maximal Provision Model seeks to provide comprehensive dental care to all children enrolled in the day care center through direct dental services.

Responsibility of Parent

To instill habits of good oral hygiene and mouth care by encouraging the brushing of teeth after meals at home

Responsibility of Center
1. To provide direct dental care services to all children in the day care center through providing a dental clinic, making an agreement with a hospital out-patient department, or contracting with a private dentist. Services to be provided should include:
    a. Routine examinations
    b. Routine cleanings

     c.   Treatment of dental problems
     d.   Application of topical fluoride (with written parental permission)
2.   To arrange for the dental consultant to conduct a program for children, teachers, and parents emphasizing the need for good mouth hygiene and preventive dental care
3.   To provide each child with a toothbrush at the center and instruct him in its use so he can brush his teeth after meals

Modal Provision Model

The Modal Provision Model encompasses a wide range of program possibilities whereby the responsibility for dental care of the children in day care is shared by both the parents and the center.

Examples

In France, dental services are available to all children under the state system of socialized medicine. In Paris, children enrolled in day care are brought to the main consultation center in groups of twenty for yearly dental examinations and treatment as necessary.

From the age of three, children enrolled in day care in Sweden are given yearly dental examinations. In addition, all children use fluoride toothpaste when brushing their teeth at the center.

In Yugoslavia, dental examinations are scheduled yearly through a contractual arrangement between the day care center and a private dentist.

As there is a shared responsibility between the parent and the center for the dental needs of the child in day care, the center provides as many direct services to the children as possible and parents are asked to supplement this care through private dentist or dental clinic services. Depending upon the extent of dental services available at the center, the following responsibilities will be shared with the parents.

Responsibility of Parent
1. To arrange for routine dental examinations and treatment for their child if the center does not provide such direct services
2. To instill habits of good oral hygiene and mouth care by encouraging the brushing of teeth after meals at home

Responsibility of Center
1. To require yearly dental examinations for all children in day care if such services are not available through the center
2. To keep on file the name, address, and phone number of the child's dentist or dental clinic used for continuing care
3. To provide the services of a dentist to examine each child's teeth, apply topical fluoride (with written parental permission), and refer child for treatment to his family dentist or health clinic
4. To have the dental consultant conduct a program for children, teachers, and parents emphasizing the need for good mouth hygiene and preventive dental care
5. To provide each child with a toothbrush at the center and instruct him in its use so he can brush his teeth after meals

Social Services

Minimal Provision Model
The Minimal Provision Model attempts to provide for the social service needs of children in day care and their families through the use of center staff personnel with additional assistance provided through referrals to community service agencies.

Responsibility of Parent
1. To seek information regarding the location of day care services in their neighborhood and the requirements for their child's eligibility
2. To work closely with the teachers and inform them of

any change or crisis in the home which might affect their child's well-being or behavior in the center

3. To become actively involved in the parent group at the day care center, sharing problems and offering suggestions

Responsibility of Center

1. To review all applications and interview prospective children and their parents.
2. To obtain information regarding the following:
    a. Reasons for seeking day care services
    b. Family background information
    c. Pertinent developmental history
        1. Complications of pregnancy and birth (if any)
        2. Eating and sleeping habits
        3. Toilet training
        4. Physical health
        5. Emotional well-being, i.e., fears, mannerisms, etc.
        6. Social relations (with adults, peers, strangers, etc.)
        7. Previous group experiences
        (See Appendices, pages 312-314, Record Forms)
3. To explain the services offered by the center:
    a. Hours of operation
    b. Fees
    c. Policies
    d. Admission process
    e. Responsibilities of parents and responsibilities assumed by the center for:
        1. Health and medical care
        2. Dental care
        3. Social services
        4. Psychological services
        5. Nutritional services
    f. Child care program

4. To refer to community agencies problems noted at home or at school which cannot be resolved by the center
5. To keep parents informed of child's adjustment and experiences in the day care program and to work closely with parents to insure optimal integration of home experiences and day care program

Maximal Provision Model

The Maximal Provision Model seeks to provide direct social services to families of children enrolled in day care. Day care centers should have social work as one of its integral components. Through the services of a social worker, both the children in day care and their parents are helped with individual and family problems and are able to make the best use of available community resources and services.

Responsibility of Parents
1. To seek information regarding the location of day care services in their neighborhood and the requirements for their child's eligibility
2. To work closely with the teachers and the social worker and inform them of any change or crisis in the home which might affect the child's well-being or behavior in the center.
3. To participate actively in parents meetings, sharing problems and offering suggestions

Responsibility of Center
1. To provide the services of a social worker to:
   a. Assist in the development of forms and records
   b. Review all applications
   c. Interview parents and children
   d. Obtain pertinent information regarding family background and the child's developmental history *(See Minimal Provision Model. Responsibility of Center, No. 2)*

e. Explain the services offered by the day care center *(See Minimal Provision Model, Responsibility of Center, No. 3.)*

f. Work closely with parents to insure the well-being of each child at the center *(See Minimal Provision Model, Responsibility of Center, No. 4)*

g. Provide family counseling as necessary and refer problems unable to be handled at the center to appropriate community service agencies (i.e., child guidance clinic, family counseling service, legal aid, welfare rights, etc.)

h. Assist center staff and parents in coordinating their care and adjustment of each child

i. Observe individual children and help teachers and parents understand the meaning of behavior

2. To provide the opportunity for parent participation in the day care center. *(See Modal Provision Model, Responsibilities of Center, No. 6)*

Modal Provision Model

The Modal Provision Model attempts to assist the parents of children in day care through use of a consultant social worker who advises the center on social policies and gives direct assistance to families in case of emergency.

Responsibility of Parent

1. To seek information regarding the location of day care services in his neighborhood and the requirements for his child's eligibility.

2. To work closely with the teachers and inform them of any change or crisis in the home which might affect the child's well-being or behavior in the center

3. To become actively involved in the parent group at the day care center, sharing problems and offering suggestions

Responsibility of Center

1. To provide the services of a consultant social worker to:
   a. Advise in developing forms, records, and policies at the center
   b. Assist through direct counseling and use of referrals in case of emergency (i.e., battered child, impending separation or divorce in family, lack of financial resources, etc.)
2. To review all applications and interview prospective children and their parents
3. To obtain pertinent information regarding family background and child's developmental history. *(See Minimal Provision Model, Responsibility of Center, No. 2)*
4. To explain the services offered by the day care center *(See Minimal Provision Model, Responsibility of Center, No. 3)*
5. To work closely with parents to ensure the well-being of each child at the center *(See Minimal Provision Model, Responsibility of Center, No. 4)*
6. To provide opportunities for parent participation within the classroom, determining policies, setting up agenda for meetings, etc.

Psychological Services

Mental hygiene encompasses the whole child; his physical, emotional, social well-being and that of his family. The classroom program itself can do much to nurture the psychological development of children through a child-centered program sensitive to their needs and abilities. Thus one can view "psychological services" as an integral program component.

There are three main aspects of mental hygiene which can be promoted within the classroom. The first is the establishment of an intangible quality called atmosphere. Love is perhaps the most vital ingredient in this feeling tone which affects the child so greatly. But loving care alone is not enough to produce positive psychological growth. The reassurance of firm but kind adult guidance is needed, as is a discipline which builds the inner strength and social awareness of the child. Under no circumstances should adults resort to chastisement, corporal punishment, or ridicule. These forms of discipline are exceedingly detrimental because they undermine the child's sense of worth by causing humiliation and frustration. Redirecting the child's attention and removing him from the group until he has regained control are two methods of discipline which promote healthy psychological growth and therefore are positive methods of discipline.

Good teacher-parent relationships are the third ingredient necessary to enhance the psychological development of the child in day care. As the child is part of his family constellation, the day care staff should work with parents to promote healthy family relations. Sometimes harmful attitudes can be changed through patient counseling of parents.

Minimal Provision Model

The Minimal Provision Model for psychological services assumes that it is the parents' responsibility to provide special psychological services for their child. The role of the center is to provide a healthy environment for emotional and mental growth.

Responsibility of Parent
1. To introduce the child slowly to the day care program and understand his needs and the feelings produced by separation
2. To work cooperatively with the day care center relating any information and ideas which might help the child feel more secure
3. To secure any special services required to promote the psychological development of the child

Responsibility of Center
1. To create a warm, loving child-centered atmosphere responsive to the needs of individual children

2. To work closely with parents in order to better understand the child and his needs
3. To arrange for a psychiatrist and/or psychologist to speak at a parents' meeting to explain some of the components of child growth and development, and answer any questions
4. To help parents find private or community psychiatric or psychological service agencies if necessary

Maximal Provision Model
The Maximal Provision Model seeks to provide direct, comprehensive psychological care services to the child in day care and his family.

Responsibility of Parent
1. To work cooperatively with the day care center staff in order to understand more clearly the needs of their child and provide for his care
2. To relate any information or suggestions which might be of assistance to the center staff in caring for their child

Responsibility of Center
1. To create a warm, loving, child-centered atmosphere which is responsive to the needs of individual children
2. To work closely with parents in order to understand better the child and his needs
3. To provide the services of a psychologist to:
    a. Observe the classroom groups and follow-up individual children periodically
    b. Study the progress records kept by the nurse, doctor, dentist, and teachers on each child enrolled in the center
    c. Periodically test children in order to record developmental gains and evaluate the care program components
    d. Organize staff conferences to coordinate the associated service inputs and evaluate their effect on individual children

    e.   Speak to parents in groups in order to discuss some of the components of child growth and development and answer any questions

    f.   Arrange conferences with parents to discuss their child and his progress

    g.   Refer children and/or their parents for psychiatric evaluation and treatment as necessary

4.   To provide the services of a psychiatrist to:

    a.   Consult with the staff regarding the mental health aspects of child care and offer specific advice concerning children with behavior or personality problems

    b.   Make referrals for evaluation and treatment of child and/or his parents when indicated and such care cannot be provided at the center

Modal Provision Model

The Modal Provision Model seeks to promote additional insight into the psychological needs of children by providing the services of a psychologist and/or psychiatrist on a consultation basis.

Responsibility of Parent

1.   To work cooperatively with the staff at the day care center to understand better the needs of their child and provide for his care

2.   To relate any information to the staff which may be of assistance in designing the program of care for his child.

Responsibility of Center

1.   To create a warm, loving, child-centered atmosphere which is responsive to the needs of individual children

2.   To provide the services of a consultant psychologist and/or psychiatrist to observe individual children and assist the center staff in designing a program of care

3.   To arrange for the consultant to speak at parents'

meetings in order to explain some of the components of child growth and development and answer any questions the parents may raise
4. To refer children for psychological testing if necessary
5. To refer child and/or his parents for psychiatric evaluation and treatment if necessary

Nutritional Services

Introduction
Proper nutrition has a critical role to play in the physical, mental, social, and emotional development of children. Studies indicate malnutrition not only affects physical health and growth patterns, but also mental development and intellectual ability. Therefore, centers which care for children during the day should assume the responsibility for insuring the children suitable, nourishing meals.

The nutritional responsibilities of the center do not conclude with the provision of an adequate diet. Care must be taken to insure that food is simply prepared and attractively served so children will enjoy eating.

Food carries an emotional impact to children. Familiar foods link memories of home to mealtime at the center and promote security and feelings of belonging. Eating can also be a learning experience for children; therefore, they need time to try new tastes and textures and learn to enjoy a variety of foods. Mealtime, therefore, should be unhurried and pleasant — a time for enjoying the food served and exchanging conversation with others.

Food Requirements
Children enrolled in day care usually receive a substantial part of their daily food requirements at the center. Depending upon the length of time a child spends in the center, snacks and sometimes meals need to be provided. The variety and amount of food to be served should meet the National Research Council Food Allowances for children in day care.

For a child in half-day care (under four hours) a

midmorning or midafternoon snack of milk or juice and bread or its equivalent is sufficient. Children in care five to eight hours require one third to one half of their food needs for the day be served at the center in one regular meal (not counting breakfast) and one or more snacks. For children in care longer than nine hours, two thirds of their food requirements for the day need to be provided through two meals and one or more snacks.

The minimal amounts of foods to be served at meals depend upon the age of the child. Formula and diet schedules for infants should be prescribed by a doctor and conscientiously followed at home and in the center. Individual diet cards for young infants need to be kept on file and revised frequently by the doctor as the infant matures.

The Special Food Service Program for Children in each state receives donated (surplus or commodity) foods from the Federal Department of Agriculture and makes arrangements for such foods to be distributed to needy families and service institutions for children such as nonprofit child care centers. They suggest the following minimum amounts of component foods be served at meals:

Age one up to three
Breakfast: 1/2 cup of milk; 1/4 cup of juice or fruit; 1/2 slice of bread or equivalent or 1/4 cup of cereal or an equivalent quantity of both bread and cereal.
Lunch or Supper: 1/2 cup of milk; 1 ounce (edible portion as served) of meat or an equivalent quantity of an alternate; 1/4 cup of vegetable or fruits or both consisting of two or more kinds; 1/2 slice of bread or equivalent; 1/2 teaspoon of butter or fortified margarine.
Supplemental Food: 1/2 cup of milk or juice; 1/2 slice of bread or equivalent.

Age three up to six
Breakfast: 3/4 cup of milk; 1/2 cup of juice or fruit; 1/2 slice of bread or equivalent or 1/3 cup of cereal or an equivalent quantity or both bread and cereal.

Lunch or Supper: 3/4 cup of milk; 1 1/2 ounces (edible portion as served) of meat or an equivalent quantity of an alternate; 1/2 cup of vegetables or fruits or both consisting of two or more kinds; 1/2 slice of bread or equivalent; 1 teaspoon of butter or fortified margarine.

Supplemental Food: 1/2 cup of milk or juice; 1/2 slice of bread or equivalent.

Reimbursement

Section 13 of the National School Lunch Act, as amended in 1968, provides funds for reimbursement to service institutions in connection with meals served to children. Such "service institutions" include child care centers which provide day care services to children from poor economic areas or neighborhoods where there are large numbers of working mothers.

Reimbursement rates are determined by the State Office of School Lunch when application is made. Maximum rates of reimbursement per child for meals are as follows: breakfast, 15 cents; lunch or supper, 30 cents; and supplemental foods, 10 cents.

Funds are also available to pay 75 percent of the purchase or rental of equipment for storage, preparation, transportation and serving of food to children.

For further information on reimbursement possibilities consult the State Office of School Lunch Programs in your vicinity.

Refrigeration and Storage

Whether the nutritional program utilized the Minimal, Modal, or Maximal Provision Model, there must be some provision for the refrigeration and storage of food supplies. Milk and all perishable foods should be stored in a refrigerator maintained at 45° F. or below. Food supplies not refrigerated must be kept in clean, covered containers which are inaccessible to insects, rodents, and other vermin.

Sanitary Procedures

Persons preparing and serving meals should submit to the

center a health certificate signed by a physician stating they are in good health and free from any communicable disease which might be passed on to others via food products. They should maintain good sanitary practices at all times: wash hands thoroughly with soap and warm water before preparing food; wear a clean, washable uniform, apron, or dress daily; handle food with clean utensils in a sanitary manner, etc.

All eating and drinking utensils should be free from cracks or chips and be maintained and stored in a sanitary condition. Utensils used in the preparation, serving, and eating of food should be washed with soap or detergent in warm water and then sanitized by immersion for at least one minute in hot water (over 170°F.) or immersed in an approved bactericidal solution such as chlorine. Equipment should be air dried since bacteria can accumulate on dish towels and be spread from one utensil to another.

Minimal Provision Model

The Minimal Provision Model seeks to insure that food brought from home for the child's use in the center is adequate for his needs. The nutrition program seeks to assist parents in learning how best to provide for the nutritional needs of their child.

Responsibility of Parent
1. To send daily to the child care center food to be eaten by their child during the day. Such food may include: sandwiches, fruit, milk, etc.
2. To see that food sent is properly wrapped and brought in a covered container such as a paper bag or lunch box
3. To send nutritious, well-balanced foods which their child enjoys eating

Responsibility of Center
1. To provide refrigeration for all perishable foods sent from home for the children to eat during the day
2. To put child's name on bag or container when it arrives to ensure each child received his own food
3. To assist parents in learning how to provide the proper

foods for their children through arranging for a nutritionist to speak at a parents meeting; conducting demonstrations using surplus foods; menu planning with parents either individually or as a group

4. To provide milk or juice if possible to supplement food brought from home

5. To provide a pleasant relaxed atmosphere at mealtimes so children can enjoy eating and share conversations with others

6. To provide vitamin supplements if possible (with written parental permission).

Maximal Provision Model

The Maximal Provision Model seeks to provide a comprehensive nutrition program which ensures adequate food is provided to all children in the day care center.

Responsibility of Parent

1. To ensure their child receives an adequate diet at home when he is not being fed at the day care center

2. To consult the posted menus at the center to avoid duplication of meals served at home

Responsibility of Center

1. To provide all meals and supplemental snacks as necessary to the children enrolled in the day care center

2. To assist parents in learning how to provide the proper foods for their children *(See Minimal Provision Model, Responsibility of Center No. 3)*

3. To plan meals and supplements so they are well-balanced and in accordance with the National Research Council Food Allowances for children in day care

4. To utilize the services of a nutritionist for menu planning and supervision of kitchen staff

5. To post menus weekly so mothers can plan for meals at home accordingly

6. To provide a kitchen where food can be properly prepared and stored. The kitchen should be separate

from the classrooms and used only for the preparation and storage of food, and the washing, sanitizing, and storage of eating utensils and equipment. The kitchen should be kept clean and orderly and have adequate lighting and ventilation. In addition, sinks with hot and cold running water, refrigeration, cooking range, and shelves for storage should be provided

7. To utilize surplus and wholesale foods in order to reduce food costs
8. To receive reimbursement if possible for food and equipment costs from the National School Lunch Act
9. To provide a pleasant relaxed atmosphere at mealtimes so children can enjoy eating and share conversations with others
10. To provide vitamin supplements (with written parental permission)
11. To ensure all staff working with food submit a report from a physician stating that they are in good health and are free from any communicable disease which might be passed on to others via food products. The report of a negative intradermal tuberculin test should also be required
12. To ensure all staff follow prescribed sanitary procedures regarding the preparation and storage of food and the sanitizing of equipment and utensils *(See Sanitary Procedures, page 114)*

Modal Provision Model

In the Modal Provision Model, the role of the center is to provide simple food services in order to supplement the responsibilities of the family in adequately meeting their child's nutritional needs. The amount of supplementing by the center varies for the individual program.

Responsibility of Parent
1. To send daily to the center food to be eaten by his child if such food service is not provided by the center

2. To wrap all food sent to the center securely, place it in a covered container, and label it with child's name
3. To send nutritious, well-balanced foods which the child enjoys eating

Responsibility of Center
1. To provide all supplemental foods for snacks, and meals if possible
2. To provide refrigeration for all perishable foods whether sent from home or provided at the center
3. To assist parents in learning how to provide the proper foods for their children *(See Minimal Provision Model, Responsibility of Center, No. 3)*
4. To plan meals and supplements so they are well-balanced and in accordance with the National Research Council Food Allowances for children in day care
5. To utilize the services of a consultant nutritionist for menu planning
6. To post menus weekly so mothers can plan for meals at home accordingly
7. To provide a kitchen area where food can be properly prepared and utensils sanitized and stored
8. To receive reimbursement if possible for food and equipment costs from National School Lunch Act
9. To utilize surplus and wholesale foods in order to reduce food costs
10. To provide a pleasant relaxed atmosphere at mealtimes so children can enjoy eating and share conversations with others
11. To provide vitamin supplements (with written parental permission)
12. To ensure that all staff working with food are in good health *(See Maximal Provision Modal, Responsibility of Center, No. 11)*
13. To ensure that all staff follow prescribed sanitary procedures regarding the preparation and storage of food and the sanitizing of equipment and utensils *(See Sanitary Procedures, page 114)*

CARING FOR CHILDREN

Curriculum

We use the word *curriculum* to include the theory, practice, and objectives of both the educational and caretaking aspects of your day care program. It is a crucial issue discussed throughout the book and can be defined as the sum of all the parts of your program.

Traditionally, the word *curriculum* implies a standard set of requirements which must be completed during a given course, program, school year, grade, etc. With that in mind, the question, "What can you teach preschoolers?" is frequently asked, and the asker is always quite sure the answer is "nothing." We would like to suggest an alternative to tradition to help clarify why there is a necessity for preschool curriculum planning and what preschoolers might learn. Curriculum, to us, is *any deliberate effort at creating a learning situation within the context of the day care center.*

Children are always learning. They are explorers, discoverers, seekers, reachers, and testers with insatiable curiosity. Therefore, virtually anything can afford them an opportunity to learn; yet not everything is part of a curriculum. Only that which demonstrates a conscious recognition of the needs, capabilities, and learning processes among children is part of the preschool curriculum. However, we urge that teachers consciously define all classroom activity as a curriculum resource they will deliberately utilize as a learning situation. Often, learning situations appear to be just "play" in practice, but why must learning be "work"? When a child dresses up and plays house in the housekeeping area, it is play, but it is also a crucial element of his learning experience. Any good teacher will recognize the value of a housekeeping area as a tool of socialization through which children build their self-concepts and learn to understand the roles and behavioral expectations of our society. So, too, for a water-play table or block corner. Both are fun, and both are invaluable vehicles for learning science and social studies, for socialization in group activity, and for learning basic principles of arithmetic.

Recognition of the children's needs and learning processes leads preschool educators to create a classroom environment encouraging children to explore and learn in a way most satisfying to them. With supportive adult supervision which offers suggestions, guides explorations, and encourages discussion and inquiry, the effects of the classroom as a learning environment are maximized.

Educators and psychologists tell us that the first three years of life are the most crucial for future intellectual, social, physical, and emotional development. Five years of age is the outer range of this crucial period. It is known as "preschool" in the United States, but it is certainly not prelearning.

With an understanding of the role of the preschool years in cognitive development, one can begin to recognize the responsibility a day care center has to offer an educationally sound program as well as to provide all of the caretaking services of a good baby-sitter. The educationally appropriate objectives for any preschool program are to expose children to the widest possible variety of experiences in order to arouse their curiosity, challenge their physical and intellectual abilities, and encourage self-expression. In effect, the first "school" experience should be one which develops a sense of joy, wonder, and curiosity in the world around us. Children should feel confident that they can and should ask questions, try new ideas, and, most importantly, feel good about themselves. Indeed, one of the most important objectives of a good preschool program is to begin to develop a positive self-concept among all the children. When children feel good about what they can do, when they understand their role as son, daughter, friend, brother, or sister, when they recognize the love and friendship of teachers and children, and when they have confidence in themselves, they will be far more receptive to the learning opportunities of any experience than if they are feeling angry, hurt, alone, confused, shamed, or rejected. Thus, when someone asks what do preschool teachers teach, the answer is they teach mathematics and science, music and reading, dexterity and cooperation in the context of productive exploration and experience and in an atmosphere of warm support for each child rather than through arbitrary schedules, group tasks, and synthetic assignments and evaluations.

Perhaps the reasons for our feelings about an appropriate curriculum should include some mention of the books which influenced them. Each is a theory of learning and development directly relevant to the preschool program. First, is *Origins of Intelligence* by Jean Piaget. Piaget is a prolific writer whose studies of children from birth through adolescence present concrete analyses of the stages of growth and development and the processes of intellectual maturation in children. Briefly, he suggests that human beings are born with only very few reflexes (sucking and grasping being among the most important) and from those limited raw materials all else must be learned. He posits three major periods of development during roughly the first fifteen years of life. (While there are rough approximations of age correspondence, Piaget is not concerned with age relationships so much as developmental stages.) These in turn are divided into sub-periods and stages, each representing prerequisite skills and knowledge for stages that follow. In addition to defining the stages of development, Piaget also suggests the processes or mechanisms for development from the basic reflexes. Again, very briefly, the process he suggests is one of both assimilating into the child's inventory of skills the serendipitous occurrence of variations on old experiences and accommodating old skills to new experiences or circumstances; these are then reinforced through repetition.

The important variable for development, according to Piaget, is not the kind of formal instruction a child has; rather, it is the quality and quantity of opportunities he has to respond to stimuli with his limited but ever-increasing inventory of skills. The most important implications of this theory for the preschool curriculum, then, are to provide a stimulating environment which allows and encourages children to respond with and develop their skills rather than a formal, regimented schedule of instruction; and to recognize the extreme importance of the nonacademic pursuits among children in the classroom.

Because Piaget writes in detail which is often tedious or difficult to read easily, several excellent books have been written to summarize, paraphrase, and elucidate his work. Two of the best we've found are *The Origins of Intellect, Piaget's Theory*, by John L. Phillips, Jr. (W.H. Freeman and Company, 1969), and *The Developmental Psychology of Jean Piaget*, by John H. Flavell (D. Van Nostrand Company, 1963). The Phillips book is a brief, explanatory outline of Piaget's theory while Flavell goes into considerably more detail. Both books include extensive bibliographies of other books on Piaget.

The second book influencing our suggested focus for curriculum is *Organization of Behavior*, by D. O. Hebb. It describes the neurophysiology of learning in relatively simple language. Hebb clearly illustrates how early learning differs from adult learning. The latter is "insightful," due to the network of neural connections developed during the early learning period which, unlike adult learning, is slow and repetitive. When educators understand the process of learning and of learning to learn as Hebb defines it, they can begin to teach children more effectively. Similarly, once a day care staff recognizes the difference between early and adult learning, the desirability of a stimulating environment in which children can respond to materials freely becomes increasingly apparent; so does the need for patience in having to repeat over and again the myriad things that children learn only through repetition; and, finally, an understanding of Hebb's theory makes apparent the importance of nonacademic elements of the preschool curriculum just as Piaget's theory does.

Both Hebb and Piaget help us understand how children learn, what they can learn, and the limitations on that learning. There are of course, bookstores full of other theories, concepts, hypotheses, and experiences relevant to the learning process and preschool curricula, but for a start, Hebb and Piaget are most useful.

With the theories of Hebb, Piaget, and developmental psychologists in mind, we can begin to delineate principles for developing the daily and long-range program. The important elements are such things as the size and composition of your classroom discussed in Chapter 2, the classroom environment discussed in Chapter 6, and the curriculum which includes curriculum objectives, teaching techniques, scheduling, and caretaking procedures.

Curriculum Objectives

While many parents feel that preparation for public school is the most important objective for a day care center or other preschool program, we find that such preparation will be a ready by-product of other experiences. Except perhaps for the older children who will enter public school the following year, there is no need for deliberate public school preparation. Children will learn to be away from home, to work with other children, and to abide by rules of behavior regardless of the preschool program they are in. Beyond that, we see no purpose in imposing other kinds of preparatory experience, such as the very rigid rules of behavior characteristic of many public schools or such formal academic requirements as being able to say the alphabet. For older children, it would be helpful to take field trips to the public school, to develop longer attention spans, and to devote more time to developing reading, writing, and number concepts; however, all children should not be expected to proceed at the same rate or, indeed, to leave their preschool program with a set of required skills.

Instead of numbers, letters, and obedience, we prefer to see preschool programs concentrate on observation skills, language skills, physical strength and coordination, a sense of process (how final products come about), providing many and varied experiences, and developing a positive self-concept which allows children, among other things, to be self-motivated in their pursuit of learning. Whether you work with infants or with five-year-olds, these will remain appropriate objectives for a preschool curriculum.

Teaching Techniques

The teacher's responsibility with respect to both the curriculum objectives and theories that motivate them is to provide appropriate opportunities and materials in the context of an open, supportive, cooperative atmosphere. The careful observation of children, not a predetermined list of requirements, should prompt teachers to stress or avoid any given learning experience.

Although the teacher does not require participation in specific activities, he or she cannot expect that children will recognize many activity possibilities. For example, a child will rarely ask to learn about jungle animals unless there is someone (an adult or another child) who can stimulate that kind of curiosity. A good teacher will provide pictures, models, books, trips to the zoo, displays of animal skins, and opportunities to discuss observations and ideas about animals if that is a subject he or she would like to introduce into the classroom. (See page 212.) Once teachers have provided such stimuli, their role is one of adviser, supervisor, companion, and experienced grown-up participant to whom children can turn for help, guidance, and conversation, and in whom they can place their trust and respect. In other words, the teacher must begin with some ideas about a topic that will interest the children, follow through with a variety of stimulation relevant to that topic, and continue to be an active, enthusiastic participant and supporter of the children's pursuits.

If there is a label in conjunction with this approach to teaching, it is "child-centered." That is, rather than the teachers' presenting themselves as authorities from whom classroom activities, controls, and decisions must come, a sense of the importance of the children and respect for them as people with the right to voice or demonstrate their feelings must predominate.

The range of teaching styles for this approach is broad, but attitudes towards children and curriculum objectives should not vary. Rather, there is a continuum of control or structure appropriate for this approach. Thus, both a teacher who feels the need to plan each day according to a schedule of activities and one who prefers a more open, unstructured classroom can be successful in a child-centered classroom. We stress again that attitudes toward children, curriculum objectives, and an active understanding of how children learn are the most important aspects in good teaching.

It may be that the teacher's preferred style will be inappropriate for some children. If this is the case, the teacher must compromise in order effectively to create a productive environment for emotional and intellectual development. Examples include a classroom of children who, for whatever reason, are boisterous and rowdy when asked to be self-directed, who need instead a more gradual introduction to freedom. Similarly, children who are very shy and inhibited will need more directed, structured activity before they feel able to be self-directed. Expect, too, that no class will be homogeneous with respect to the need for structure or independence. The teacher-child ratios we recommend elsewhere take this into consideration and allow for some teachers having to work with certain children on a one-to-one basis, while the rest of the teaching staff supervise activities for the other children. Our ratios can be raised as long as the teachers are capable of handling more children and are not overwhelmed by the responsibility to provide adequate supervision, effective stimulation, and time for one-to-one interaction for all children as well as plan and prepare daily activities.

A word about discipline in the child-centered classroom is in order because all too often people confuse freedom, independence, and choice with license. In fact, a child-centered classroom in no way avoids the question of discipline. Safety and courtesy considerations are never ignored. It is felt that when anybody (children notwithstanding) has a say in what he does and how he is treated, his sense of courtesy, safety, and fair play is more acute. He is more willing to abide by rules because he understands them. In effect, discipline is a more demanding task in the child-centered classroom, because teachers are not free to make rules that suit just them; everyone has a hand in making rules. Of course, teachers are responsible for stopping dangerous, cruel, or unfair behavior, which inevitably occurs, but the emphasis is not on punishment so much as developing an understanding of why such behavior is inappropriate. Regardless of what a child has done, there is never any verbal or physical abuse. Furthermore, an effective teacher will make every effort to understand what motivates a child to misbehave, especially if the misbehavior is chronic, and will then determine the best way to help the child overcome his problems.

Schedule

While the actual schedule of any day is not as important as the teaching approach, the environment, and the curriculum objectives, it often helps to have at least a rough outline of how the day will proceed, especially if teachers are unable to deal with the kind of chaos that results from even a brief moment of boredom. The sample schedule we present can become highly structured with a specific limitation on activities, materials, and general time allotments; or, conversely, it can be very loosely structured with no specific time allotments or expectations. So long as any schedule is seen as a flexible tool with which to facilitate your objectives, it is appropriate.

Typically, a day will progress so that from the time the first child arrives to about one-half hour after breakfast there is free play with an emphasis on the activities relevant to the five basic curriculum areas and any other activities which do not necessarily require elaborate preparation. The time following free play and preceding lunch includes a snack, often accompanied by an assembly or meeting in which the whole class gathers to discuss the day, introduce some new or unusual materials, have show and tell, or simply chat. This block of time is either maintained as one activity period or divided in two, with a different array of activities during the two blocks of time. Children who don't want to participate in activities specifically planned for that time can have a free play period if they do not disrupt or choose to do something severely limiting the number of teachers available to supervise other activities.

Water play, cooking, music and dance, at least one art project, carpentry, and science projects are all appropriate for this time, as are outdoor play and field trips. While many of these activities do not necessarily require elaborate plans, at least two and often more are presented with a well-planned variation on the standard activity in mind. Whatever activities are presented during an activity period, they will probably be more successful if materials are gathered and set up in advance. (See page 215 on Stimulation.) It is important to introduce activities effectively, and teachers should give children enough warning about the end of an activity for them to finish what they are doing and clean up without feeling frustrated.

The first activity period is followed by lunch and naptime. The remainder of the day proceeds in a manner similar to the prelunch time, and the period following supper is devoted to activities which can be ended quickly when parents come to fetch their children. Often a full day care program develops so that morning hours are used for more academic pursuits and the afternoon for less structured play. However, there is no set rule, and all teachers must be able to redefine their schedule as the events of the day indicate.

Caretaking

Although we have emphasized the need to maximize the educational benefits of your program, we don't mean to ignore the extreme importance of providing effective caretaking services in a manner which will offer security, behavior models, and educational advantage as well as serving the more obvious functions of eating, sleeping, and toileting.

Eating

Mealtime can significantly affect children's behavior during the rest of the day as well as the more basic feelings they have about themselves and others. In fact, the infant's earliest feelings of comfort or discomfort, trust or mistrust, center around the satisfaction of his hunger. It is important both from health and development standpoints that a pleasant environment characterize mealtime at the day care center.

Insuring a positive, accepting attitude toward eating is an important caretaking objective. Following are some basic suggestions for developing positive mealtime attitudes:

1. Provide child-sized tables, chairs, and utensils. Children will enjoy eating more if they are comfortable and able to manage on their own. If tables have been used for other activities, they must be cleared and cleaned. Often, children will enjoy helping to clean and set up tables.

2. Ideally, set tables and have the food ready to serve before the children sit down. Young children just sitting and waiting quickly become restless. In many programs, children help clean up the room, wash their hands, and then participate in a quiet group activity such as a story just prior to eating. This helps children calm down after active play. They will enjoy their food more as well as participate in mealtime discussion.

3. If possible, have at least one adult per table not only to supervise the children, but also to provide a role model. Children learn through imitation. Therefore, an adult who enjoys a wide variety of foods, expresses pleasure in eating, and uses appropriate table manners can do much to teach

children appropriate mealtime behavior as well as encourage pleasurable associations with mealtime experiences.

4. Give small servings to young children. If first servings are small, the hungry child can ask for more and the child without a large appetite will not be overwhelmed by too much food.

5. Use family-style service whenever possible. It is preferable to standard cafeteria food service. Not only is the amount of food more likely to reflect the individual child's needs, but family-style service is more homelike, more apt to encourage conversation and a sense of enjoyment during meals.

6. Simple foods that "look good," contrast in color, and are attractively served are enjoyed by most preschool children.

7. Never deprive children of food as a punishment for unacceptable behavior occurring at other times during the day.

8. Encourage children to assist in cleanup after meals, whether simply putting dirty dishes in a specified place, or more detailed responsibilities.

9. Be consistent and firm in your expectations for mealtime behavior, so that children learn to consider it as important as the rest of the day.

Most states have rules and regulations governing food preparation and feeding in the day care setting. Be sure to check the requirements in your state. (See pages 112-118 for additional information.)

Sleeping

Naptime is something most preschool children require but often resist. Children find it difficult to leave an exciting, stimulating environment to rest quietly or actually sleep. The teacher must feel confident that a nap period is important for children if he or she expects to convince them that it's necessary.

The means of maintaining limits at naptime may

support and reassure a child or undermine his sense of self. Through quietly whispering a reminder or reassuring a child with a smile, teachers are better able to help a child settle down to rest than by using such negative tactics as frowning dissapprovingly or threatening reprisal. Expressions of disapproval may be taken to mean general disapproval of the child as a person. By making a child feel uncomfortable and/or angry, a teacher may inadvertently encourage resistance and rebellion, especially at naptime.

These suggestions may help to make naptime more pleasant.

1. Young children like the security of routine, so nap time will be more successful if it occurs at the same time every day. Most centers find children are ready for sleep immediately after lunch.

2. Each child should have his own cot and blanket clearly marked with his name. Not only is this a good health practice, but such labeling also affords children reinforcement of expectations of nap time.

3. Cots should be put in the same place for nap period each day so the children know where they belong at that time. There should be adequate space alloted between cots (at least two feet) to allow for good ventilation and to prevent children from disturbing each other. Those who have trouble resting should not be placed next to one another. When possible, a separate room or area of the room should be used for children who are apt to bother others.

4. Darkening the room will generally assist children in falling asleep.

5. Usually, preschool children require no more than an hour or two of rest at naptime. A child who continually sleeps longer than two hours or who falls asleep at other times during the day should be referred for medical follow-up.

6. There should be a regular procedure for ending naptime. In some centers, as children awaken, they are assisted in putting cots and blankets away and directed

toward a quiet activity. When most of the children are awake, or a sufficient number are available to join a small group activity, one or more teachers will take the group outside or to another area in the center, if possible. However, at least one teacher must remain with the sleeping children at all times to insure safe supervision and assist waking children.

Children in an all-day program need a regular rest time daily. Teachers can do much to help children gain the required relaxation and sleep through supportive reassurance and patient understanding of children's needs. A teacher should not attempt to force a child to sleep, but should nevertheless expect him to respect the rights of other children who may want to sleep or rest.

Toileting

Toilet training may promote feelings of self-confidence and worth or develop feelings of failure. Such feelings affect many aspects of behavior. Often excessive negativism in a child is based on rigid early toilet training procedures. Various inhibitions which may affect spontaneity and creativity can also be traced to this source. Loss of self-confidence is a further result of overly strict toilet training.

Fortunately, many children are allowed to become toilet trained at their own rate as they develop physical and emotional maturity. Such children are rewarded for their successes rather than penalized for failures.

Here are some constructive procedures regarding toileting practices at the day care center:

1. The physical setup plays an important role in helping build positive feelings. The room itself should be pleasant, well lighted, and attractive. Furthermore, the setting should help the child feel safe and comfortable. Heavy doors shutting children off from others during toileting can produce anxiety and fear. Such doors should be removed entirely or replaced with latticed or free-swinging booth doors. Separate toilet facilities for girls and boys are not necessary in preschool; the toileting arrangement should be casual and matter-of-fact at this age.

2. If children are to learn to care for themselves independently, they need equipment well suited to their use. Many children are afraid of falling into an adult-sized toilet; therefore child-sized toilets are preferable for use in the day care center. If such equipment is too expensive, you can build steps so children can easily reach the seat and their feet are supported while sitting. You may also construct a new toilet seat to prevent children from falling in.

When converting adult-sized toilets for children's use, include a step platform made to fit in front of the toilet. This arrangement provides easy accessibility, and children feel more comfortable and safer when they can rest both feet on a firm surface.

3. Washroom facilities should be located in or near the toileting area to encourage good hygiene habits. Children should be encouraged to wash their hands after toileting and especially before eating.

Sinks can be lowered to a height easily reached by young children, or step platforms constructed so they can reach the basins without assistance. A mirror should be hung securely over washbasins to help children see the results of their washing.

Soap and paper towels should also be provided in the washroom area, as well as a waste basket. A word of caution: paper towel dispensers should be placed as far away from the toilets as possible. Children often enjoy stuffing paper down the toilet and then watching it flush away. However, paper towels do not flush easily and can clog the toilet drain.

4. In an all-day program it is necessary for each child to have his own facecloth and towel. Each should be clearly marked with the child's name and hung on a separate hook placed so cloths and towels do not touch each other. When used frequently, and especially during the summer months, all wash cloths and towels should be laundered daily.

Extra washcloths come in handy for cleaning children after "accidents." Naturally such cloths should be laundered after use and never reused afterward for washing a child's face.

5. Ideally, each classroom should have toilet and washroom facilities immediately adjacent. This arrangement provides the optimum ease in accessibility and supervision. If access to toileting areas is safe, and the children are mature enough and feel secure, they can attend to their toileting needs independently.

A set toileting schedule often does not meet individual needs, and every attempt should be made to avoid such patterning. However, most teachers find it helpful to suggest toileting for all children around midmorning, before lunch, and after naptime.

Problems in toileting often occur at the day care center due in part to earlier training procedures initiated at home. Since feelings and behavior are closely linked with toileting, a sensitive, understanding teacher can promote self-confidence and encourage independence in this area. "Accidents" should be handled matter-of-factly and every attempt made to discover the cause of repeated episodes. When teachers are relaxed and supportive of toileting procedures, children can feel comfortable, too.

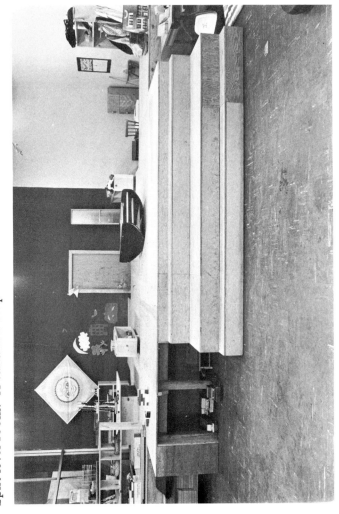

Split-level room. A variation on platforms

Homemade tables and chairs, for children and adults

Library Area

Library Area has many functions

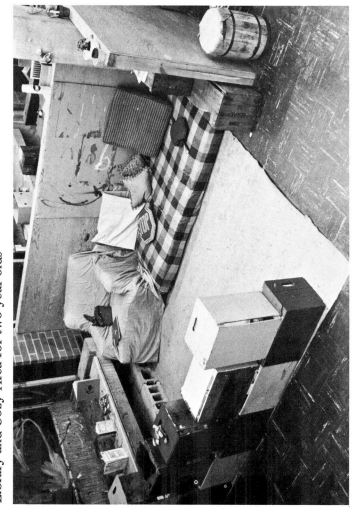

Library and Cozy Area for two-year-olds

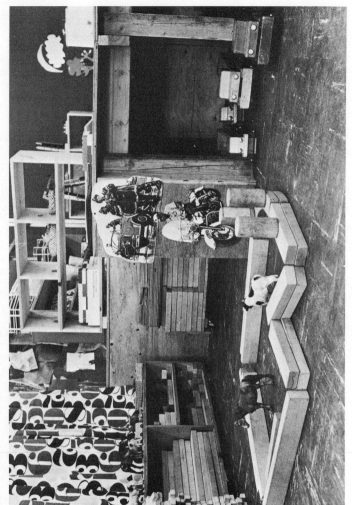

Blocks Area with trucks stored nearby

Puzzles and table games (all parts are portable)

Sunken Housekeeping Area (all parts are portable)

Old crates are good for cubbies and general storage

Art Area with easel made from tri-wall in background

Sand Area

Windows and railroad ties make sand area exciting

Platforms and storage shelves allow more work space in a small room

New ideas for platforms

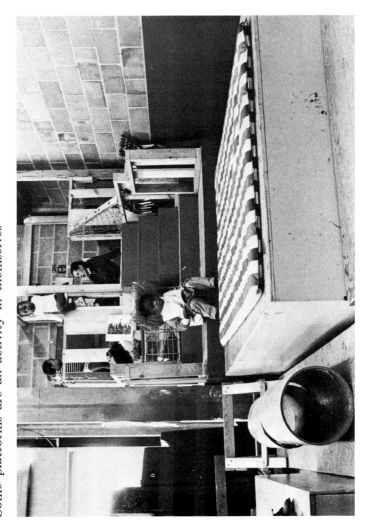

Some platforms are an activity in themselves

Elevated observation booth for good visibility and storage

Climbing structure from old railroad ties

Playgrounds are changing

Teacher Greg Tobias with Ann Johnson

DEVELOPING THE CLASSROOM: FIVE BASIC CURRICULUM AREAS

Definition

A curriculum or activity area is a section of the classroom defined by specific materials and physical boundaries. Classrooms are divided into areas to order the room, limit chaos, and encourage children to pursue an activity that excites their interest for a maximum length of time and with minimum distraction or interference from other activities or children.

When setting up activity areas, important points to keep in mind are (1) the relative noise levels of activities, (2) patterns of traffic within and among areas, (3) the potential for interfering dirt or mess from surrounding activities, (4) the number of children likely to participate in an area at a given time, and (5) the need for adequate storage space. These points are especially important when deciding where to locate areas. A beautifully designed library, for example, is considerably less effective if noisy, sawdusty carpentry is located on one side of it, and active, boisterous large-muscle activity on the other side. An art area located far from the water supply will cause traffic problems.

Good room planning must include a measure of flexibility. As teachers learn about the children, the teaching styles of their assistants, and the other realities of functioning

155

within a specific classroom, they will want to rearrange their rooms to suit newly recognized needs. This should be possible with little expense and effort. Rearranging classrooms is not only inevitable, it's good teaching. It is one approach in dealing with activity areas which are either overused or ignored. For example, a new room arrangement re-creates the feelings of the first few days of school when everything seems new and different and children just *have* to explore all they see. Rearranging also allows a teacher to accommodate the changing needs and abilities of children. For example, the first several weeks of school are often difficult for children because of the painful separation from home. The housekeeping area then becomes an immediate attraction because it represents a link to home. During that time, a teacher may want to have a more elaborate housekeeping area than is required during the remainder of the year. Similarly, an extensive language or number area may not be needed at the beginning of the year, but toward the end many children may have developed skills enough to merit rearranging the room to include language and number areas for daily use.

Flexibility should be a primary objective in developing classrooms. It can be achieved with movable storage (whether "junk" crates or elegant wood units); portable easels; light-weight tables and chairs; and careful planning of such permanent areas as an indoor sandbox or fauceted water-play table. Flexibility is creating a room with portable, inexpensive, functional parts so that teachers and children, not weight and money, determine what the room will be.

Rarely will you find a facility capable of housing the full variety of areas appropriate for a preschool classroom. Rather, teachers should choose those areas which will be a permanent, though versatile, part of the classroom, those that can be assembled from readily available materials in storage. The areas you choose should be selected on the basis of teaching style, the known and anticipated needs of the children, and the physical givens of the classroom.

Basic Curriculum Areas

Although selecting curriculum areas is a matter of individual choice and circumstance, our experience leads us to recommend that housekeeping, blocks, library, art, and puzzle and table-games areas are basic and essential. They are basic because almost all the educational objectives of a day care center can be met through them. Activities in those areas address the physical, social, emotional, and intellectual needs of adequate growth and development more thoroughly than any other combination. Furthermore, they represent the kinds of activities children will want to participate in daily and span the full range of sophistication, supervision, and group size. Finally, they can be effective during both free play and more structured activities. This should by no means suggest that your day care center be limited to the five basic areas. Rather, it should not exclude any of these basic areas, regardless of what else is included.

Housekeeping area

For children of any age, the housekeeping area is both a source of security and an invitation to dramatic play. It is a place where children develop an understanding of the roles of son or daughter, brother or sister, mother or father, and those of a variety of community workers. It is an opportunity for them to explore and act out the roles of people they see, to understand the logic of the society in which they are growing up. It is not the only area that elicits dramatic play, but it is the only area which will surely do so. Any teacher will learn more about his or her children by paying attention to their activity in the housekeeping area.

Materials. The basic materials for the housekeeping area are dolls, a good-sized mirror, household furnishings, and dress-up clothes. Beyond that, let your imagination be your guide. Dolls should be of both sexes, all races, and in a variety of sizes (However, dolls smaller than ten inches high don't function well and often become little more than knick-knacks, if they aren't lost right away.) Our preference is for rubber dolls that bend easily and can be washed without damage. Children may dislike baths and hair washing themselves, but they love to impose them on their dolls. On occasion, bring a basin of sudsy water to the doll corner for an interesting variation on standard activity.

Although toy companies sell dolls that do everything but read and write, we prefer dolls that can be whatever children want them to be because they are just dolls. Plain dolls — the kind that don't walk, talk, wet, or cry real tears — really do become whatever children want them to be because the givens of the doll don't direct children's imagination.

A variety of clothing for dolls is nice but not absolutely necessary. One or two outfits is minimal, but it can be sufficient. Do any of your teachers sew or knit? If so, you may find their talents well used in creating doll clothes from simple patterns. It is not only economical to have homemade doll's clothes, but often homemade creations are more exciting and useful to children than store-bought ones. Be sure children can manipulate whatever clothes are available. If buttons, snaps, and styles are complicated, you will be playing with the doll clothes more than the children. Two's and young three's will, for the most part, be unable to manipulate doll clothes and will probably be uninterested in them, anyway. Four's and five's, on the other hand, will delight in being successful at changing clothes. Dress-up clothes are your old clothes — or any clothes children don't ordinarily wear. High-heeled shoes, long skirts or dresses, neckties, hats of any shape (including helmets), and purses are standard dress-up items. For a new dimension, consider wigs, uniforms, jewelry (only a little; children will make their own jewelry and should be encouraged to do so), clothes from exotic places, fans, shawls, and beards or moustaches.

The mirror mentioned earlier comes in here. Nobody can resist seeing what he looks like when he dresses up. But beyond children's sheer delight in seeing themselves as mommy, daddy, or doctor, the mirror has important value. Body parts generally and "my" body parts specifically are discovered in the looking glass with new understanding. So is a sense of what it is like to be mommy as opposed to a four-year-old. The mirror need not be located right in the housekeeping area, but it should be accessible to children playing dress-up.

Furniture for the housekeeping area can be as simple as several cushions and a turned-over carton painted to look like a stove, or as elaborate as store-bought, child-sized replicas of grown-up's furniture. If you have limited funds, this is one area where you can cut several corners. Any furniture will do. Is there an old arm chair in a junk yard that you can disinfect and use? Does someone have a cradle ready to be thrown out? You shouldn't have to *buy* much furniture for the housekeeping area. Rummage sales, Goodwill stores, and used furniture sales are perfect places to look for inexpensive items.

Generally, the two areas of a house that should be represented are the kitchen and bedroom. They are both the easiest to contrive and the greatest source of identification for the children. Tea sets, utensils, dishes, pots and pans, brooms, mops, and dustpans are the basic materials for the "kitchen." Again, they can be donated, bought used, or furnished more expensively from curriculum materials suppliers. Stoves, sinks, refrigerators, tables, and chairs can be obtained from the same sources.

Child-sized and/or doll-sized cradles and beds are the mainstay of the "bedroom." Whatever tables, chairs, or cushions you have can be spread throughout the area. For two-year-olds, several carriages and/or wagons to carry dolls (and anything else) are valuable assets. Older children enjoy using these vehicles too, but often they are more appropriate in the large-muscle activity area where older children can use them with more vigor. For all children, some combination of cradles, cribs, high chairs, and rocking chairs are welcome additions. These items, like the others mentioned, need not be specifically for dolls. Real cradles, cribs, and high chairs in small sizes work just as well. How much doll furniture you include is less important than whether you've got so little that children fight over it, or so much that the area inevitably becomes crowded and chaotic when even a few children are there.

Setting Up the Housekeeping Area. For a classroom of twenty children, the housekeeping area should be large enough to accommodate at least six children. However you delineate the area, it is generally best to avoid making maximum closure. Because there is often a lot of productive interaction between the housekeeping and other areas, the children should not be limited to a confined space. If you have actually created a small "house" in the housekeeping area, there should be many windows and sufficient room and light for children to stand and interact as well as sit. And there should be room at the entrance for housekeeping activities to spill out of the house.

Consider too, that the place where teachers keep hot plates and other kitchen materials is a logical extension of the housekeeping area. Many teachers have also found that locating housekeeping near the block area benefits both activities. Boys who limit themselves to block play find integration into the myriad housekeeping activities easier because they can build something that can be part of housekeeping; and girls who find block play distasteful are more apt to change their minds when blocks can be part of more familiar territory.[1]

Teachers also find that animal cages, terraria, and carpentry areas function poorly in conjunction with the housekeeping area — one or the other usually dominates.

Dress-up clothes can be stored on hooks, on shelves, in shallow crates, or on a low rack, but they should be accessible and visible, wherever stored. They can be part of the housekeeping area per se, or part of their own dress-up area. Try different combinations until you discover which works best for you.

---

[1] We want to emphasize that the stereotyped roles of boys at blocks and girls at housekeeping are not being endorsed here. Rather, many children come with such prejudices, and we are suggesting ways of gradually changing them.

Library Area

In the library area, books, stories, language development, quiet play, and general enjoyment of literature are emphasized. It should be comfortable and cozy, but not so limited in size that children can't comfortably gather to hear a story, look at the pictures, or talk noisily in one corner without disturbing a silent reader in another part of the area.

It isn't essential or even desirable to read stories or have books only in the library area.

Materials.   Basic materials for the library area are shelves, seats, books, and pictures. While pictures may seem optional rather than basic, in fact they are generally essential in making the environment appealing. Books are often the least visible element in the library, so something else must attract children to explore the area. That "something else" is the atmosphere created primarily through the furniture and pictures.

Books should be varied. Many teachers make the mistake of including only children's storybooks. They are important, but by no means all a library should hold. In addition to storybooks, have several picture books without much text: picture books of animals, geographic and other natural phenomena, including stars, people, plants, bugs, prehistoric animals, and sea life. Picture books on virtually any topic are appropriate. They do not require the assistance of an adult to be understood, and they encourage questions and provoke discussion. They elicit information children already know and are proud to tell. And this makes teachers more aware of the levels of sophistication among their children. A rich variety of wall pictures serves the same function, with the added advantage that they can be changed frequently to meet changing interests at little or no additional expense.

Try to include a good number of storybooks children can relate to personally. For example, *Peter's Chair*, by Ezra Jack Keats, is very well suited to preschoolers because it deals with the problem of sibling rivalry. *Will I Have a Friend?*, by

Miriam Cohen, tells about a child's fear of going to a new school. Some of the older children will face the same fear soon and should have the opportunity to express that fear and deal with it. Many such feelings are first coped with at a day care center in a variety of ways, not the least of which is through stories and discussions evolving from them.

Other stories for preschoolers should introduce people of many different locales and countries, especially if your class has children from other nations. Stories should portray both reality and fantasy. We find, however, that many books of fantasy are not really appropriate. Imaginary monsters, for example, often get confused with reality. Horror stories should be avoided until children are older, more able to discriminate fact from fancy.

In addition to picture books and storybooks, some reference books written on the children's level are very useful. Cars, boats, airplanes, dinosaurs, volcanoes, and people are sources of great fascination. It's impossible for any teacher to have the answer to all the questions children ask, but with references right there, teachers and children together can tackle questions and develop an awareness of the process of obtaining information.

Finally, all preschool libraries should include several books children make themselves. Many children enjoy re-creating their experiences with paints or crayons. Did they take a trip? have a party? catch a frog? or build an exciting block structure? Do they talk about their families? or their Christmas presents? These are the kinds of topics which can be drawn or painted, and the teacher can write the stories children tell about their drawings or paintings to complete the book. Bind all the pictures from the class or all the pictures of an individual child with yarn, ribbon, staples, or clips to make a book for the library. This same technique is equally effective with photographs of the children and their experiences. Both kinds of books delight children and give them a sense of accomplishment as well as an awareness of process, of how final products come about.

Books that appeal to the senses are valuable in a

classroom for two-year-olds. These are the books with textured pictures, with pictures that can be manipulated to make sound, with pop-out pictures, and with pages which in fact are part of the construction of a particular object. Children can interact with these books without having to concentrate on a story line.

If you have the funds, any age group will enjoy listening to records or tape recordings of stories, or of their own conversations and made-up stories. Such recordings can be in the library area or in a separate section of the room. Another, less expensive, story companion is a felt board. Any sturdy flat surface wrapped in felt is a felt board. Pictures relevant to stories can be cut from felt and will adhere to the felt board with no other adhesive necessary. For paper pictures, tape some sandpaper to the back and they, too, will adhere.

Books are expensive, and children's books are no exception. However, you need not purchase all the books you need in order to have a well-stocked library. In addition to buying used books at reduced rates, look for publishers offering liberal discounts to educational organizations. But the greatest savings will come from extensive use of public libraries. They not only have a large selection you can use free, but they generally offer extended borrowing schedules to schools and can help you decide on the list of books you do want to own.

Setting Up the Library Area. Use your imagination to make the library attractive — more than just a storage area for books. You can, for example, avoid using shelves to define its boundaries. Do something inventive like using large plants, mobiles, tubes, or plywood walls for boundaries. Shelves can then be used as a central focal point, or more functionally, to subdivide the library area. You might also avoid hard-back chairs and use cushions, stuffed chairs, pillowed alcoves, raised benches, and/or rugs for seating. One very imaginative center used an old front car seat (replete with seat belts too!). Decorate the walls of the library with children's artwork, posters, magazine cutouts, and photographs. A display table for new or forgotten books is generally effective; other tables are not necessary if the floor space is comfortable.

If space allows, consider having different sections of the library area for different kinds of activities. One section may be for noisy group activity; another for more quiet, individual activity; still another for whatever miscellaneous activities children create. The sections can be marked in a variety of ways. One obvious method is to use bookshelves to partition the larger area. Another possibility is to have platforms of several different heights and sizes to indicate different activity sections, or you can use the plants and mobiles and walls suggested earlier. Finally, you can simply let your seating arrangements indicate the kinds of activities and the numbers of children appropriate for different sections.

When deciding where to locate the library, keep the need for good light in mind. A window is not necessary if there is adequate reading light. Typically, the library area functions best with maximum closure or separation from other activities. The neighboring activity areas should offer a minimum of loud noise or distractions. Puzzles and table games generally work out well as a library neighbor. In fact, only art, carpentry, water play, and musical instrument areas should be deliberately avoided.

Block Area

Perhaps the one universal area in preschool classrooms is the block corner. It's an area where most elements of the preschool curriculum can be addressed, thanks to the catalytic function of blocks. Dramatic play, for example, is often as lively in the blocks area as in the housekeeping area. Children build boats and become sailors; they build planes and become pilots. Does someone want to play store? Simple. Just build a storefront from blocks and see how high-pressure a salesman can really be.

Number concepts are also a ready by-product of block play. With a standard set of nursery school blocks, children can deal with such questions as, "How many of these (a four-inch block) will you need to make one of these (a twelve-inch block)?" Because they can visualize such questions in the context of an interesting activity, developing number concepts will be painless. Furthermore, learning the vocabulary of relative size and shape as well as how to work with others, articulate ideas, and plan projects can result from block play.

Materials.   Unit blocks — the nursery school blocks mentioned above — are the standard, most basic blocks. Although expensive (about $100 for a full nursery school set and $50 for a half set), they are essential and not readily made by even your most talented do-it-yourself teacher. The other side of the expense, however, is that they last. Unlike most other materials, you won't have to worry about damaging blocks. Unit blocks are the most versatile, appealing, and standard blocks, but other kinds make good additions to the range of block play. There are four major varieties: hollow blocks, cardboard blocks, Jumbo Lego Bricks, and table blocks.

Hollow blocks are much larger than nursery school blocks. They generally look like yellow crates, and children can build life-size structures from them. While they are perhaps too heavy for two's and three's to use, four's and five's will enjoy the challenge of larger, heavier blocks. Because structures built with hollow blocks are large, children will want to climb on, walk through, and sit in them. The blocks you buy should therefore weigh at least two pounds each — light enough for children to handle and heavy enough to support them.

Cardboard blocks are especially nice for younger children. They come flat and are easily folded and secured. They are usually brightly colored with geometric designs, or made to resemble bricks. And they have the decided advantage of being light enough for two-year-olds to build large units without being hurt by toppling structures or carelessly tossed blocks.

Jumbo Lego Bricks are plastic red, white, and blue rectangular interlocking blocks, four inches long. Although used in the same way as construction sets in the puzzles and table games area, they require a lot of floor space on which to collapse, because Lego Brick structures are large and towering. The smaller school set of Lego bricks, on the other hand, belong in the puzzle and table games area. These are only an inch long and require the same space as other puzzles and table games. Do not confuse them with Jumbo Lego Bricks.

Table blocks fall more readily into the category of puzzles and table games, but their name confuses people. We include them in this section because they function well as an introduction to block play for children who are intimidated by standard blocks or by the more aggressive social interaction that generally characterizes the block area. Table blocks are small and literally require only a table for use.

In addition to blocks per se, a variety of props stored with blocks completes a well-equipped block area. Props representing animals, cars and trucks, trees, street signs, and community people provide further incentive to discover, build, and act out, a bit more of the world in which children live. Props are generally listed with blocks in supply catalogues and come in a variety of materials and sizes. Unfortunately, not all props are stable enough to stand without support. It is worth a few extra dollars to buy props which stand securely. We prefer rubber props to metal or cardboard because they last longest, cause fewest accidents, and don't chip, break, or wear easily. When you decide which props to buy, beware of the tendency to overstock the block corner with them. Children are generally extremely imaginative and creative with only a few materials.

Setting Up the Block Area.   The two prerequisites here are easy visibility of blocks when stored and sufficient floor space to build large structures. Anticipate that three to six children will be at the block area at any given time and they will want to keep their structures up for a long while after they are built.

Store blocks in low shelves according to size and shape so that both size and shape are easily recognizable. Shelves may be used to mark the general boundaries of the block area but not to fully enclose it. The opportunity to build out as well as up should be preserved by having one side at least partially open-ended. An alternative to using shelves for boundaries is to use old railroad ties or a narrow, raised platform. Then the shelves of blocks can be flush with the wall.

Partially carpeting the blocks area with a short-haired rug will muffle some of the noise inevitably accompanying block play, but noise can never be prevented completely. It is important to consider noise level when locating blocks in the room. As mentioned earlier, the library area would suffer neighboring the block area, while the housekeeping area would benefit from the added impetus to dramatic play. Although puzzles and table games are generally more sedentary and quiet activities than block play, they do not suffer from neighboring noise as long as there is an adequate partition between the two areas. In classrooms for younger children it is unwise to locate blocks near animals in open-air cages. They are neither old enough to be careful of animals while using blocks, nor sophisticated enough to use blocks well with animals. The older children, on the other hand, may be careless or even cruel at times, but they are more aware of the dangers of hurting animals with blocks, and, with a little encouragement, can develop elaborate mazes or ultramodern cages for the animals. Finally, neither a sandbox nor a water-play table makes a very good neighbor for blocks. In short order, the blocks will be either warped by water or buried in sand.

Art Area

The art area is the most diverse of the five basic areas. Painting, drawing, cutting, pasting, collage, clay, and papier-mâché modeling are only the most obvious art activities. In fact, there is almost no end to the number and variety of projects an art area yields. Often, more than one art activity will be going on at the same time, or perhaps a single activity will be popular enough to include all children simultaneously. For these reasons, it is best to have an area with direct access to a large open space.

Although a good preschool art program has many objectives, it is perhaps necessary to point out that developing technical skill should not be one of them. Rather, exposure to a variety of media should be emphasized. Children should have considerable opportunity just to mush, squish, scribble, and experiment with art materials, both to enjoy the range of things that can be done with them and to know how it "feels" to use different materials.

A good teacher will recognize that art activities encourage nonverbal communication and provide an outlet for tension and hostility or fear. In light of this, the teacher will not impose ideas about how something should look, how it should be made, or what a child should paint or draw. This is not to say that all requests for assistance should be refused. Rather, children should be encouraged to use their own imagination and to feel that whatever they do will be acceptable. Again, that does not mean that teachers must give indiscriminate praise to all artwork. There will always be children who are more adept than others, and their skills should be recognized. However, there will always be something truly praiseworthy about any honest effort, if it is only the effort itself. If you create an atmosphere which encourages free expression, the children will generally have quite a bit to say about their paintings or drawings. Relating their comments to the actual drawings can be invaluable in revealing the emotions of each child and his needs.

It is helpful for teachers to be familiar with the developmental stages of drawing so they can understand what appears to be just scribbling or misperceived representations. When teachers recognize the differences in ability level, emotional motivation, and perception skills, they can begin to make productive use of children's artwork without making serious mistakes in judgment.

Finally, art activities can be both a catalyst for and a by-product of many other activities. In fact, art can integrate the entire inventory of activities available in your classroom: carpentry projects can be painted; block structures use homemade scenery; library books are illustrated; dramatic play utilizes costumes and puppets; parties need decorations; and puzzles can be constructed.

Art seems to be the most pervasive preschool activity, but it can be overused. Indeed, it's important to recognize that many inexperienced teachers are not familiar enough with the full complement of activities appropriate for preschoolers, that they consistently cling to the most obvious and readily exciting kind of activity — art. As they become more experienced, they will be able to put their art time in better perspective, but until then, they will need a more elaborate art area than more experienced teachers who will not translate all other activity areas into art area satellites.

Because of the great range of teaching styles with respect to art activities, it is most difficult to determine the variety and quantity of art supplies you will need. Thus, the policy of ordering supplies several times during the year is quite appropriate. With each successive order you will learn more about teachers' needs without suffering over an extended period from mistakes made in early orders.

Materials.   Be wildly imaginative in finding materials for the art area. Don't limit yourself to prepackaged stuff even if you have unlimited funds. An enormous range of activities require only "beautiful junk" scavenged throughout the community at no cost. Using beautiful junk is not just a way to save money, it is also a way to insure a high-quality art program. See page 223 for the kinds of junk to look for and places they might be found.

The store-bought materials come in almost as great a variety as beautiful junk, but we have found that basic materials are as follows:

PAINT

Tempera. You can get premixed or powdered paint, or both, but if you choose the latter, be sure your teachers don't try to economize by making paint thin and watery. Nothing is more frustrating than drippy, runny paint. A wide range of colors is always appropriate, but minimally you will need the primary colors and black and white.

Finger Paint. Again, you will need the three primary colors minimally, but a large selection of colors is best.

PAINTBRUSHES

Brushes come in all sizes, but you will rarely need more than three sizes. At least half should be about one inch wide, with the other half a mixture of wider and narrower brushes.

PAPER

Brown Paper. Buy a roll and spend a bit more money to get a dispenser with a cutting edge. This kind of paper is invaluable for murals and miscellaneous projects, like body tracings. Although it comes in many widths, it is best not to buy a roll narrower than 30 inches wide.

Construction Paper. Buy this in all colors. If you are able to, buy it in several different sizes, otherwise, 18 by 24 inches is the most versatile size, and it can always be cut into smaller sizes.

Finger Paint Paper. Highly glossy white paper specifically designed for finger painting. Buy the 18-by-24-inch size. Glossy shelf paper is an inexpensive substitute which works well; so does a formica top when children don't want to take their paintings home.

Heavy Drawing Paper. Not all drawings need be on this paper, the most expensive you need. However, children should have an occasional opportunity to work with it. This is the most appropriate paper to use in making children's books discussed under library area materials. Again, 18 by 24 inches is best if you can buy only one size.

Newsprint. Most easel painting can be on newsprint of the standard 18-by-24-inch dimensions. It is the least expensive paper in the classroom, a mainstay of many activities. It also comes on a roll.

Oak Tag. Shiny, thin cardboard sometimes known as tagboard. It comes in many different colors and should be bought in at least five or six colors.

Tissue Paper. One of the most beautiful and pleasurable art projects for children and adults is tissue paper collage. It is done with torn pieces of colored tissue paper and watered-down glue. The colors run to make new colors and interesting designs, and the overlapping paper makes a collage of textures as well as color.

EASELS

While you can get along without easels by using tabletops or walls, we find the freedom and perspective provided by easels, especially upright floor easels, is worth the expense and, except under the most limited budget, should be considered essential. They are easy and inexpensive to make, as well as available at a variety of prices.

CLAY

Clay comes in many grades and colors. We recommend moist clay in the standard gray color and inexpensive grade. If you anticipate extensive work with clay, or really want the variety of clay available, supplement the basic gray with both Plasticine and colored clay. You may also want a few clay-work tools, but for the most part only the older children will use them, and the most basic tools listed in catalogs will be all that is necessary. Play dough, on the other hand, is all that any classroom really needs. It can be made at almost no cost with flour, oil, salt, and food coloring, or bought ready-made from curriculum suppliers.

Additional supplies are clay boards and containers. The former serves both to protect table tops and to allow maximum portability. Both functions can be served at no expense by covering tables with an oilcloth tablecloth or by having children work on oilcloth-covered or shellacked boards of scrap wood. The clay containers allow you to buy large quantities of clay without fear of its drying and hardening. Any large container lined with a sealable, heavy-duty plastic bag can serve the same function, but never as well as an airtight container.

CRAYONS

Buy lots of crayons. They are used by both children and teachers in dozens of ways and are a classroom staple. Any one of the many crayon varieties will do with the exception of those less than one half inch in diameter, too narrow for the limited small-muscle control of preschoolers. Pick whichever shape suits your fancy and buy in a large assortment of colors. If you buy sets of six to eight crayons, you will find them less likely to be lost and broken than large-quantity packages of sixty to eighty crayons each.

GLUE

Glue, much more than paste, is another staple in the preschool classroom. A room of twenty children can easily use a gallon a month. Almost anything can be glued, and gluing projects always appeal to children. Although there are many brands, we have found that Elmer's glue is substantially better than others we have tried.

CHALK

Kindergarten chalk. A very thick brightly colored chalk which usually makes both hands and clothing brightly colored, too. Children love to use it, and it is valuable for outdoor play, especially if you contend with cement and concrete rather than grass and trees.

Charcoal. Many teachers have found charcoal a well-received addition to the classroom, but it is not essential.

White chalk. If you have a chalkboard, you will of course need chalk. Almost any classroom can put a chalkboard to good use, but it is not essential to have one.

CHALKBOARD
See white chalk.

MAGIC MARKERS
These are the felt-tip pens which come in many sizes, colors, and points. Children especially like the thick-pointed variety and will use them at every opportunity. There's something very satisfying and controllable about Magic Markers that makes them so popular. However, they are very expensive, especially since they do not last long and have a way of getting lost or dried up, thanks to easily lost tops. Because Magic Markers are expensive, many centers limit them to teacher use only.

POPSICLE STICKS AND TONGUE DEPRESSORS
These can be glued, pasted, nailed, painted, and modeled in dozens of different projects. They are simply a nice material to have for little extra expense.

PIPE CLEANERS
Not only do these help develop small-muscle control, they are also useful in almost any art project. Puppets, dolls, mobiles, sculpting, and collaging are only the most obvious kinds of projects making good use of colored pipe cleaners.

In addition to pipe cleaners, many teachers find thin lengths of colored wire very useful. It can be bought from curriculum suppliers or scavenged as beautiful junk from electricians and telephone companies.

PAPER CUTTER
There should be at least one paper cutter available to teachers and preferably one per classroom. They are

extremely dangerous and cannot be operated safely by children.

SCISSORS

Although younger children (up to three years old) cannot use scissors, they should be given an opportunity to try on occasion. Many older children will still have difficulty using them, but for the most part all enjoy them. A classroom of twenty older children should have between ten and fifteen children's scissors; younger children need about five scissors unless many are already skilled in using them. In addition to small children's scissors, you will need adult's scissors, a wire cutter, and, on occasion, a pinking shears.

STRING AND TWINE

With string or twine, a piece of paper can become a cape or wings; macaroni can become a beaded necklace; and all art activities multiply in range of possibilities. All sizes and weights are useful.

WIRE

Many projects, especially making mobiles, benefit from pliable wire. A good supply of wire can generally be scavenged as beautiful junk.

YARN

Sewing with yarn is a good way to begin developing small-muscle control. It serves many of the same functions as string and wire and should be used in conjunction with them to add color and texture.

STATIONERY GOODS

Masking tape, Scotch tape, paste, pencils, pens, erasers, pads, labels, and other gummed stuff; hole punchers, staplers, and thumbtacks always have a productive place in the preschool. They are especially good for free-play activity, but they can also be incorporated into more formal activities. A good supply of each item should be available to all classrooms.

Setting Up the Art Area. The three kinds of activities an art area must accommodate are table, floor, and easel work. Because of the space needed for each of these categories, it's important to have a large area facing an open space so activities can spread.

In addition, you should assume that at least two different table activities will often be going on simultaneously. Appropriate planning for this includes separate tables for different activities and allowing for the possibility that different table activities may have to be separated.

In a classroom of twenty children, four to eight children may be easel painting at the same time. Most standing easels accommodate two and often four children. Therefore, you will need two to four easels with paint containers. Locate easels so they do not reduce available floor space and are away from distractions.

Because of the enormous variety of art materials, it is especially important to give careful thought to storage. You should store materials so you can put your finger on any item quickly. Teachers' and children's materials should be effectively separated.

We suggest that teachers locate storage facilities near the areas they serve. Paints, painting paper, brushes, and smocks, for example, should be stored near easels.

Large rolls of paper should be out of reach of children but readily available to teachers. Other paper for table work should be stored according to size, color, and variety in a way that gives teachers access to the whole supply while both children and teachers have small quantities available on a daily basis. Generally, it is helpful to build units with low, open shelves for children, and higher shelves with doors and locks for teachers. However you store paper, all paper cutters and adult scissors must be kept out of children's reach.

Beautiful junk is often a serious storage problem. For

large items or large quantities of junk, it is probably best to decorate cartons and either label them or draw pictures of the contents on them. For example, fabric scraps can be kept in a box painted gaily with the word *Material* on it or a fabric collage attached to indicate the contents. Similarly, excelsior, styrofoam, carpet, tile, and cardboard tubes may be in separate cartons.

Small items — beads, buttons, popsicle sticks, etc. — can be stored in muffin tins, tin cans, and jars. Again, these should be stored out of children's reach, with only small quantities made available to children. In that way you can set limits to activities and save your supply from instant exhaustion.

There are several possibilities for creating boundaries to the art area. Some teachers find that using storage shelves, tables, and easels to define general boundaries is sufficient. Others use raised platforms for delineating both the different sections of the art area and the general art boundaries. Still others have found no real need for boundaries as long as all equipment is highly portable, including storage shelves. They feel free to arrange and rearrange the art area as the day's activities require. Finally, those teachers who find art a pervasive element of their daily curriculum often choose not to limit art equipment to one area of the room; they punctuate the entire room with various materials and equipment for art. Keep in mind the need for water. Minimally, the easels should be near the water supply. Other areas benefit from proximity to water, but if you choose to scatter the art areas, then the priority should be for painting to be near water.

Puzzles and Table Games Area

This is perhaps the most difficult area to arrange effectively, yet it requires the least adult supervision and results in some of the most educationally productive activity, both formal and informal. Number concepts, abstract reasoning, small-muscle control, group cooperation, individual concentration, shape and size concepts, observation skills, and all varieties of language development are addressed in the puzzles and table games area.

Materials.   Deciding which materials you want to include in this area is difficult. There is almost no end to the number and variety available, and each item you look at will probably seem better than the last. When perusing catalogs or browsing through toy stores, it will be obvious which items belong in a place labeled "Puzzles and Table Games"; less obvious is which items are appropriate for which age group. Two-year-olds do not have the attention span, the coordination, or the abstract reasoning that four's and five's have. Their games should therefore be considerably less complex, abstract, and time consuming. However, the two's should be given the opportunity to develop all of the skills mentioned above with materials you provide. In many instances, they will just do simpler tasks with the same materials you provide for older children, but many items are best suited for one age group rather than another.

We make distinctions between older and younger children rather than between specific age groups because the sophistication levels of specific age groups vary and three-year-olds seem to be in no-man's-land with respect to puzzles and table games. Some will be quite content with the two-year-old's games, and others will want more sophisticated equipment. If you have a classroom of just three-year-olds, equip it with more advanced puzzles and table games for two-year-olds and less advanced materials specified for four's and five's.

PUZZLES

Puzzles should have large pieces and bright colors. (Many come equipped with small knobs on each piece for developing small-muscle control. They are good, but children won't use them consistently.) For two-year-olds, it is best to have puzzles consisting of several one-piece pictures on the same board. One-piece pictures can be varied objects (clock, boat, dog, umbrella), classes of objects (animals, shapes, school items), or part of a larger scene (children throwing a ball at the beach might have a removable boy, girl, ball, pail, shovel, and pet dog). Parts of a whole should be discernible parts so that a whole head, for example, not part of the head, is removable. Whatever is depicted, realism is a virtue here. Children should recognize on their own what any given part is rather than discover it in the context of the whole puzzle.

Puzzles with pictures on the backs of pieces are newer, and appropriate for many ages. One puzzle, for example, shows a house with the rooms logically located behind each piece, drawn on the back of that piece. Discovering the picture behind the puzzle piece delights children and encourages them to discuss the functions relevant to each picture.

A more active kind of puzzle is one teachers make themselves. Cutting letters, shapes, or objects from thick cardboard creates puzzles of excitingly large dimensions, especially if the cardboard is the size of a child, or preferably, larger. The trick to making a good puzzle of this sort is to leave one-quarter of the thickness uncut in order to have a firm base.

For four's and five's, puzzles with eight to fifteen pieces are appropriate. You need only a few of the object puzzles which the two's use, because older children are more able to recognize pieces as parts of a whole and should have opportunities to develop their observation skill. Many new puzzles for older children are, in effect, two puzzles. For example, one side might depict a mother animal in her habitat and the other side, the mother and her babies. Only a few of these are useful; they require abilities many four's and five's don't have until later in the year, if at all.

PEGBOARDS

There are two kinds of pegboards. One has several rows of holes and children simply put dowels or other shaped pegs into the holes. The other kind has several rows of pegs around which children can put rubber bands in any design they choose. Both can be bought or homemade, and both are useful for all age groups. To make the latter, hammer several rows of nails into a board one to two inches apart, allowing sufficient room to wind string, rubber bands, or other materials around the nails with ease. The other kind of pegboard is more difficult to make, because you must be sure that the holes you make fit the pegs you supply.

GIANT ATTRIBUTE BLOCKS

Giant attribute blocks are colorful plastic blocks in large and small, thick and thin, red, yellow, and blue triangles, squares, circles, and rectangles. There is almost no end to the variety of activities these blocks suggest. They are so versatile that infants and math scholars alike can enjoy and be challenged by them. We especially like them for preschoolers because they can be used by one or many children and help develop the most basic early learning skills.

CONSTRUCTION SETS

The most well-known construction sets are Tinkertoys and Erector Sets, but toy makers offer dozens of variations of this theme in bright stimulating shapes and colors. Children enjoy these both as blocks and as a game of precision skill. Several varieties should be available in each classroom.

LOTTO

Lotto games are matching picture card games. Teachers can easily make their own lotto games, but many prepackaged sets are designed for developing specific skills at various developmental levels. Only the simplest lotto games are appropriate for two's. Older children will probably become skilled with several different sets by the end of the year.

STRINGING STUFF
　　Beads, large macaroni, empty spools of thread, rubber
　　washers, and drilled bottle caps are only a few of the
　　many items children can string to make jewelry or just
　　to have the satisfaction of combining materials. Both
　　small muscle control and eye-hand coordination are
　　developed in this activity.

TABLE BLOCKS
　　Table blocks were mentioned earlier as a good intro-
　　duction to block play for more intimidated children.
　　But they also serve a much broader function. They help
　　develop observation and perception skills, small muscles,
　　and number concepts. Try to include at least six or
　　seven varieties over the course of a year with older
　　children. Younger children need three or four varieties
　　during a year. Parquetry blocks, geo blocks, small Lego
　　blocks, colored cubes, and sets called "table blocks" are
　　all appropriate.

PUZZLE AND TABLE GAMES ESPECIALLY GOOD FOR
TWO-YEAR-OLDS
Shape Sorter. The shape sorter is a container with geometric
　　or other shapes cut out of the sides and pieces to match
　　those shapes. The object is to find the piece that
　　matches each cutout so that one can put the piece into
　　the container through the cutout.
Stack Puzzles. These toys help develop relative size
　　discrimination — whether a smaller object must be
　　stacked on a larger object or put inside a larger one, and
　　so on. Since there is only one order for stacking, these
　　puzzles frustrate misperception and reward accuracy.
Pounding Benches. The standard design is a reversible
　　workbench-type frame with colorful dowels that can be
　　pounded down with a mallet. Other varieties serve the
　　same function; all are listed under manipulative mate-
　　rials in supply catalogs.

Lock Box. These have different kinds of standard locks, latches, knobs, and handles. They are small and loose enough for children to manipulate and are set on the same base board for ready comparison. The lock box is excellent for developing small-muscle control and increasing familiarity with the adult world.

ESPECIALLY FOR FOUR'S AND FIVE'S

Abacus. There are many specifically styled for young children and the math concepts they are ready to understand.

Threaders. Wires in a variety of convolutions attached to a base, accompanied by beads or other threadable items, are called threaders. They are especially effective in helping children develop both small-muscle coordination and self-confidence.

Setting Up the Puzzles and Table Games Area. There will probably be several different activities going on here at once, and the range of need will include quiet and seclusion as well as open space and freedom to be noisy. To accommodate such diverse needs, simply have different tables with different materials arranged according to the kind of activity they suggest. The materials can be limited to whatever has been set out on those tables each day; or storage shelves can be used to divide the area into smaller sections for different activities. Other possibilities include creating a network of carpeted, multi-leveled platforms. The platforms may be divided by storage areas. Some teachers even have several areas in different sections of the room to accommodate the various needs of puzzles and table games.

There is no standard breakdown for subdivisions in this area, but the following are possibilities: puzzles and manipulative toys which can be done by one person in a small space; group puzzles and table games in a larger space; materials requiring a lot of space on a table (table blocks) or on the floor; and finally, materials used in more direct instruction. The spaces in the puzzles and table games area should be reorganized to reflect the increasing sophistication of the children's skills. It is important that materials ordered for puzzles and table games have a wide range of skill level so that even at the end of the year children are both challenged by more difficult materials and rewarded by immediate success with easier materials.

Don't display all available materials at once. Rotate them to maximize the life-span of each item. Both the children's interest and the benefits they derive will increase if all items are not always at hand. And from a practical standpoint, you will overcome, to some extent, the major difficulty of puzzles and table games: *they get lost easily.* By limiting the available materials and providing specific storage areas for each item, you'll minimize loss and damage.

DEVELOPING THE CLASSROOM:
OTHER DESIRABLE CURRICULUM AREAS

We consider the five basic curriculum areas essential elements of a preschool program for both their versatility and appeal to children. If you must severely limit the design of your classroom, these basic areas are the minimum.

In this section we will outline six more curriculum areas we feel have an important place in the preschool classroom. They are "desirable" rather than basic for two reasons: first, they don't require a permanent place in the room and can be set up on a temporary basis without difficulty (with the exception of the sand area), and second, the activities can, in many respects, be incorporated into the five basic areas. The distinction between basic and desirable areas is made primarily for determining priorities. We encourage you to include as many of both the basic and desirable areas in your classrooms as possible.

Water Play
Water is not only the most universal solvent, it is very nearly the universal instructor. When children begin to explore water, they will simply splash and slosh, pour and bubble; they will do little conscious exploration. But once they are familiar with the water-play table, they will begin a seemingly endless quest for experience.

As a science resource, the water-play table develops a

sense of sinking and floating, categories and sets, solubility and insolubility. It is a medium for discovering the world of color and optics, weight and volume relationships. Surprisingly complex power systems are devised and set to work with only a few waterwheels and tubes. Language skills, both conversation and vocabulary, develop as children talk among themselves and with their teacher about what they're doing, the problems they've devised, and the answers they've discovered. Where else do children interact with water? At the beach? In the rain? In the bathroom? The kitchen? Discuss these experiences; display pictures of them; and learn about them in conjunction with the water-play table for a productive social studies activity.

Materials. Obviously the most essential water-play materials are a water container and water. The container may be hooked up to a faucet, or it can be virtually any container that won't leak. Several large plastic basins will do as will a homemade wooden box covered with several coats of waterproofing. Sturdy plastic wading pools, large toy rowboats, a large bassinet, an old trunk, or an elegant water-play setup available through classroom suppliers will do as well as the fauceted sink. Unfortunately, only a table with faucet and drain avoids the time-consuming problem of filling and emptying the table, but children can help in both processes, and if plumbing isn't involved, the water-play table can be moved from place to place or removed altogether with little effort.

The materials to use in conjunction with water play are virtually limitless. Here is a partial list:

Buckets
Corks
Washers
Funnels
Strainers
Tin cans (with and without holes drilled on the sides)
Plastic, metal, rubber, and spray-topped containers of all
    shapes and sizes

Tubing of all lengths, widths, and convolutions
Clay
Waterwheels
Bubble pipes
Straws
Soapsuds
Food coloring
Eyedroppers
Plastic egg cartons
Ice cube trays
Sponges
A variety of fabrics for varied absorbency levels
Rubber gloves
Boards with all sizes of holes
Any objects which can be tested for floating and sinking
Waterproof balances
Paintbrushes
Boats
Small hoses
Etc., etc., etc.

The teacher's responsibility is to determine which items are appropriate at what times. If he or she is just introducing water play, only a few basic containers and tubes, soapsuds, and food coloring are necessary. If, on the other hand, a consideration of floating and sinking is the object, it is wise to omit the waterwheels, tubes, and food coloring. Even if the teacher just wants to maintain interest over a long period of time, he or she should keep some materials out of sight so they can be introduced gradually and offer a new perspective. Although not essential, it is generally a good practice to provide waterproof smocks for water players. These can be store-bought, homemade of oilcloth, or created out of plastic garbage bags with three holes cut for head and arms.

Many curriculum suppliers prepare several items especially designed for effective water play. They are good and shouldn't necessarily be dismissed; however, if you are anxious to save money, this, like the housekeeping area, is one place to do so. Homemade and "found" materials work just as well.

Setting Up the Water-Play Area.   If you are going to have a fauceted table, where you set up will be determined by where you can connect the faucet. If you are going to supply water with human labor, then you are freer to choose any site you wish, but keep in mind the distance between the table and the water source. You will minimize mess and effort if you locate the water table within easy access of the water supply. If you keep the table and the surrounding area bright and stimulating with pictures, mobiles, and an interesting array of materials, the water-play table will undoubtedly be a favorite area. Since it will attract several children at a time, you'll need a large enough table to accommodate about ten children. You might keep the table in another room, or limit the number of children who play there by introducing water play along with other very popular activities and making the water area somewhat isolated.

Many of the materials for water play will be stored away from the table and accessible only to adults. However, there should be some choices open to the children. Pegboards on a nearby wall serve as convenient, efficient storage for water-play equipment. So will shallow shelves in the water-play area, or sailcloth pockets attached to the table. If you are building your own table, you might consider shelves under it as both a storage unit and a stand to elevate the table to the appropriate height for your children. There's no need to create closure or even suggest closure around the water-play table because by definition the activity is confined to the area immediately surrounding the table.

Sand Play
While sandboxes of all shapes and sizes are standard outdoor equipment, they are rarely found indoors. It's unfortunate because sand play, like water play, is as versatile and popular an activity and teaching device as one could hope for. Wet sand as well as dry sand is effective, and children of any age or personality find satisfaction in using both of them.

Materials. Sand-play materials are almost identical to those for water play. Funnels, sifters, strainers, containers with holes, scoops, spoons, cups, and anything else that can contain sand, let it pour, spill, and be shaped is good. We have found the best sand areas created directly on a floor which is protected by tarpaulin or durable plastic. The sides can be built up with old railroad ties, a very sturdy wood or brick wall, or with cinder blocks, You can also buy or build self-contained sandboxes with their own base and sides. However, one effective method for dealing with the "mess" is to leave one side of the sand box open so that you need only a broom to replace sand that inevitably leaves the box.

The sandbox should be large to inspire the full range of activity possible. You might also add climbing structures in the sandbox. For two's and three's this is perhaps one of the most effective ways of developing coordination, balance, and strength without a corresponding number of bumps, cuts, bruises, and scary spills. If the sand area is large enough, the climbers and the castle builders need not interfere with one another.

A sandbox should be large enough to accommodate between five and eight children. The sand should be minimally eight inches deep within a enclosure six inches above sand level. Eighteen inches is the outer limit for the depth of sand. It is wise to wet your sand frequently. This cuts down dust and offers variety in sand activity. Have as varied an array of materials as you do for water play, limiting and changing materials as necessary and appropriate. If you live in a climate where it snows, sand play can double as snow play. Food coloring is very effective for both.

Setting Up the Sand Area. Sand is messy. Avoid close proximity to animals, plants, library, and cooking, if possible. If you can't avoid being near these areas, set up high boundaries to squelch the temptation of seeing how well animals survive in sand or how Jello tastes with a sandy topping. Although sand, like water play, fares best in isolation, it can be effective near blocks, the housekeeping area, a science corner, or puzzle and table games because neither the noise nor mess of any one of them will disturb the others if boundaries are sufficient. If you don't want to leave sand-play materials in the sandbox itself, low shallow shelves or pegboards work very well for storage as well as for defining boundaries.

Carpentry Area

Often carpentry is viewed with horror by adults who feel it's too dangerous and difficult for preschoolers. Ironically, the best way to avoid danger is by buying not children's tools but adult tools *and* by demanding that they be treated as tools, not toys. By limiting the number of children at the carpentry table and by providing adult supervision at all times, you can feel sure that children will not be in danger — they will learn to handle tools in and out of school with safety and success.

No more than four children should be at the carpentry table at any one time. It's not necessary to demand that children "make something." Just nailing two boards together or sawing a piece of wood in half is productive. If children want to make something and ask you for ideas, simple boats and airplanes can be done easily, but abstract creations emerging from the carpentry area are equally important and should never be discouraged.

Once children feel they have successfully built something, they can move to the art area to paint or otherwise decorate their creation. The feeling of accomplishment they derive from starting with raw materials and completing a decorated product is perhaps unequalled in any other activity, no matter what the final product is. Moreover, carpentry is invaluable in developing eye-hand coordination, small-muscle control, and an awareness of some basic physical phenomena.

Materials. A sturdy worktable with vises attached, hammers, saws, nails, and wood are the basic carpentry materials. Sandpaper is not essential, but is fun for children to use and solves the safety problems of splintered wood. Hand drills are also useful as basic equipment. Screws and screwdrivers might be added, but they are more difficult for children and often get ignored in favor of easier materials.

Four's, five's, and many three's will use the carpentry table extensively and successfully, but younger children cannot be expected to show any skill here. Standard carpentry materials should therefore be excluded from their classroom. Offer instead, activities which encourage the same carpentrylike skills. Toy pounding benches require less strength, coordination, and concern for safety than nailing wood with a hammer, but they utilize the same muscles and energies. A good homemade substitute for carpentry is pounding golf tees into hard clay with a mallet. For those children just about ready to use hammer and nails, you can offer several layers of cardboard glued together instead of wood so nails will penetrate easily.

Simply designed carpentry tables can be bought or homemade. If you make your table, be very sure you make it sturdy enough to withstand misguided hammers and nails and have room to attach a vise.

Pegboards with traced outlines of tools are probably the best means for storing materials. Individual containers for nails, screws, and small miscellaneous items are better than a single container with separate compartments. Wood can be stored in crates, a trunk, or a special wood rack, but it should not be left lying loose on the floor. If you have a large supply of wood, try to limit the supply directly available to children so they won't spend more time selecting their wood than working with it. On the other hand, avoid having so few pieces that there is no choice at all. It's important and fun for children to make this kind of decision.

Setting Up the Carpentry Area.   The noise and sawdust mess of the carpentry area helps determine where to locate it. It doesn't require a large area; like water and sand play, the activity itself limits the space required. Art is probably the area which most complements carpentry. Plants, animals, and the library are least neighborly here. Consider, too, that you don't want children to walk or run with tools, and the best way to avoid this is to make it difficult or uninteresting to do. Keep the carpentry area away from other tempting activities, and enclose it enough so children know they are expected to stay put until they finish a project.

Science
Science covers so much of a preschooler's activity that even if you do have a formal science area, it will be only one of several places used for science. Indeed, a formal science area best functions as a catalyst to experimentation. It should be a place where children interact with materials or get ideas that might lead them anywhere else — in or out of the classroom. Plants and animals are part of science, but shouldn't necessarily be located at the science area. A sound table, for example, may be set up temporarily so children can discover the hows and whys of sound by feeling, observing, and experimenting with many "things" that make sound. The sound table need not be part of the science area per se. Rather, the size of the exhibit, the objectives for having it, and the kind of activity it stimulates should determine its location. The same holds for any special exhibit, regardless of curriculum label.

Materials.   Below are some of the basic materials for the science area. Starred items are optional because they are not essential and are most appropriate for older children.

*Bones for a Skeleton (store-bought or from a carefully carved turkey or chicken)
Eyedroppers
Flashlights and Batteries
Hand mirrors, including concave and convex mirrors
Inclined plane (This can be made with any flat surface propped against two objects of different heights. Books on the table or floor will do, and a piece of board can be the plane.)
Magnets, magnetic and nonmagnetic materials
Magnifying glasses
*Pendulum
Prisms

Reducing glasses and materials to reduce
Rocks and a hammer for cracking them (rocks should be cracked in a towel or bag for protection against flying debris)
*Scales and balances, including a seesaw
*Simple microscopes and objects to view through them
*Stethoscope
Test tubes
Transparent color paddles

Animals. It's always nice to have animals for children to play with, observe, and understand; however, the decision about what animals to have, and indeed whether to have animals at all, should be made carefully. Some of the more important considerations are as follows:

- Animals need a lot of attention. Feeding and cleanup are obvious, but supervising children with animals, caring for baby animals, and tending sick animals are also realities of animal care. Remember, too, that care must continue on weekends and holidays.

- Children may be squeamish, scared, or inconsiderate if animals they handle make sudden movements. Many children will be frightened by any animal.

- A teacher who is nervous around animals must decide whether she can overcome her fear or at least function with that fear without encouraging children to be afraid, too.

- Death will inevitably come to at least one of your animals while the children are there. It is by no means an impossible situation to handle, but it may be something you should avoid if the prospect upsets you.

If you do decide to have animals, the following are appropriate for the preschool classroom:

Chicks	Guinea pig	Rabbit
Fish	Hamster	Snake (lizard
Frog	Insects	or iguana too)
Gerbil	Mice	Turtle

Birds, dogs, and cats may be very good household pets, but they are inappropriate for the classroom. All animals mentioned above are suitable with three- to five-year-olds. Two's and toddlers will be most happy with fish, a guinea pig, and a rabbit. The younger children will delight in observing any animal, but don't expect them to play with, care for, or even be kind to animals.

If one animal had to be singled out as the most successful preschool pet, we would vote for the guinea pig. Baby guineas are born almost ready to take care of themselves; food is both inexpensive and easy to provide; guineas never overeat; they're not prone to sudden, jerky movements; they don't smell; they can't climb; and they are very likely to stay where you put them. They will not bite unless fingers are put directly in front of the mouth in an irritating way, and they come in a variety of colors and hair lengths. While guinea pigs cannot be dropped without a good chance of breaking their small, frail legs, they aren't more fragile than most animals of their size.

Fish, too, are attractive to all children, but there is more to worry about with fish. Not only do they overeat if you overfeed them, but they will eat each other if the tank gets crowded or you select incompatible fish to share the same tank. The tank must be kept clean, well heated and lit, and appropriately set up; it takes time to care for fish. It is also important to have a lid for the tank because children are very likely to drop all sorts of foreign objects into the tank and contaminate it. In light of all these disadvantages, we recommend goldfish for classroom use. They are colorful, hardy, and do not require elaborate heating, filtering, or controlled water conditions.

When trying to decide which animals to have, be sure you get only those you can care for properly in ALL of the following respects:

Cage: What size, location with respect to heat and light, special needs, and cleaning schedule are necessary?

Food: What must the animal eat, in what quantity and according to what schedule? What is the price of the food? Are there any feeding problems?

Handling: What kind of handling will be intolerable to the animal? Can you expect children to avoid that kind of handling?

Babies: Which if any parents must be removed from the cage when babies are born and for how long? What kind of care must you provide for babies and for how long?

Health: Does the animal need any shots? How many, how often, and at what cost? Can people be hurt from a bite, scratch, or other affliction from the animal? Are children likely to be allergic to the animal? Are any of your children known to be allergic to the animal? What kind of health difficulties can you expect, and what is the remedy?

Whatever animals you decide on, be sure to get as much information about their care and handling as possible.

Bugs, ants, worms, and insects are fun to catch and fun to keep. Don't overlook them as a cheap and profitable addition or substitution for classroom animals. They can be kept in jars and require little care. Frogs, toads, and turtles are slightly more difficult. Toads and frogs need flies and insects to eat, and all three are prone to illness or disease when moved to the artificial environment of the classroom. But children love them. They are free, and they can be let loose when you no longer want them.

If you can afford them, chicken egg incubators are exciting. Nothing fascinates children or adults more than the birth of a living thing. However, the problem of what to do with growing chickens should be considered before hatching them. Chicken farms rarely accept classroom hatched chicks because of possible disease or contamination, and full-grown chickens are not well suited for a preschool, except perhaps for those in rural areas with facilities to care for chickens.

Cocoons, nests, and hives are also suitable and relatively inexpensive if they can't be found easily. All these can be shared among several classrooms and have long-range activity and educational values.

You will rarely have to buy any of your animals. With animal shelters in virtually every city, there will always be rabbits, mice, gerbils, guinea pigs, and hamsters to be given away. Furthermore, existing preschool and kindergarten classrooms generally have animals who have babies which teachers are only too happy to give away. Cages can be homemade from scrap materials. Only tropical fish tanks must be bought from a store.

Plants: Potted plants, germinating seeds, and a terrarium are the materials for a plant area. While most preschool classrooms have a terrarium and/or an outdoor garden for vegetables and flowers, too few have potted plants around the room. Philodendron are almost indestructible, and they make a cheerful, attractive, and effective means for defining areas, stimulating interest, and just perking up the classroom.

Flower markets also give away flowers when closing. Our own center is always decorated with a variety of cut flowers because teachers go to the flower market regularly. And flowers are more than just pretty to look at and smell. They can be pressed, observed through the magnifying glass or microscope, strung, arranged, mobiled, collaged, and taken home as gifts.

Many curriculum suppliers sell ready-made terraria, but we prefer the homemade kind. Any box at least six inches deep and of any size is adequate, provided you've remembered that it will be watered often. Fill the box (or a floor area similar to the sandbox, but smaller) with good, rich soil. (Just any old dirt won't do.) Then plant your garden. Any kind of bean seed, quick-growing flower, vegetable, or grass seed will work well. You never have to limit a terrarium to one kind of plant, but try to have plants with similar moisture, light, and heat needs. Children should be responsible for planting, watering, and tending the plants, but of course the teacher has to supervise so that plants won't be overwatered, planted too closely, or uprooted. Two's and three's are able to work with a terrarium under close supervision. They may prefer "soilless garden" — wrapping several seeds (lima beans work best) in moist paper toweling. Keep the towel moist and store it in a dark place. Every day for three to six days, observe the new developments. When they sprout, you can plant the seedlings in a pot. They will last only several days, but that's about all the interest you can count on from the two's. Older children might like to germinate seeds this way, too.

To water plants buy child-sized watering cans, or use paper cups with several pin holes in the bottom, a plastic squeeze bottle with a sprinkle top, or any other container.

However you create your plants area, encourage children to observe them and to become aware of their need for water, air, sunlight, and soil to grow.

Setting Up the Science Area.　The best arrangement for a science area is one *displaying* materials, rather than just storing them, and offering enough table and floor space for both individual and group experimentation. You can arrange separate shelves and tables by subject, or create individual areas of both display and work space. You might also simply set materials out on the tables where children can work with them. However you set up the area, try to provide materials for many possible contingencies.

It is also a good idea to include appropriate picture books, children's reference books, and blank books with crayons along with the science materials. This holds for the terrarium and animals as well. Prisms, mirrors, and magnifying glasses make excellent additions to a fish tank.

Large-Muscle Activity

Although the outdoors is the most common place for large-muscle activity, it's necessary to have indoor equipment for large muscles, too. Foul-weather days keep you inside, but the weather won't affect the children's desire to be active. Even on nice days you may be unable or unwilling to take children outside to play, but they will still need and want an opportunity to be active. How you accommodate these needs depends on how much space and money you have.

Materials.   Below is a list of basic equipment.

BALLS

For infants through two-year-olds, soft, furry, light-weight balls about eight inches in diameter are excellent introductions to ball play. Older children will prefer large rubber balls and smaller throwing balls. Try to avoid balls less than five inches in diameter in the classroom; they can be thrown faster and harder than large balls and cause more painful accidents.

*BICYCLES

You should have, at the very least, four tricyles for a class of twenty four- and five-year-olds. Younger children need smaller-sized bikes. Nothing causes tears and fights more easily than too few bikes. Seven bicycles would be ideal.

*CLIMBING STRUCTURE

Usually a jungle gym, ladder, or a maze of sturdy crates of different heights. We've even seen a marvelous, abstract structure built of old railway ties joined asymetrically to dimensions of 5 by 5 by 6 feet. Anything children can climb on is a climbing structure.

HULA HOOPS

If children can't gyrate well enough to keep the hoops on their hips, they can always find some other use for them. Their imagination and the need to be active will be sufficient. It may be they just want to walk in and out of the loop while holding it, or jump in and out of the hoop on the floor. However children use hoops, they will be active and creative with them.

PUNCHING BAG

A punching bag or some other punching object makes a good outlet for aggression, excellent exercise for large muscles, and an inexpensive, space-saving, easily stored addition to your large-muscle equipment.

ROCKING BOAT

Catalogs use this name to describe an apparatus holding four to six children in a rowboat-shaped rocker. When the boat is turned upside down, it is a two-sided, three-step stairway joined by a platform.

SEESAWS

A seesaw can be part of the science area as a balance, as well as part of the large-muscle area. It requires very little space, can be stored easily, and used in a variety of ways. One of the most popular variations is to make an inclined plane for children to walk up and then jump from. Or add another base for the board, creating an elevated walking board.

SLIDES

Small store-bought slides are adequate, but we prefer the more portable, homemade slide described in *Cardboard Carpentry*, a booklet put out by Education Development Center, 55 Chapel Street, Newton, Massachusetts.

*SWINGS

Although swings with their own frame can be bought

anywhere, we prefer securing swing seats to two heavy chains hung from the ceiling (if possible). This requires considerably less space, offers greater flexibility, and allows for easy storage.

TUMBLING MATS

Children of all ages, including toddlers, benefit from tumbling mats. With careful supervision and several mats, you can involve the whole class in tumbling at the same time.

*WAGONS AND PUSH OR PULL CARRIAGES

Young children love to use these, and the youngest children especially love them. However, wagons and carriages, like bicycles, are a constant source of trouble if you have too few of them. If you make them available to older children, be sure to have adequate space for them really to travel with their wagons.

Items marked with an asterisk require plenty of open space for both use and storage. The other items require minimal space, can be stored easily, and many can remain in the room on a permanent basis.

Setting Up the Large-Muscle Activity Area.   Many day care centers and nursery schools utilize a separate room for large-muscle activity. Some even include all noisy activities — sand play, water play, and carpentry — in this room. Regardless of what you include, we think it's an excellent idea to separate large-muscle play from the other activities. You avoid conflict between boisterous children and those seeking quieter pursuits. You also remove the temptation to ride bikes or wagons or throw balls where other children are working. Teachers can worry less about damage to equipment, and children can feel unhampered. Several teachers can share the large-muscle activity room, but they should work out a schedule so all children are not brought into the room at once.

If your facilities don't allow a separate room, try reserving a specific section of the room for large-muscle activity. If you can't isolate large-muscle activity, select equipment for the space you do have, and clear other materials away to make space for very active play. Don't omit all materials for which you have no indoor room — you still have the outdoors.

Materials you choose for indoor use need not be kept in the room at all times. Rather, select a few items daily, and store others until needed. You may find the rocking boat, punching bag, tumbling mats, and climbing structure so popular that teachers will want to have them on a permanent basis.

Music

Children chant, sing, swing, and move to the rhythm of their activities quite spontaneously. The teacher's function is never to demand that children sing well, or perfect their dance, but to encourage self-expression in a variety of ways.

You don't need a specific part of the room for music, only storage space for instruments and a home for the record player.

Materials.   Contrary to popular opinion, a piano is not essential for a good preschool music program, nor should teachers necessarily be adept at singing or playing an instrument. Both would be definite assets, but they are by no means a must.

If you have a good record player meant for adults only, be sure it is out of children's reach. However, if possible, offer the children the opportunity to select and play records. This experience not only helps them respect the equipment, it also offers the child who feels like being quiet something productive to do and encourages children to be more aware of music they hear.

What kind of records should you use? Not just Mother Goose and fairy tales. Classical, rock 'n' roll, exotic music, and adult folk songs are also good. No form of music is more legitimate for children than any other.

Records, like books, are expensive, but they can be borrowed from libraries or donated. And they can be shared among several classrooms.

Following is a list of instruments you might have for two different-sized classrooms. The starred items are optional if your budget is tight.

If you really have money to spend on music, consider buying some Karl Orff rhythm instruments. They are exciting to look at, use, and listen to, but also expensive.

INSTRUMENT	QUANTITY	
	10 Children	20 Children
*Autoharp	1	1
Bells		
Wrist	3 pr.	3 pr.
*Stick	3 pr.*	3 pr.
*Scale	1 set*	1 set*
Drums		
Hand	2	4
Congo	1*	1*
Bongo	1*	1*
Other	1*	1*
Cymbals	1 pr.	2 pr.
*Gong	1	1
*Guitar	1	1
Kazoos	3	6
Rattles		
Maracas	1 pr.	2 pr.
*Other	1 pr.	1 pr.
*Piano	1*	1*
Rhythm Sticks	3 pr.	5 pr.
Tambourine (6"-10")	1-2	2-4
Tone Blocks	1 pr.	2 pr.
Triangles	2	2
Xylophone	1	1

Homemade Instruments

DRUMS

Use kegs, cheese boxes, wooden mixing bowls, oatmeal boxes, large cans, or coconut shells for the body. The drum head can be made from strong animal skins, tight shellacked cloth, rubber inner tubes, or from regular drum heads available at musical instrument repair shops. The plastic tops on many coffee cans make the cans ready-made drums.

If you use skin or cloth for a drum head, it should be wet before it is fastened to the body for maximum stretch and tightness. Use thumbtacks to fasten the head to the body, if possible. You can use cord where thumbtacks won't work.

A small spool padded with cloth and fastened to the end of a stick makes a good drum stick; so do spoons and dowels. Children or teachers can decorate the drums as they wish.

BOTTLES

A series of bottles filled with varying levels of water the higher the water level, the higher the pitch makes a good percussion instrument. Any wooden or metal object serves as a mallet to"play" the bottles.

FLOWER POTS

Different-sized flowerpots make nice sounds when hung upside down from a bar. Run the string through the hole and attach to a stick slightly larger than the diameter of the hole.

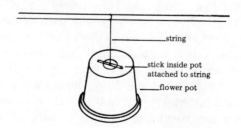

RATTLES

Gourd maracas. Soak gourd, scrub it with steel wool, and dry before using. Remove seeds and put nice small pebbles or large seeds inside the gourd, then cover the hole with tape. These can be painted if you wish.

Shakers. Put seeds, pebbles, rice, paper clips, nails, etc., into a small box. Put a stick through the box as a handle. The handle can be made more secure with tape if necessary. Children can paint the box.

TAMBOURINES

Attach bells to shellacked paper plates and fasten the paper plates so that the concave sides are together. Another method: attach small bells or bottle caps to a tin lid.

BELLS

Wrist bells. Sew Christmas or dime-store bells to a piece of elastic, and sew the ends of the elastic together so that it makes a bracelet small enough for children's wrist.

Stick bells. Attach the elastic to a stick with a stapler.

Much more elaborate homemade instruments are described in a booklet called *Musical Instrument Recipe Book*, which the Education Development Center publishes. (See page 219.)

Language, Numbers, and Social Studies

Each of these aspects of preschool curriculum will pervade all classroom activity; it is unnecessary to create specific areas for them. For example, if children are having cantaloupe for snack, a teacher could ask: How heavy is each cantaloupe? Which is biggest? How many pieces must it be cut into to serve everyone? How can those pieces be cut equally? It may be snacktime, but consideration of size, shape, equality, and division are directly relevant, as are such social studies points as where cantaloupes come from, how they get to us, or a reminder that not everybody in the world eats the same food. The descriptive vocabulary which is part of snacktime is excellent for developing language skills. These opportunities abound every day, and can be directed at any age or skill level.

Puzzles and table games areas are often the most appropriate home for language, numbers, and social studies, but a little imagination and awareness of ways children develop their understanding of these subjects will enable teachers to include them in every other curriculum area as well. The purpose for doing this is not to save space, but to encourage language, number, and social studies skills in a context children enjoy.

Language Materials. Some objectives for selecting language materials: to develop both active and passive vocabularies; to develop conversation skills and ability to articulate needs and ideas; and, finally, to develop skills necessary for reading and writing. Language development depends on conversation, and the best materials are those that stimulate conversation and allow new vocabulary to be introduced into conversation easily.

None of the objectives require a special language area nor very special materials. The best homemade devices for developing vocabulary and conversation are pictures, interesting objects, and a mystery box containing an unknown object which must be felt and described to determine what it is. You can use posters, photographs, reprints, and magazine cutouts, carefully selected to evoke conversation. Their arrangement is crucial. If, for example, a teacher wants to introduce the notion that different words name different groups of things, it's helpful to have pictures depicting those words together, e.g. a *herd* of cattle, a *crowd* of people, a *flock* of geese, and a *bunch* of bananas.

The interesting objects you provide should be selected and arranged with equal care to provoke lively conversation.

Among store-bought materials for vocabulary and conversation skills are picture lotto, giant attribute blocks, and picture attribute blocks, mounted picture series of everyday experiences and extraordinary experiences, children's books (like those by Beatrice de Regnier, who writes in heroic couplets leaving out the last rhyming word for children to supply), and concept-matching cards. Of course, all library area materials are perfect for language development, too.

While many parents are most concerned about reading and writing skills, and feel cheated if a preschool classroom has no formal instruction in reading and writing, it's not really necessary to aim for letter recognition or simple writing skills, even among older children. Rather, exposure and experience encouraging children to *want* to learn to read and write are important. A rich variety of written stimuli in the classroom is very helpful. Supermarket sale signs are free, bold, attractive, and effective; so are labels for objects throughout the room. Pictures with labels, names on artwork, and word collages are also good.

Typewriters are effective for children who are beginning to recognize letters and want to write before they are able to; and for children who are beginning to write, you can provide paper with letters, words, and names to be traced and/or copied.

Since the process of reading and writing requires acute observation skills to discriminate small differences in letters, you should have materials to help develop these skills. We suggest lotto games and puzzles requiring children to put pieces in the order in which pictures they depict are likely to occur.

The most important point to remember is that learning to say the alphabet is perhaps the least important skill in learning to read and write. The alphabet is simply an arbitrary ordering of symbols which represent sounds. Recognizing the symbols' correspondence to particular sounds is the important skill, and developing it requires close observation and familiarity with the symbols.

Numbers Materials.   According to developmental psychologists, there are two prerequisites for dealing with number concepts. The first is an understanding of a one-to-one correspondence between objects. The second involves the conservation of matter — recognizing that changing shape does not necessarily affect quantity. These understandings come with time, experience, and general cognitive development. They cannot be "taught" per se. Rather, the teacher should provide repeated exposure to experiences illustrating these concepts. In water play, for example, filling different-shaped containers with the same equal volume of water illustrates conservation of matter. One-to-one correspondence can be demonstrated by simply setting one juice cup per table setting or showing how many children can use swings by matching one swing to one child.

In addition, there are many possibilities for developing the vocabulary of numbers and recognizing relative size, shape and weight. The block area illustrates the basic principles of fractions as does cooking, even using simple recipes.

If you would like to include some attractive pre-packaged number materials, try to be aware of the concepts they represent. Puzzles, geo blocks, counting cubes, parquetry blocks, and domino games are among many that help develop number concepts.

Social Studies Materials. Social studies at the preschool level is simply an awareness of people, places, and customs. It teaches tolerance of different races and ethnic groups, as well as an understanding of the roles various community workers and family members have. In short, it is an introduction to the social world of which children are a part. Materials for social studies might include maps, globes, pictures of exotic and local places and people; exotic artifacts like dolls, or musical instruments of other cultures; and the equipment various community workers use on their job. These are supplemented by field trips to the post office, fire department, library, zoo, docks, a farm, a factory, subways, or any special building.

Field trips are the most dramatic way to show children many different ways of living, places to live, and the variety of jobs people have. And social studies is such things as having Chinese, Spanish, and Italian food as well as American food on your menus. It is playing exotic music and singing foreign folk songs or songs from other parts of the country. It is seeing a zebra at the zoo and then finding the place where zebras come from on a map.

In fact, social studies, like language or numbers, should be thoroughly integrated into the total classroom activity. If you have a specific area for social studies, it should function primarily for displays which will encourage questions, arouse curiosity, and suggest activities.

Social studies may be the label which best summarizes the curriculum objectives of any good preschool program. It helps children develop a strong self concept, an awareness of the various societal roles with which they interact, and effective interaction within those roles.

OUTDOOR PLAY AREA

Young active preschool children need an exciting outdoor environment giving them opportunities for creating, exploring, discovering, and learning. In that environment they need to invent and to improvise, to build and to destroy, to make things work and to learn how and why. While children enjoy excursions to nearby parks and playgrounds, these cannot replace an outdoor area of their own.

A good outdoor play area will fulfill children's needs for:

— Space
— Safety and Supervision
— Physical exercise
— Problem solving
— Learning through play
— Practising skills: doing and redoing
— Creativity

Materials and Equipment. Elaborate, expensive equipment is not necessary. All the needs of young children mentioned above can be met by the following raw materials for learning out of doors.

SAND

Children enjoy sand because it is malleable. By using only his hands, a child can dig, pile, sift, build, tunnel, mold, and design with sand. An outdoor sandbox should be large (at least 100 square feet). An assortment of inexpensive implements (spoons, cups, cans, sifters, scoops, shovels, bowls, pans, molds, etc.) will give children many hours of pleasure. It's often wise to have a shady sandbox area. An awning will do if trees are not available.

WATER

Water is probably the most popular of all natural play materials. Children are fascinated by it and enjoy exploring its many properties. Water can be poured, squirted, sprayed, and splashed. Toys can be floated, sunk, whirled, or dropped in water — each producing different results. You can use tubs, plastic pools, or water tables and a wide variety of inexpensive clear plastic bottles, syringes (naturally, without needles), watering cans, varying lengths and widths of plastic tubing, short lengths of garden hose, an assortment of brushes, soap for making bubbles and washing doll clothes, food coloring, toys, cups, spoons, cans, cork, wood, metal, etc. — all for experimenting with water.

DIRT

An outdoor space should have grassy areas, shrubs, plants, and trees. And an open space for digging and one for gardening is enjoyable for children. By tending a garden they can watch one of life's greatest mysteries unfold. Too often adults forget the wonders of nature and how important it is for a child to experience them. And living plants bring bees, butterflies, and other insects — all fascinating for study, guaranteed to arouse a child's curiosity. Rakes, hoes, shovels, trowels, watering cans, a garden hose, wheelbarrow, etc., should be provided for gardening and just experimenting with the properties of earth and mud.

BUILDING MATERIALS

Children are doers; they love to create, dismantle, and rebuild anew. Simple materials, such as odd lengths of wood, boards, barrels, hollow blocks, cartons, large spools, packing crates, boxes, sticks, pieces of metal, stones, string, old tires, rope, and cloth, can be used by children to create new and exciting worlds in dramatic play.

CLIMBING STRUCTURES

Healthy children have strong needs for mobility, release, and noisy, dramatic action. They enjoy climbing all sorts of structures, especially those they make themselves. Large packing crates, ladders, and sturdy planks are excellent, and they offer far more variety than a sterile jungle gym. Children can create new structures geared to their interests and abilities if they have the proper tools.

If you have permanent structures, they should be easily adapted to children's changing purposes. For example, an outdoor house might be constructed with stairways, outside ladders of both wood and rope, wide rope mesh for climbing, different platforms and floor levels. Hang swings from extension arm of the playhouse. Children will use the building as a house, fort, castle, store, etc., for dramatic play and physical exercise.

A large mound or grassy hill is excellent for climbing, running, and sliding or rolling down. You can use a large sewer pipe to make a tunnel through the hill.

WHEELED VEHICLES

Part of the outdoor area should be paved. If you can surface a ten-foot-wide space next to the building and build a roof over the area, it can be used year round in all kinds of weather. A paved, winding walk or roadway starting at this point and curving through the rest of the play yard lends variety and lessens traffic congestion. The roadway should be wide enough to allow such wheeled vehicles as tricycles, doll carriages, carts, wagons, wheelbarrows, trucks, and pedal cars to pass by.

OTHER OUTDOOR ACTIVITIES

Weather permitting, almost every activity inside the classroom can be carried on as well or even better outside. You can read stories under a shady tree or awning, and children should be free to choose books to look through on their own.

Often children feel freer, less inhibited working with art materials outside. Painting need not be confined to paper; painting on windows can be fun, too. "Painting" with water is another exciting variation.

Woodworking, applied science, music, creative movement, singing, and dancing are naturals outdoors.

Storage. A storage shed can be attached to the playhouse, main building, or be a separate unit. Suggested size: 10 by 12 feet with a 7-foot ceiling. Door openings should be wide enough to easily admit large wheeled toys. Inside, you will need shelving, 2-to-3 feet wide, to store boards, outdoor hollow blocks, and portable ladders; snap hooks for garden tools; baskets for water- and sand-play toys, balls, etc; and bins for assorted "junk" such as ropes, hoops, pieces of wood, and cloth.

Size, Safety, Supervision. Many states require a minimum of 75 square feet per child. We feel this is a bare minimum; at least 150 square feet per child should be allotted, if possible. However, the size is not as important as ingenious arrangement for optimal use.

Safety must be ensured. Enclosing the play yard with a 4-to-7 foot fence allows children to play without going out of bounds and makes adult supervision easier. Safety and responsible supervision go hand in hand. Some safety suggestions to keep in mind:

— Be sure to have a soft landing surface (sand, dirt, rubber mat, etc.) at the end of the slide. The safest slides are built into hills or mounds so a child cannot fall off the top or sides. Free-standing slides need fenced-in top platforms to prevent falls.

— Place swings away from busy play areas. Plastic discs, rubber tires, canvass or leather seats are preferable to conventional hard wooden or metal swings.

— Don't use hard surfacing, such as concrete and asphalt, under climbing structures. Grass, sand, or rubber-mat surfacing helps prevent injuries from falls.

— Keep all materials and equipment in good repair — free from splinters, jagged edges, and the like.

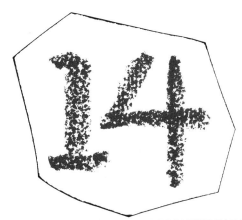

FINDING CURRICULUM MATERIALS

You'll discover a perennial Christmas feeling when you begin to open cartons of materials ordered for your center. However, the process of selecting materials is every bit as frustrating, time consuming, and uncertain as shopping for just the right gifts. Catalogs attest to the countless merits of every item. Everywhere you turn you'll find items hailed as "educationally valuable," "delightful for children," "money-saving" and "a must for your classroom." It is up to you to make decisions about materials and the functions you want them to serve.

It is almost impossible to determine everything you will need in advance because teachers and children will be unique in classroom interaction and therefore unique in their needs. Only they can determine what is really necessary; but you may have to order materials before you know who your teachers and children will be. The best plan, therefore, is one left intentionally incomplete. It begins with classroom necessities and continues only a bit further so you will have second and third orders as the year progresses. Try to anticipate needs for three to six months, and one to two months before that time is up, confer with your teachers and decide what materials you want for the next four to six months. The more frequently you order, the more appropriate your equipment will be. However, it is rarely necessary to order more than once every four months. Petty cash should be sufficient to fill in gaps which arise before the next ordering period.

When you do begin to make decisions about materials for your classroom, keep these considerations in mind:

Can You Afford Them?

Sometimes this does not mean simply, Do you have the cash for an item? You must also consider how big a chunk of available money goes for a particular item, thereby limiting the quantity and/or quality of other things. And consider durability. If an item breaks easily, can it be repaired easily at a low cost, or will it be a constant source of frustration and expense?

Can They Be Shared with Other Classrooms?

Some very expensive equipment becomes less costly when people recognize it does not have to be bought in one-to-a-classroom quantity. We've found that tape recorders, records, movie and slide projectors, teaching machines, microscopes, egg incubators, musical instruments — all expensive items — can be readily shared among several teachers.

Other, less expensive items can also be shared success-fully if the rotation is less frequent. Puzzles, table games, books, dress-up clothes, toy trucks and cars, animals and cages, and water- and sand-play materials belong in all classrooms, but all can be circulated. Don't plan to have materials shared, however, without discussing it with your teachers. They will want their daily schedules to reflect the materials available.

The other side of sharing is frustration. All teachers must be especially conscientious about keeping materials in good condition.

Will the Materials Excite Children's Curiosity, Imagination, and Creativity?

Try to find materials that really stimulate children. Trucks with opening doors, removable trailers, and sizable compart-ments for actually transporting goods, for example, are superior to trucks with all the details painted on them. Often, the former are much more expensive, but we feel the extra money is well spent (even if you are forced to buy fewer trucks) for the extra educational and interest mileage you will get from them. So too for magnifying glasses that *really* magnify and magnets that *really* attract. They actually do excite interest and curiosity, whereas the "toy" magnets and magnifying glasses bring little more than frustration after only a moment of interest and curiosity.

But we don't mean that only expensive items are educationally sound. For example, why buy a fully grown plant when the process of planting and nurturing seeds is much less expensive and much more valuable in terms of education and the length of time children are likely to be interested in it? The point is not how much something costs, but how well it can be used.

Are the Materials Versatile?
Not all materials have to be used in 101 ways to be acceptable, but it's always wise to consider that the best results come when teachers can adapt to specific children and circumstances. We've found many puzzles, for example, are not worth buying because individual pieces are so abstract and stylized they cannot be used for discussions, for simple language and observations games, or even for tracing or color identification. They are at best only puzzle pieces. Similarly, consider whether only a limited number of children can use an item or whether there's a wide range of possible uses.

Giant attribute blocks are an excellent example of a versatile item. Some children will use them as colorful blocks only, others will be able to consider the attributes of color, size, shape, and thickness; still others will delight in the many problem solving games for which they were especially created. The level of "play" ranges from infantile to mathmatically sophisticated, and they can be used by only one child or by as many as five or six.

Needless to say, not everything will be as versatile as attribute blocks. But when you shop, keep in mind the educational range, variety of uses, and number of children various items accommodate.

Are the Materials Stimulating?

Consider all levels of sensory stimulation when selecting materials. Are they colorful and otherwise visually interesting? How about an interesting texture or smell? Do they make any funny sounds or have parts to pull, push, turn, twist, shake, or poke? Some materials may be so stimulating they don't invite constructive, deliberate play. Others can be so single-purposed they are left on the shelf because children get bored by them. Typically, puzzles and games designed to develop number concepts are guilty of this. Materials for the most part should look as if they'll be fun.

Can Children Use Them?

Remember that children, not adults, are the primary user of the materials you get. Therefore, their abilities and behavior should be considered carefully. Are they light and sturdy enough for a specific age group? Can they withstand children's abuse, lack of coordination, and often inappropriate experimentation? Are manipulative toys actually manageable for children in terms of their hand size and limited small-muscle coordination and strength? And, of course, are they safe?

Teaching Considerations

In addition to the above, keep the following questions in mind when ordering materials:

— Are the parts of a toys so small they will inevitably be lost?
— What kind of storage is required? Can I make the materials accessible to children, or must I store them out of children's sight and reach?
— Will children just fight over this item if I have only one? Bicycles are the classic example of toys that cause more harm than good if not bought in quantity.
— Is extensive adult supervision necessary with these materials?

If the answer to these questions is yes for many materials, you will probably find you are creating a tense situation for your teachers. However, by making several curriculum orders during the year, you'll learn from your mistakes.

Sources for Curriculum Materials

Some curriculum supply companies may be less expensive than their competitors, but they may also be extremely slow or inept in delivering. Another company may be expensive, but its discount for bulk orders may make it better than a seemingly inexpensive company. If you deal with curriculum suppliers, first write for catalogs and compare prices, quality, and variety. Ask salesmen candid questions about delivery. Hopefully, you'll be able to find a supplier near you who can bring samples and to whom you can easily return defective materials. It's always wise to deal with as few companies as possible. Your own bookkeeping will be significantly streamlined, your discount increased, and the headaches of ordering, receiving, and distributing materials will be lessened if you limit the number of firms. The following is an alphabetical list of major curriculum suppliers:

Childcraft Education Corp.
964 Third Avenue
New York, New York   10022

Child Life Specialties
Highland Street
Holliston, Massachusetts 01746

Community Playthings
Rifton, New York 12471

Creative Playthings
Princeton, New Jersey 08540

Crowell, Collier, and Macmillan, Inc.
Threshold Program and Materials for Early Learning
         Centers   (From the following nine addresses,
                  choose the one nearest you.)

School Materials, Inc.
2124 W. 82nd Place
Chicago, Illinois   60620

School Materials, Inc.
200 W. First Street
Austin, Texas   78701

American School, Inc.
2301 Black Street
Denver, Colorado   80205

American School of New Mexico, Inc.
3204 Candelaria Road, NE
Albuquerque, New Mexico   87107

Arts and Crafts, Inc.
9520 Baltimore Avenue
College Park, Maryland   29741

Cambosco, Inc.
342 Western Avenue
Boston, Massachusetts   02135

Standard School, Inc.
1945 Hoover Court
Birmingham, Alabama   35226

Standard School, Inc.
2966 Old Schell Road
Mobile, Alabama

Standard School, Inc.
5817 Florida Avenue
Tampa, Florida   33604

J. L. Hammett Co.
Educational Supplies and Equipment
Hammett Place
Braintree, Massachusetts   02184

165 Water Street
Lyons, New York   14489

2393 Vaux Hall Road
Union, New Jersey   07083

Box 4125
Lynchburg, Virginia   24502

Houghton-Mifflin Company
53 West 43rd Street
New York, New York   10035

3108 Piedmont Road, NE
Atlanta, Georgia   30305

6626 Oakbrook Boulevard
Dallas, Texas   75235

777 California Avenue
Palo Alto, California

110 Tremont Street
Boston, Massachusetts   02107

McGraw Hill Co.
8171 Redwood Highway
Novato, California   94947

Manchester Road
Manchester, Missouri   63011

Princeton Road
Hightstown, New Jersey   08520

Xerox Corporation
P.O. Box 381
Beacon, New York   12508

3330 Wilshire Avenue
St. Charles, Missouri   63301

7225 S.W. 109th Terrace
Miami, Florida   33156

29670 Harvester Road
Malibu, California   90269

Tri-Wall Containers, Inc.
1 DuPont Street
Plainview, New York   11803

SEE (Selective Educational Equipment)
3 Bridge Street
Newton, Mass.   02195

In addition, you might also consider using the same firms which supply your local public school. Often schools use places offering liberal discounts, but do some comparative shopping to determine whether prices are really lower after the discount. Art and stationery supplies are usually less expensive through these companies, but other items may be more expensive because of the special needs of the public schools.

Other sources for materials:

Tri-Wall Containers, Inc. Tri-Wall is reinforced corrugated cardboard from which sturdy, portable, versatile, and inexpensive equipment can easily be made. If you use the Education Development Center's *Cardboard Carpentry* for design ideas, you will find that major equipment costs are significantly reduced.

Hardware Stores. Carpentry items, kitchen and doll corner materials, sand and water play equipment, and many science materials are often expensive from curriculum suppliers because they are nicely packaged and styled for children; but equally functional, durable, and appropriate materials can be found at any well-stocked hardware store.

Five and Dime Stores.   Books, dolls, and materials for the areas mentioned under hardware stores are often very inexpensive in the five and dime. The only drawback is many of the items are inexpensive because they don't work well or because they break easily. If you have time to make the effort to check, five and dime stores may be a valuable source of savings.

Community Activities.   If there are rummage sales, charity sales, auctions, etc., in your community, check into them. There's a good chance you'll find items of significant value at insignificant cost. Unfortunately, these affairs cannot be relied on, but they are an additional source for interesting, instructive materials.

Schools.   Try commissioning local shop and arts and crafts classes to make items you need. Sewing, woodworking, and any number of other crafts are taught and practiced in public schools, colleges, adult education and vocational schools, and philanthropic organizations. You may have cabinets built, dolls and doll clothes made, tables, chairs, and doll furniture constructed by at least one or two of these classes so your expenditure of both time and money is kept at a minimum.

Donations.   If you take time to figure out what household items you would like in your classrooms and make a list for distribution throughout the neighborhood, you are likely to get everything on the list — from books, records, and furniture to "beautiful junk"   — at no cost. If you add businesses to the list of community resources for possible donations, you'll find a veritable gold mine of free materials available. Here is a partial list of "beautiful junk" which can be procured from residents, businesses, or from scavenging in junk yards and garbage heaps:

BOXES, CRATES, CARTONS

Literally any size, shape, or material is appropriate. Hatboxes, egg cartons, food containers, and crates for any packing purposes should be sought. Homes, grocery stores, shipping companies, hardware stores, and restaurants, as well as any business which receives it's shipments in boxes, cartons, or crates, should be considered potential resources.

PAPER AND PAPER PRODUCTS

Again, anything goes. Wallpaper catalogs for cutting and pasting and collage are marvelous; magazines, newspapers, and newsprint, paper bags, paper boxes, paper napkins, paper towels, and tubes from various rolls of paper products have unlimited activity potential. Wrapping paper, tissues, tissue paper, and corrugated cardboard are just a few more paper items to be included.

WOODEN MATERIALS

The most obvious source of wooden"junk" is a lumberyard where wood scraps, wood shavings, sawdust, and other items are available free in quantity. Tongue depressors, railroad ties, wooden barrels, wooden spools, and wood clothespins are among the many other wood products to be considered.

HOME FURNISHING SCRAPS

Try carpet stores for their samples and tile or linoleum stores for theirs. Paint stores may not have paint to give away, but they will have paint color cards, which have a valuable place in the classroom, especially for matching games, identification games, and collage. Wire screening, venetian blinds, and telephone wires (in many colors), cable spools, and just plain old telephones are other home furnishings available through business offices.

MATERIAL AND FABRICS

Whether you seek scraps from families, tailors, textile mills, or stores, or from other sources, all materials in both small and large scrap sizes can be useful. Braiding, eyelet, ribbons, felt and flannel, and leather are often forgotten as part of the material category. More obvious possibilities are burlap, muslin, wool, velvet, and synthetic fabrics. Whether they come as old clothes, curtains, linen, or scraps, they are useful.

NOTIONS

Buttons, safety pins, yarn, string, straight pins, sewing needles, thread, snaps, tacks, tape, rubber bands, and small ornaments are among the wealth of materials which come under this category. People can generally find large quantities in their homes, but both retail stores and manufacturers should have large supplies to be given away.

CONSTRUCTION SCRAPS

Old tires and inner tubes, sewer or other cement piping, cinder blocks, bricks, nail kegs, and machinery parts are some of the larger items which a bit of imagination can make useful. They are especially appropriate for outdoor or other large-muscle activity, but need not be limited to that.

AUTOMOBILE PARTS

You may have passed by auto heaps for years and thought of them only as eyesores. However, once you think in terms of classroom activities, you gain a whole new perspective. Steering wheels, car seats, tires, inner tubes, engines, mirrors, floor mats, and, indeed, a whole car, can both furnish part of your room and offer materials for a wide array of activities.

MISCELLANY

Once you and your teachers have become attuned to classroom possibilities, you will discover that only very few items of "junk" cannot be put to use. In addition to old clothes and jewelry, furniture and appliances, and books, records, and pictures with obvious functions, consider the following very partial list which can be retrieved from the garbage and made useful once again:

Aluminum foil
Bottles and bottle caps
Brushes: hairbrushes, toothbrushes, scrub brushes
Candles
Cellophane
Chains
Chalk
Clocks
Dolls and puppets
Eyedroppers
Excelsior
Fans
Hoses or other rubber tubing
Jars, jugs, tin cans
Plastic bags, cups, tubes, and squeeze bottles
Pots and pans
Rope
Seeds
Sequins
Shoe laces
Simple machines
Soap
Sponges
Steel wool
Styrofoam
Televisions (with or without the tube, working or not)
Typewriters, etc., etc., etc.

While scavenging is not a method you can rely on, remember that once you and your staff begin thinking about everything in terms of what children and teachers can do with it, you will discover that not everything of value comes in a beautiful package.

PART

IV

PLANNING A BUDGET

The budget is a list of every item connected with the program for which cash payments may be made. For some items, cash payments may not in fact be made, as when staff volunteer their services, but they should nevertheless be included in the budget and assigned a monetary value of zero. In that way, the budget becomes both a description of your program and a summary of its cost. In our sample budgets, we will always assume that every item must be paid for.

The projection of specific costs for a particular program is impossible because costs for any given budget item will vary from one area of the country to another, sometimes by thousands of dollars, and because some budget items will not be included at all in some programs. However, a general budget analysis which compares the costs of programs of roughly equivalent quality is useful. The important questions for such an analysis are, What are the different ways of providing service on a roughly equivalent level? and, How much does each cost?

The most widely quoted figures on operating costs for a day care center that we have seen are the Standards and Costs for Day Care which were developed by the Office of Economic Opportunity in 1968. Although these figures are now being revised, they remain the most recent analysis of the subject. The document is included as Appendices, pages 315-316. According to the OEO budget, the annual cost for a child in day care which is of "desirable quality" is almost $2,500. Our total low budget cost for a high quality program is roughly the same.

Keeping this general estimate in mind, we must go on to say that the specific numbers assigned to each item in our sample budgets are the least important part of this chapter. Our budget figures, for example, are based on usual costs in a large Northeastern city, and therefore, as actual cost projections they will be inappropriate for many parts of the country. Thus, we want to emphasize that the main objectives of this chapter are to show you how a budget is set up and what items go into making a budget, how to read and understand a budget, and how to reduce costs by the substitution of inexpensive service equivalents. Our discussion will hopefully serve as a framework for your budget planning.

There is a standard format for a program budget which is widely used and which you should learn, especially for proposal writing purposes. In this format, costs are presented in the following categories: Staff Salaries and Fringe Benefits; Consultant Services; Equipment; Supplies and Materials; Travel; Food; Space Costs and Utilities; Other Fees (insurance, health payments, license payments).

All of the costs for your program can be described within these categories. Below is a description of what each category covers.

Staff Salaries and Fringe Benefits.   Staff salaries will include personnel from many different program components. Here you will list all personnel, from the director to the teachers to the social worker to the maintenance man, whoever is working in your program who could be paid a salary. When reading a staff salary budget, you will be able to tell what the quality and scope of the social service, health, parent counseling, training, and transportation components are by noting the presence or absence of relevant staff. You will usually be able to judge the quality of the classroom program as well, by noting the number of teachers who are hired and what their salaries are.

Fringe benefits refer to all of the services the program will usually make available to staff and will pay for. Fringe benefits might include social security, retirement, unemployment insurance, medical insurance, sick leave, and vacation payments. A standard estimate of costs is 10 percent of salaries.

Consultant Services. Listed here will be all of the people who are contributing to the program but who are not actually "on staff." They are usually working on an infrequent schedule, and it is simpler to pay them on a per diem basis.

Consultant services could range from a physician who consults for an equivalent of one half day a week, being "on call" to the center, to an early childhood educator from a nearby college who conducts a training session for teachers one afternoon a week, to an artist who is invited to give one lecture to the staff on teaching art to very young children. In order to evaluate a program, the consultant services budget must be read in conjunction with staff salaries. For example, a staff salaries budget which does not list any highly trained teachers may lead you to conclude that the program has a weak educational component, but under consultant services, you may find several professionals who contribute to the program on a regular basis and overcome this apparent deficiency.

Equipment. Equipment includes all those items acquired by the center which are fairly permanent, that is, which are not regularly used up. Like all of the budget categories, equipment cuts across many program components, ranging from educational toys to typewriters to garbage pails. In our sample budgets, we break down equipment into the following subcategories: educational or curriculum equipment (such as blocks, books, easels); caretaking and housekeeping equipment (such as cots, brooms); office equipment (such as desks, furniture for staff and parents, office machines); and kitchen equipment (such as stove, pots and pans). By reading an equipment budget, you can often tell how strong an educational or training component is by noting whether the needed items have been provided.

Supplies and Materials.   The supplies and materials budget includes all those items which are used up in the process of running the center, and which are constantly being replaced. Such things as blankets, curtains, and assorted children's clothing are usually included here too. Supplies and materials, like equipment, can be broken down into subcategories for easier comprehension. The subcategories are curriculum supplies (art supplies are the only item included here); caretaking and housekeeping supplies, such as sheets, blankets, diapers, medical items and cleansers; and office supplies, such as paper, typewriter ribbons, stamps. Food is treated as a separate category.

Travel.   Transportation includes travel arrangements for children to and from the center, travel arrangements for children and teachers for field trips, and travel for staff. A glance at the transportation budget will tell you a good deal about a program. If a center does not budget money for a bus, then you know that it is not providing pickup and delivery service, and is probably located in the middle of the community it is serving. If a center does not budget money for field trips, there will be no sources of enrichment outside of the classroom. If there is no money for long-distance travel, the staff will have no opportunity to increase their learning and teaching skills through visiting other programs or attending conferences and meetings on relevant subjects.

Food.   The food budget should give the number of meals and/or snacks served at the center and the cost. It can give you a good idea of how adequate the center's meal service is.

Space Costs and Utilities.   The budget should include the number of square feet of space and the total cost of that space. By reading this budget item you will know immediately how adequate the space is for the number of children in the program.

Other Costs. Each center may have additional miscellaneous costs. Licensing fees for day care centers vary from state to state. Some programs will pay for health services when parents cannot afford to or will have medical insurance for all of the children. Some centers will have insurance, such as fire and theft, or accident, while others might find that in their area of the city insurance is so expensive that they must do without it. We will therefore leave this budget element as a catchall and not attach to it any sample cost.

After you have written your program budget, it will be helpful to break it down into operating and start-up costs. The latter will tell you how much money you will have to spend, and therefore have on hand, before the program for the children actually begins. Start-up costs include one-time expenditures such as the down payment for your building, renovation costs, and equipment. In addition the salaries of the staff who are planning the program and hiring other staff might be included, along with the salaries of the entire staff for a few weeks while they are participating in an orientation program or in preservice training.

The budget for the second year (and beyond) will be cheaper than the original budget due to the elimination of start-up costs. Some percentage of these costs will have to be added, however, because walls will have to be repainted and equipment will be broken or lost and will have to be replaced. For equipment replacement costs, 10 percent of the original costs can serve as a guide.

Now that we have delineated the basic elements of a budget and given you an idea of how a budget can be read and used, we will discuss the alternative costs involved under each budget element. Our discussion unless otherwise stated, is based on the costs for a hypothetical day care center located in Boston which serves sixty children between the

ages of two and five and a half years old. There are twenty
children in each of three classrooms, one for two-year-olds,
one for three's, and one for four's and five's. Unless the
difference in age entails a difference in cost for a particular
budget item, we will talk about the general program cost or
the general classroom cost.

The budget analysis compares a program in which
money is no object with one in which it is important to cut
costs as much as possible. Our aim is to present two budgets
for a program of the same general standard of quality. The
high budget does not include any items which are really very
extravagant. It includes items which we would really recommend if you do have the money. Similarly, the low budget
does not exclude any items which we consider necessary to a
good program just for the sake of saving money. Both
budgets are workable for good programs.

The standards on which the budgets are based come
from discussions in other chapters in the book, and you
should refer to these chapters if you have not already read
them so that you will understand why particular items or
staff positions are included.

Bear in mind that these budgets are just samples. We do
not present these budgets as gospel. Rather, they are a
framework from which you can learn how to plan your
budget and how to cut costs.

Staff Salaries and Consultant Services

We will begin by departing from our budget format and
combining the two elements of staff salaries and consultant
services. This will make the comparison of costs easier to
understand, because both salaried staff and consultants will
be involved in a program component, such as teaching or
health services, and what you really want to know is, What
are the comparative costs for such a component? But before
getting to sample budgets, the general issue of professional
and salary standards for center directors and teachers must
be discussed.

Because day care in this country has not been considered a profession and has not been well developed, there are virtually no standards for qualifications, for salaries, or for appropriate teacher-child ratios in the classroom. Differences among existing programs are enormous. Salaries for teachers are by far the largest chunk of any day care budget. Included in this book are many pages listing alternative kinds of equipment and supplies that day care centers might have, and yet the range of difference within that budget element is only a few thousand dollars. The addition or deletion of just one teacher would be more than that. To give you an idea of the possible range in costs we are talking about, we have compared below the differences in cost between a program paying high "professional" salaries to the director and teachers and using a low teacher-child ratio with one paying very low salaries and using a high teacher-child ratio.

Director and Teacher Salaries for a Program of Sixty Children

Teacher-Child Ratio = 1:5

Teachers Needed = 60/5 = 12. If each teacher works six hours in the classroom and the center is open for ten hours, you need 12 x10/6 =20 teachers.

Position	No.	Salary	Total
Director	1	$10-14,000.	$ 12,000.
Head Teacher	3	7-9,000.	24,000.
Teacher	17	7,000.	119,000.
Total			$155,000.

Director and Teacher salaries for a Program of Sixty Children

Teacher-Child Ratio = 1:10

Teachers Needed = 10

Position	No.	Salary	Total
Director	1	$ 7,000.	$ 7,000.
Head Teacher	3	6,000.	18,000.
Teacher	7	4-6,000.	35,000.
Total			$60,000.

The salaries for the first program are almost three times as much as those for the second.

Differences of this magnitude do exist in day care programs, and the differences do not even correspond to different levels of skill or education on the part of staff. We know of teachers with master's degrees who work as head teachers for four or five thousand dollars simply because they need jobs and that is what they are offered. Other teachers with less educational background receive salaries which are more than double this amount, and our program pays unskilled and untrained assistants a minimum of six thousand dollars. Similarly, we know of programs which maintain a 1:5 ratio for five-year-olds, and others which maintain a 1:10 ratio for three-year-olds. In short, the actual situation right now is one of chaos, in which no one knows what a teacher or director *should* earn, or what a teacher-child ratio *should* be. (Unfortunately, these issues are often decided simply on the basis of what a program can get away with.)

In order for us to be able to talk coherently about these salaries, we have to set up our own standards for competence and for salary scales which reflect this competence. We will not take into consideration the possibility of finding highly trained and experienced staff who want to volunteer their services or be underpaid. Rather, we will begin by assuming that the better the teacher or director, the higher the salary will be. With this assumption we can take another look at the two budgets. Budget one now becomes the professionally staffed program, and two, the nonprofessionally staffed program. In our opinion, both of these are unreasonable budget alternatives: the first is extravagant, and the second is skimpy. The standards on which we will base our suggested budgets maintain both a high-quality program and living wages, as follows:

Teacher-Child Ratios. (See Chapter on Teachers.)

— Children age 2: 1:5
— Children age 3: 1:5 to 1:8
— Children age 4-5: 1:8 to 1:10

The ranges allow for differences in the skill and training of the teaching staff. Experienced and skilled teachers will be able to work with a larger number of children than will nonprofessionals, unless of course, the nonprofessionals happen to be extremely gifted and "natural" teachers. Since there is no way of accounting for this in planning, we must assume that education and experience will produce a more competent teacher.

Salaries.   Our base salary level will be six thousand dollars. In comparison to programs which pay nonprofessionals three or four thousand dollars, this is a very high figure. But in view of the present cost of living this is, in our opinion, a minimum decent wage. Therefore, in the budget, nonprofessional teachers without training or experience will receive this salary. Professional teachers having an A.B. or M.A. degree in a field of early-childhood education or a related field will receive anywhere from seven to nine thousand dollars, the range depending upon the responsibility of the position (head teacher or assistant teacher) and upon teaching experience. This salary range seems inordinately high to some people when they think of a preschool teacher, but that is because they think of it as unskilled baby-sitting rather than as the demanding and difficult job it really is. A director having a master's degree in a relevant field and experience in directing a group program for children will receive a salary ranging from ten to fourteen thousand dollars. A nonprofessional director with no relevant education or supervisory experience would receive much less — a range might be from seven to ten thousand dollars.

Given these salary levels and teacher-child ratios, what kind of staffing pattern is the most economical within the framework of a high-quality program? At first glance it would seem that a program staffed by nonprofessionals would be, but remember that the professional teacher is capable of working with a larger number of children. Also, the professionally staffed program would not need much in the way of additional staff or consultants for training and supervision. Supervision would be given by the head teachers on the job, and additional supervision would be part of the director's job. In the program with nonprofessional staff, however, neither the head teachers nor the director would be able to provide this training. Outside consultants or part-time training and supervisory staff would be a hidden cost in using lower-paid staff. Training costs could amount to as much as five thousand dollars a year. A comparison between the two staffs, one professional and the other nonprofessional, looks like this:

Professional Director and Teacher Salaries for a Program of Sixty Children, Three Years of Age

Teacher-Child ratio = 1:8

Teachers Needed = 12

Position	No.	Salary	Total
Director	1	$10-14,000.	$12,000.
Head Teacher	3	7-9,000.	24,000.
Teacher	9	7,000.	63,000.
Total			$99,000.

Nonprofessional Director and Teacher Salaries for a Program of Sixty Children Three Years of Age.

Teacher-Child ratio = 1:5

Teachers Needed = 20

Position	No.	Salary	Total
Director	1	$ 7,000.	$ 7,000.
Head Teacher	3	6,500.	19,500.
Teacher	17	6,000.	102,000.
Total			128,500.
Training Consultants			5,000.
Total			$133,500.

The fully professional staff turns out to be cheaper than the nonprofessional staff when you try to preserve an equal program quality.

The most economical staffing pattern that would preserve a high program quality is one which combines features of both patterns above. A combination of a professional director and head teachers and nonprofessional assistant teachers allows you to save on teacher salaries and maintain a higher teacher-child ratio since the director and the head teacher in each classroom can supervise the inexperienced teachers. The all-professional staff would be our suggested high-budget staffing pattern, and the pattern below would be our suggested low-budget arrangement.

Mixed Professional and Nonprofessional Director and Teacher Salaries for a Program of Sixty Three-Year-Olds.

Teacher-Child ratio = 1:8

Teachers Needed = 12

Position	No.	Salary	Total
Director	1	$10-14,000.	$10,000.
Head Teacher	3	7-9,000.	21,000.
Teacher	9	6,000.	54,000.
Total			$85,000.

We can now turn to a discussion of other staff and consultant costs.

Administrative Staff

In addition to the nonteaching director whom we have discussed, a program for sixty children would need a combination secretary-administrative assistant, who could also function as a bookeeper. The secretary would receive a salary of seventy-five hundred dollars minimum. Costs for administrative staff salaries will not vary between programs, and will come to about $21,500.

Teaching Staff

As we have seen, head teachers' salaries will range from seven to nine thousand dollars, and teachers' salaries will range from six to seven thousand dollars. Taking the extremes of these ranges, we find that teacher salaries can vary as follows in our hypothetical center:

	High Budget	Low Budget
3 Head Teachers	$ 27,000.	$ 21,000.
11 Teachers	77,000.	66,000.

(The classroom for 2's requires $6\frac{2}{3}$ teachers; the classroom for 3's, 4 teachers, and the classroom for 4's & 5's requires $3\frac{1}{3}$ teachers.

Total	$104,000.	$ 87,000.

HOUSEKEEPING AREA (*See page 157 of Curriculum Areas*)

Item	Amt.	Cost	Low Budget	Amt.	Cost
1. Kitchen set: stove, sink, refrigerator, cabinet	1 set	$120.	Made from heavy cardboard, crates, wood	1 set	$ ——
2. Small kitchen table	1	30.	Heavy cardboard or plywood	1	——
3. Chairs at $10 each	5	50.	Made from paper tubes (the cardboard rolls paper companies use)	5	——
4. Dishes and utensils at $8 per set	3 sets	24.	Donated by staff, parents		——
5. Doll's high chair	1	10.	Omit		
6. Doll's carriage	1	25.	Omit (wagons can be used)		
7. Full-length mirror	1	15.	Same	1	15.
8. Bedroom set: bed (for dolls and children), chest of drawers	1 set	50.	Bed made from large blocks or box, with pillow and blanket; chest of drawers — cardboard facsimile	1 each	——
9. Dolls at average of $6.	6	36.	Make 3 homemade rag dolls Buy 3	3 3	—— 18.
10. Doll clothes at average of $3 a set	4 sets	12.	Made out of donated materials		——
11. Dress-up clothes (donated)		——	Same		——
12. Cleaning set: brooms, mops	1 set	5.	Donated Materials for construction		10.
Total		$377.			$ 43.

LIBRARY AREA (*See page 161 of Curriculum Areas.*)

	Item	Amt.	Cost	Low Budget	Amt.	Cost
1.	Books: (figured on the basis of two per child)			Books are borrowed from the library and donated by parents and staff		
	25 story books at about $4 each	25	$100.		25	$—
	15 picture reference books at about $10 each	15	150.	Same as above	15	—
2.	Tape recorder with microphone	1	60.	Omit		
3.	Tapes or cassettes at $2 each	10	20.	Omit		
4.	Furniture			Furniture		
	Bookshelves to hold about 60 books		50.	Bookshelves made from lumber and bricks		—
	Table for 4 or 5 children at $40	2	80.	Table made from cardboard or wood		—
	Chairs or cushions at $10	10	100.	Chairs made from paper tubes or donated cushions.	2	—
	Carpet at $5 per square yard	3 yds.	15.	Donated, or omit	10	—
				Materials for construction	10	10.
	Total		$575.			$ 10.

BLOCK AREA *(See page 164 of Curriculum Areas.)*

	Item	Amt.	Cost	Low Budget	Amt.	Cost
1.	Blocks					
	Unit blocks: a complete nursery school set of about 350 pieces for older children (4's and 5's) about 40 large	1 set	$100.	One quarter of a complete set: about 90 pieces	¼ set	$ 25.
	Hollow blocks	40 pcs.	(150.)	Omit		
	or					
	for younger children (2's): large cardboard blocks	72 pcs.	(45.)	Omit		
2.	Block Accessories					
	Sets of people, animals, trains, signs, cars, containing 4 to 6 pieces each at $5 to $10.	4 sets	30.	Sets at $5	2 sets	10.
				Donated or homemade items	2 sets	——
	Wheeled vehicles at $6 each from toy stores	10	60.	Cheaper versions at $2	10	20.
3.	Storage shelves for blocks & accessories		50.	Homemade storage shelves from crates, wood Materials	10	—— 10.
Total	(For older children)		$390.			
	(For younger children)		$285.			$ 65.

ART AREA (See page 167 of Curriculum Areas.)

Item	Amt.	Cost	Low Budget	Amt.	Cost
Equipment					
1. Table for 4 or 5 children	2	$ 80.	Made from heavy cardboard or plywood	2	$ ——
2. Chairs at $10	10	100.	Made from cardboard tubes	10	——
3. Easels: standing type which serve two children	2	40.	Wall or standing easels made from heavy cardboard or plywood	2	——
4. Assorted equipment: scissors for adults and children, stapler, paper cutter		60.	Same Materials		60. 35.
Total		$280.			$ 95.
Supplies		*Gals.*			*Gals.*
1. Paint (in gallons)	20	$140.		10	$ 70.
Tempera at $7 per gallon	4	28.	Half the amount	2	14.
Finger at $7 per gallon		*Sheets*	Half the amount		*Sheets*
2. Paper (in 18" x 24" sheets)	1,000	20.		1,000	20.
Newsprint	500	3.	Same	250	1.50
Finger paint			Half the amount		
Construction (assorted colors)	500	15.	Same	500	15.

Heavy drawing (white construction)	1,000	30.	Same	1,000	30.
Oak tag (assorted colors)	100	6.	Same	100	6.
Tissue (assorted colors)	400	8.	Same	400	8.
Brown wrapping paper, in A roll of 300 yards x 30"	1	9.	Same	1 roll	9.
Other		5.	Same		5.
3. Clay					
Modeling at 15¢ per lb.	200 lbs.	30.	Same	200 lbs.	30.
Plasticine at 50¢ per lb.	10 lbs.	5.	Omit		
Play dough at 50¢ per lb.	10 lbs.	5.	Homemade	10 lbs.	—
4. Chalk, crayons, Magic Markers at $2 per doz.	5 doz.	10.	Omit		
5. Assorted: pipe cleaners, popsicle sticks, felt, thumbtacks, glue, paste tongue depressors		25.	Same		25.
Total		$339.			$234.

PUZZLES, GAMES, AND MANIPULATIVE TOYS *(See page 176 of Curriculum Areas.)*

Item	Amt.	Cost 2's	Cost 4's,5's	Low Budget	Amt.	Cost 2's	Cost 4's,5's
1. Puzzles:							
for 2's: very large puzzles at $5 each	10	$50.		Buy half, and make half out of heavy cardboard	5		$25.
puzzles with small pieces at $3	5	15.		Same	5	15.	
for 4's & 5's: at $2	15		$30.	Same	15		$30.
2. Pegboards							
for 2's: small boards at $3	2	6.		Homemade	2	—	
for 4's and 5's: 100-hole board at $6	2		12.	Homemade	2		—
3. Attribute blocks set (4 colors and 4 shapes)	1	20.	20.	Same	1		20.
4. Table block set (parquetry, geo blocks, counting cubes) at $5 a set	4	20.	20.	Rotate among classrooms	2	10.	10.
5. Lotto games (picture lotto, illustrated dominoes) at $2	3 / 6	6.	12.	Rotate among classrooms	2 / 4	10.	4. / 8.

#	Item	No. (2's)	No. (4's,5's)	2's	4's,5's	Method	No. (2's)	No. (4's,5's)	2's	4's,5's
6.	Construction toys (Tinkertoys, vinyl sticks, giant Legos, fit-together plastic shapes, etc.) at $5 a set	3	6	15.	30.	Rotate among classrooms	1	3	5.	15.
7.	Abacus	1		2.		Same	1		2.	
8.	Pounding games at $4	2		8.		Buy one game	1	1	4.	2.
						Make one game	1			
9.	Threading set (threader, bead set, spool set) at $5	3		15.	15.	Homemade	3		—	—
10.	Shape-sorting games					Same				
	Shape-sorting boxes at $5	2		10.		Buy two sets	2		10.	4.
	Stack puzzles at $2	5		10.		Make 3 sets from donated materials	2		4.	
11.	Shape-sorter boards at $3	2		6.		Same	3		3.	
	Clothing set from a curriculum supplier for zipping, lacing, snapping, buttoning	1		12.		Donated old clothes	1		—	
Total				$195.	$141.				$102.	$85.

WATER PLAY *(See page 183 of Curriculum Areas)*

Item	Amt.	Cost	Low Budget	Amt.	Cost
1. Large basin with stand from curriculum supplier	1	$50.	A "found" or constructed large waterproofed box	1	$—
2. Assorted equipment: pails, tubes, etc.		25.	Donated equipment		—
Total		$75.			$—
SAND PLAY					
1. Sand at $2.50 per ton	1	$ 2.50	Same	1	$2.50
2. Sand area (part of floor space, defined by lumber on three sides)		—	Same		—
3. assorted equipment: pails, shovels, etc.		15.	Donated equipment		—
Total		$17.50			$2.50
CARPENTRY (for older children)			One table and equipment shared by the two classrooms for older children; drill and screwdriver omitted		$27.
1. Carpentry table	1	$50.			
2. Vises at $8.	2	16.			
3. Hammer at $2.	2	4.			
4. Saw at $5.	2	10.			
5. Nails, assorted sizes		1.			
6. Lumber: "found" pieces		—			
7. Sandpaper		1.			
8. Drill		5.			
9. Screwdriver and assorted screws		3.			
Total		$90.			$27.

MUSIC *(See page 199 of Curriculum Areas)*

	Item	Amt.	Cost	Low Budget	Amt.	Cost
1.	Autoharp	1	$40.	Omit		
2.	Bells					
	Wrist bells at 50¢	3	1.50	Homemade	3	——
	Stick bells at 50¢	3	1.50	Homemade	3	——
	Scale bells (a set)	1	9.	Omit		
3.	Drums					
	Hand drums (tom-toms) at $3.	4	12.	Homemade	4	——
	Congo drums (pair)	1	9.	Omit		
	Bongo drums	1	15.	Omit		
4.	Cymbals (pair) at $4.	2	8.	Same	2	$ 8.00
5.	Rattles (pair) at $2.	2	4.	Homemade	2	——
6.	Rhythm sticks at $1.	5	5.	Same	5	5.00
7.	Tambourines at $4.	4	16.	Homemade*	2	——
8.	Tone block at 60¢	2	1.20	Same*	2	1.20
9.	Triangle at $1.	2	2.	Same*		
10.	Xylophone	1	3.	Same*		
11.	Guitar	1	25.	Omit		
12.	Piano	1	100.	Omit		
13.	Record player	1	25.	Same	1	25.
14.	Records at $5.	20	100.	Rotate between classrooms. Buy 5.		25.
	Total		$277			$64.

*Two of the four starred items are sufficient.

SCIENCE (See page 190 of Curriculum Areas.)

	Item	Amt.	Cost	Low Budget	Amt.	Cost
1.	Globe (stereo relief)	1	$12.	Omit		
2.	Magnet					
	Horseshoe and bar at $1.50	4	6.	Same	4	$6.
	Magnetic materials: iron filings		.50	Same		.50
3.	Magnifying glass at 50¢	10	5.	Same	10	5.
4.	Binocular microscope	1	60.	Omit		
5.	Stethescope	1	3.	Omit		
6.	Prism at $2	2	4.	Same	2	4.
7.	Skeleton bones (curriculum suppliers have complete skeletons of various small animals for about $15	2	30.	Carefully carve a chicken or turkey		___
8.	Mirrors:					
	Concave and convex at $1	2	2.	Omit		
	Hand at $.60	5	3.	Same	5	3.
9.	Scale	1	15.	Omit		
10.	Balances and weights with seesaw	1	1.	Homemade	1	___
11.	Egg incubator (4 eggs)	1	13.	Omit		

	Item	Amt.	Cost	Low Budget	Amt.	Cost
12.	Ant farm	1	7.	Omit		
13.	Aquarium (15 gallon) plus related equipment for 15 goldfish	1	35.	Omit		
14.	Transparent color paddles	1 set	1.50	Colored cellophane paper		—
15.	Flashlight and batteries	1	1.50	Omit		—
16.	Animals: gerbils, guinea pigs, mice, rabbits, turtles (free)			Same		
	Fish		5.			
17.	Thermometer (outdoor, indoor)	2	2.	Same	2	$ 2.
18.	Plants (free)			Same		
19.	Animal food (1 yr. supply)		12.	Same		12.
20.	Animal cages at $10	2	20.	Homemade Materials		3.
Total			$239.			$36.

LARGE-MUSCLE ACTIVITIES FOR INDOORS OR OUTDOORS
(See page 196 of Curriculum Areas.)

	Item	Amt.	Cost	Low Budget	Amt.	Cost
1.	Large climbing structure from curriculum supplier	1	$150.	Made out of "found" lumber or omit		
2.	Rocking boat	1	30.	Same	1	$30.
3.	Small indoor slide	1	25.	Made from heavy duty card-board	1	
4.	Large slide	1	100.	Omit		
5.	Climbing ropes, rope swings at $15.	3	45.	Homemade or omit	1	$15.
6.	Seesaw	1	15.	Same	2	20.
7.	Wagon at $10.	3	30.	Same	1	50.
8.	Tumbling mat (4' x 5') at $50	2	100.	Same		
9.	Punching bag on stand	1	10.	Omit		
10.	Balls (seven and thirteen inch diameter) at $3. (for 2's: texture balls)	3	9.	Same	2	6.
11.	Tricycle at $25.	4	100.	Omit Materials		10.
	Total		$614.			$131.

SUMMARY OF COSTS FOR CLASSROOM EQUIPMENT AND SUPPLIES

	High Budget	Low Budget
EQUIPMENT		
1. Housekeeping	$ 377.	$ 43.
2. Library	575.	10.
3. Blocks	340. ($285.00 for 2's)	65.
	(390. for 4's, 5's)	
4. Art	280.	95.
5. Puzzles, games,	168. (195. for 2's)	94. ($102. for 2's)
and manipulative toys	(141. for 4's, 5's)	(85. for 4's, 5's)
6. Water play	75.	
7. Sand play	18.	3.
8. Carpentry (for 2 class-rooms only)	90.	41.
9. Music	277.	64.
10. Science	239.	36.
11. Large-muscle	614.	131.
Total	$3,053.	$ 582.
Grand Total for Three Classrooms	$9,069.	$1,705.
SUPPLIES		
Art	339.	234.
Grand Total for Three Classrooms	$1,017	$ 702.

CARETAKING EQUIPMENT AND SUPPLIES

Item	Amt.	Cost	Low Budget	Amt.	Cost
Equipment					
1. Cots at $15 each, for sleeping; 2 for isolation room	22	$ 330.	Same	22	$ 330.
2. Coat lockers at $14	20	280.	Homemade out of wood, or simply hooks in the wall	20	——
3. Chairs at $10 each, in addition to the chairs already budgeted for curriculum areas	6	60.	Made from cardboard tubes	6	——
4. Tables at $40 each for eating, in addition to those already budgeted	2	80.	Made out of plywood or heavy duty cardboard	2	——
5. Shelves for equipment and supplies, some bought, some homemade	2	100.	All homemade		——
6. Pegboards for dividing areas and for storing equipment at $13 each	2	26.	Same		26.
			Materials for homemade equipment		60.
Total		$ 876.			$ 416.
Grand Total for 3 Classrooms		$2,628.			$1,248.

Item	Amt.	Cost	Low Budget	Amt.	Cost
Supplies					
1. Sheets, blankets, towels, washcloths, assorted clothing at $25 per child		$1,500.	Same		$1,500.
2. First aid supplies, powders lotions, safety pins, etc.		50.	Same		50.
3. Diapers, at $40 per child for the year, for one classroom of 20 two's		800.	Same		800.
4. Curtains, hampers, garbage pails, mops, brooms, sponges, cleansing agents, etc.		100.	Same		100.
Total for 3 Classrooms		$2,450.			$2,450.
Grand Total, Equipment & Supplies		$5,078.			$3,698.

Social Services Staff
A comprehensive social service program would require a full-time social worker, whose salary could range from six to ten thousand dollars, depending on whether you choose a nonprofessional or someone with a degree in social work. A low-budget program could eliminate this person and give the director and teachers the responsibility for parent counseling.

Health Services Staff
A comprehensive health program might budget health staff costs as follows:

Pediatric nurse, full-time at $7-9,000.	$8,000
Physician consultant for the equivalent of 2 days a month at $100 per day	2,400
Dentist consultant for 10 days at $75 per day	750
Psychologist consultant for 2 days a month at $75 per day	1,800
Total	$12,950

A low budget program offering minimal health services would eliminate this health staff. The record keeping and emergency health care would be handled by teacher and administrative staffs, so that there would be no extra costs for specific health services staff.

Food Services Staff
(See section on Food, where we include the costs of staff related to serving meals as part of the total food element of the budget.)

Training staff in Addition to the Director and Head Teachers
A professional staff would not require extensive outside consultants for in-service training. Costs for training might be:

Consultants for curriculum workshops for 12 days (once a month) at $50 per day	$600.

A nonprofessional teaching staff would require more training. Costs might be:

Consultants for 24 days at $50 per day $1,200.

Other Staff
A center for sixty children would need at least one half-time janitor. Given our minimum salary scale of $6000, this would add $3000 to the budget.

Some centers will have a driver on the staff. This expense is discussed in the Transportation section.

Equipment and Supplies and Materials
We will combine these two budget elements so that you can more readily see what the costs for "things" are for different areas of the day care center, such as the classroom or the office, and for different components of the day care program, such as caretaking.

Classroom Curriculum Equipment and Supplies
The budget for classroom equipment will come to several thousand dollars if everything is store-bought. This is an area where you can save money by using inexpensive homemade functional equivalents of the store-bought goods. In terms of the total budget, however, these savings will be nominal. We have included detailed lists of equipment, not so much because the fifty cents for rattles and the fifteen dollars for easels are crucial, but because they offer an itemized guide to equipping a center. The lists will reflect the curriculum areas described in the chapter on Curriculum Areas.

For each curriculum area, we compare the cost for equipping it using newly purchased items with the cost of equipping it using inexpensive functional equivalents when possible. The detailed lists are for one classroom of twenty children: one of the three classrooms in our hypothetical center. This will make it easier to visualize the equipment needed.

One mechanism for reducing costs is to have three classrooms share a given item. Therefore, in order to be consistent we will define the single classroom cost of such items as one third of their total cost so that the total cost for equipping the center will be three times the classroom cost, with no exceptions.

Office Equipment and supplies

Equipment   Office equipment includes all one-time expenditures, such as chairs, desks, typewriters, tables, and lamps, that you will need for the administrative, teaching, and associated services staffs, and for consultants and parents. In general, plan on a separate desk for each staff person who will be doing a great deal of paperwork or a great deal of interviewing or counseling on a one to one basis. This would include the director, the secretary, the social worker, and perhaps the head teachers. The teachers will need an area where they can write and think and meet with each other. This area, with a couple of desks or tables, can be shared. You will need an area with enough adult-sized furniture for staff meetings, training sessions, parent meetings.

You need not, however, spend a great deal of money on fancy desks and tables and chairs. As was true for most of the children's furniture, you can make inexpensive substitutions. A nice table or desk for an adult can be made from an old door or from an inexpensive piece of plywood for a fraction of the purchase cost.

A comparison of high- and low-budget costs might look like the chart on page 257.

Supplies.   Office supplies include most stationary items, such as paper, pens and pencils, typewriter ribbons, envelopes, stamps and so on. For a center of sixty children, at least $300 should be budgeted.

Grand Total. $2190 is the total for newly purchased equipment and supplies. The low-budget total is $740.

OFFICE EQUIPMENT

	Item	Amt.	Cost	Low Budget	Amt.	Cost
1.	Desk at $125 for the director, the secretary, social worker, consultants (shared)	5	$ 625.	Homemade from wood	5	—
2.	Desk chairs at $40	5	200.	Chairs at $20	5	100.
3.	Reading lamp at $15	2	30.	Same	2	30.
4.	Table (about 3' x 5') for teachers, for meetings	2	120.	Homemade from wood	2	—
5.	Bookcases at $50	2	100.	Homemade from wood	2	—
6.	Chairs (folding type) for meetings, teachers at $5	15	75.	Same	10	50.
7.	File cabinet (4 drawer)	1	70.	Same	1	70.
8.	Bulletin board (3 x 4)	1	30.	Painted cardboard or felt		—
9.	Typewriter (electric) at $150	2	300.	Same (used)	1	60.
10.	Adding machine	1	140.	Same (used)	1	70.
11.	Furnishings for parents' lounge (comfortable chairs, coffee table, lamp)	4	200.	Omit		
				Materials		50.
Total			$1,890.			$ 440.

SAMPLE HIGH-COST BUDGET FOR FIRST YEAR

Program Element	% Time	No.	Salary	Total
I. Staff				
A. Administrative				
1. Director	100	1	$10–14,000.	$ 12,000.
2. Administrative Assistant	100	1	7,500.	7,500.
B. Teaching				
1. Head teacher	100	3	7–9,000.	24,000.
2. Teacher	100	11	7,000.	77,000.
C. Social service	100	1	6–10,000.	8,000.
D. Pediatric Nurse	100	1	7–9,000.	8,000.
E. Cook	100	1	6,000.	6,000.
F. Maintenance	50	1	6,000.	3,000.
G. Driver	25	1	6,000.	1,500.
Total				$147,000.
II. Fringe benefits at 10% of salary costs				14,700.
III. Consultant Services				
A. Health related				
1. Physician at $100 per day for the equivalent of 24 days				$ 2,400.
2. Dentist at $75 per day for 10 days				750.
3. Psychologist at $75 per day for 24 days				1,800.
4. Nutritionist at $25 per day for 24 days				600.
B. Training and curriculum related at $50 per day for 12 days				600.
Total				$ 6,150.

		Total
IV.	Equipment	
A.	Educational	$ 9,069.
B.	Caretaking and housekeeping	2,628.
C.	Office	1,890.
D.	Kitchen	8,000.
Total		$ 21,587.
V.	Supplies and Materials	
A.	Educational (art)	1,017.
B.	Caretaking and housekeeping	2,450.
C.	Office	300.
Total		$ 3,767.
VI.	Food	
	For two meals and two snacks:	
	60¢ x 60 children x 260 days	$ 9,360.
VII.	Transportation	
A.	Bus rental and gasoline	3,700.
B.	Field trips	720.
C.	Local staff travel	100.
D.	Long-distance travel	500.
Total		$ 5,020.

SAMPLE HIGH-COST BUDGET FOR FIRST YEAR

Program Element	% Time	No.	Salary	Total
VIII. Space costs				
4,850 square feet at $2.50 per square foot				$ 12,125.
IX. Utilities				
A. Telephone: 2 at $30 per month each				720.
B. Heat at $60/month				720.
C. Light at $50/month				600.
Total				$ 2,040.
X. Other Fees and Expenses				
Here you might include such items as insurance, day care licensing fees, health care payments				
Grand Total				$221,749.
(per child)				$ 3,696.

Kitchen Equipment and Supplies
Because most states and cities have special regulations about the kitchens serving children in public programs, it would be useless for us to itemize a list for you. Be sure to check with the regulatory agency in your locality to make sure you will have the right kind of equipment. High-budget and low-budget programs alike will have to meet these standards. In general, costs for equipping a kitchen to serve sixty children will range from about six to eight thousand dollars.

Carpentry Workshop Equipment and Supplies
A low-budget program which will cut equipment costs by using homemade substitutions for costly purchased items will have to add the "hidden" cost of the necessary carpentry tools. In order to make the furniture and other equipment we have listed, the following workshop tools will be necessary:

Saw	$ 7.
Circular saw	40.
Saber saw	30.
Electric ¼ inch drill	25.
Assorted drill bits	4.
Electric sander	25.
Hammers (2 at $5.00)	10.
Framing square	2.50
Saw horses (4 at $1.00)	4.
(simple metal frames)	
12-foot tape measures	
(2 at $4.00)	8.
Assorted nails	1.
Paint (5 gallons at $8)	40.
Plastic varnish	
(2 gallons at $10.00)	20.
Total	$217.

Travel
If your center is going to provide transportation to and from the center for the children, then you will need to purchase or

SAMPLE LOW-COST BUDGET FOR FIRST YEAR

Program Element	% Time	No.	Salary	Total
I. Staff				
A. Administrative				
1. Director	100	1	$10,000.	$ 10,000.
2. Administrative Assistant	100	1	7,500.	7,500.
B. Teaching				
1. Head Teacher	100	3	7,000.	21,000.
2. Teacher	100	11	6,000.	66,000.
C. Cook	100	1	6,000.	6,000.
D. Maintenance	50	1	6,000.	3,000.
Total				$113,500.00
II. Fringe Benefits at 10% of salary costs				11,350.00
III. Consultant Services				
Training and curriculum related 24 days at $50 per day				1,200.00

Total

IV. Equipment
   A. Educational   1,705.
   B. Caretaking and housekeeping   1,248.
   C. Office   440.
   D. Kitchen   6,000.
   E. Carpentry   217.

Total $9,610.

V. Supplies and Materials
   A. Educational (art)   702.
   B. Caretaking and housekeeping   2,450.
   C. Office   300.

Total $3,452.

VI. Food
   For two meals and two snacks:
   60¢ x 60 children x 260 days $9,360.

VII. Transportation
   A. Bus rental
   B. Field trips
   C. Local staff travel   50.

SAMPLE LOW-COST BUDGET FOR FIRST YEAR

Program Element	% Time	No.	Salary	Total
D. Long-distance travel				
Total				$ 50.
VIII. Space Costs				
3,200 square feet at 2.50 per square foot				$8,000.
IX. Utilities				
A. telephone at $30. per month				360.
B. heat at $36. per month				432.
C. light at $30 per month				360.
Total				$1,152.
X. Other Fees and Expenses				
Here you might include				
such things as insurance,				
and day care licensing fees.				
Grand Total				$157,674.
		(per child)		$ 2,628.

rent a bus large enough for sixty, or a couple of smaller minibuses. Some centers prefer to rent so that they do not have to worry about repairs and insurance. For a large bus or for two minibuses a rental charge would be about $300 a month, or $3,600 for the year. Gas would come to at least $100 for the year.

The vehicle operator would work at least one quarter time (two hours each day), and this would add another $1,500 to your travel budget.

Another aspect of travel is field trips for the children. If your center had a bus, it would be available for trips during the day, and it would be possible for the children to visit many places not in the immediate neighborhood, such as museums, zoos, children's theaters, and parks. Since many places have entrance fees, field trips are another budget item. A good estimate is one dollar a month per child (this would probably cover two places), which would come to $720 for the center.

At least $100 should be budgeted for local staff travel, which would cover staff visits to the children's families, to day care meetings in the area, and to health and social service facilities.

If money is available, it is a good idea to budget money for long-distance staff travel, enabling supervisory and teaching staff to attend meetings and conferences on child care and to visit other centers as part of the center's training and upgrading program for staff.

At the other extreme, the travel budget can be entirely eliminated, with the exception of a small petty cash fund of about fifty dollars for local staff travel. Parents would have the responsibility of delivering and picking up their children, and field trips would be almost entirely eliminated, being limited to free places within walking distance.

Within the high- and low-budget extremes, there are many alternatives possible. You can, for example, rent a bus for one class on a daily basis for a special field trip. A comparison of the travel budget for the extremes follows:

	High Budget	Low Budget
Bus Rental	$3,700.	$——
Driver	1,500.	——
Field Trips	720.	——
Local Staff Travel	100.	50.00
Long Distance Travel	500.	——
Total	$6,520	$50.00

Food

Food for two meals and two snacks each day will cost sixty cents per child per day, or $9,360 for the center for the year. Such a meal program would certainly need a full time cook, and this would add at least another $6,000 to the budget. A nutritionist consultant who would come in to help the cook in menu planning two days a month would add another $600 to the budget.

A low-budget program could save money only by doing without the services of a consulting nutritionist, but costs would remain almost the same.

Many programs will be able to get complete reimbursement for food costs from the federal government *(see page 114)* so that this budget for the food component of a day care center will more often than not represent the "true" cost rather than the "actual" cost which the center will incur. The comparison of "true" costs for high and low budget programs looks like this:

	High Budget	Low Budget
Food Costs	$ 9,360.	$ 9,360.
Cook	6,000	6,000
Nutritionist	600	——
Total	$15,960.	$15,360.

Space

In arriving at a budget for space rental, we will assume a cost of $2.50 a square foot, which seems to be an average figure in our city. We have recommended that a center have about fifty square feet of classroom space for each child, although in most states, you can have only thirty-five square feet per child. In addition to classroom space, however, don't forget that you need space for the kitchen, for storage, for staff, for meetings, and for sick children. You might also want to have a lounge for parents and an observation area for visitors. Also, the more extensive your health and social service programs are, the more space you will need, such as an examining room, a larger room for sick children, and a separate place where the social service person can meet with parents in privacy. Because each center will have different space needs and options, we can provide only the most general of guidelines. Below is a high- and low-budget comparison of space needs and costs.

		High Budget	*Low Budget*
1.	Classroom space (from 35 to 50 sq. ft.)	3,000 sq. ft.	2,100 sq. ft.
2.	Kitchen	300	200
3.	Isolation room	150	100
4.	Examining and testing room	100	——
5.	Vestibule and hallways	100	100
6.	Storage areas	100	100
7.	Parents' lounge	200	—
8.	Observation area	100	—
9.	Workshop for making equipment	—	200
10.	Director's office area	100	multi-purpose area 350
11.	Admin. asst. office area	50	
12.	Teachers' room area	200	
13.	Counseling room area	100	
14.	Meeting room	300	
15.	Toilets	50	50
Total		4,850 sq. ft.	3,200 sq. ft.
Total at $2.50 per sq. ft.		$12,125.	$8,000.

SAMPLE ACTUAL COST BUDGET FOR A COOPERATIVE DAY CARE CENTER FOR ONE CLASSROOM OF TWENTY CHILDREN

	Program Element	% Time	No.	Salary	Total
I.	Staff				
A.	Director–Head Teacher	100	1	$7,000.	$7,000.
B.	Teacher (parents, student volunteers)	50	6		
Total					$7,000.
II.	Consultant Services				
	Curriculum and supervisory consultants: 20 days at $50 per day				$1,000.
III.	Equipment				
A.	Educational				$ 568.
B.	Caretaking and housekeeping				416.
C.	Office				100.
D.	Kitchen				200.
E.	Carpentry				216.
Total					$1,500.
IV.	Supplies				
A.	Educational (art)				234.
B.	Caretaking and housekeeping				817.
C.	Office				50.
Total					$1,101.

	Total
V. Food 1 meal and two snacks: 35¢ x 20 children x 260 days	$ 1,820.
VI. Space rental 1,000 sq. ft. (35 sq. ft. per child = 700 sq. ft., plus 300 sq. ft. for kitchen, staff room, and storage space, and toilets) at $2.50 per sq. ft.	$ 2,500.
VII. Utilities Telephone at $15 per month Heat at $12 per month Light at $10 per month	$ 180. 144. 120.
Total	$ 444.
Grand Total	$15,365.
	$ 768. (per child)
	$ 1,476. (per week)

Utilities include such items as telephone service, heat, light, trash removal, water, and sewage disposal. The latter three items are usually not paid for by the center, and we will not include them in our budget, but check to see whether you will have to. Your heat and light bill will depend upon how much space you have. Based on our space estimates, we can estimate costs for utilities for high and low budget programs.

	High Budget (4,850 sq. ft.)		Low Budget (3,200 sq. ft.)	
	per mo.	*per year*	*per mo.*	*per year*
Heat	$60.	$720.	$36.	$432.
Light	50.	600.	30.	360.
Telephone (2)	30.	720.	30.	360.
Total		$2,040.		$1,152.

RAISING FUNDS

It is very likely that within the next few years Congress will pass legislation for a comprehensive day care program serving the children of low-income families and of working mothers. When this happens, large-scale funding for day care centers for a broad spectrum of the population will become available for the first time. Until that time, funding a center is a matter of piecing together monies from a variety of public and private sources, or of serving a narrowly defined population who either can pay or can be paid for under existing legislation.

Federal Funding

We suggest that you obtain the booklet, *Federal Funds for Day Care Projects*, which is put out by the Department of Labor, Women's Bureau. This booklet describes close to fifty different federal programs which can fund some aspect of a day care center's operation. Most of these, however, are not applicable to most day care centers, and in this section we will discuss only the major sources of funds which we think will be realistic possibilities for many centers.

Funding for Day Care: *Service*

Title IVA. Title IVa of the Social Security Act provides for day care services for the children of parents on AFDC (Aid to

Families with Dependent Children) who are enrolled in training or education programs leading to employment. Grants to the states are open-ended, with the federal government matching state funds on a 75 percent to 25 percent basis. The program is administered on the state and local levels by departments of welfare.

The WIN (Work Incentive) program is the major training program covered by this title. WIN is administered by the Department of Labor and provides for people on AFDC training designed to give them employable skills, and thus enable them to leave the welfare rolls. AFDC recipients in other kinds of training or education programs with similar goals are also eligible for day care, as are people who are working part-time but still receiving some AFDC payments. Also eligible are AFDC families who for medical or psychological reasons would benefit from having their children in day care. Finally, at the discretion of each state, "former and potential" AFDC recipients may be eligible so that people with marginal incomes who cannot afford to work if they have to pay for child care can have this paid for by welfare departments.

A great deal of money is available for day care services under this title, and in past years the money has been underutilized by the states.

If you want to provide day care for eligible children, your department of welfare can pay you on a per child basis for your program. You can use these funds to pay for one child, several children, or for a whole program. To be eligible, programs must meet the federal interagency requirements for day care. *(See chapter on Rules and Regulations.)* Because comprehensive day care services and low staff-child ratios are required, payments are usually sufficient for fine programs. In Massachusetts, many programs are receiving about forty dollars per week per child.

If you are planning a day care center which will serve children from a low-income area, then it is quite probable that you would have no trouble finding more than enough children for your program who are eligible for day care services under the above criteria. Your center could then be entirely funded by the Department of Welfare. But if you do fund your entire program in this way, you will find certain disadvantages.

Your enrollment will be entirely limited to the children of families on welfare, and your program will be limited in terms of the kind of social stimulation and learning that it can provide. We prefer to see a program for children from a variety of socioeconomic backgrounds. Your program will also be limited in that it will not be able to serve the needs of the whole community in which it is located.

If you are starting a new program there is a very serious drawback to total funding of this kind, and that is that you receive no money for planning and for setting up your program because no children will be actually receiving day care services during this period. You are funded by departments of welfare on a fee per child basis rather than on a program basis. The budget for your program is broken down into a cost per child figure, and you are reimbursed for the number of children who have actually received your services.

Further, after your service program has begun, you will be reimbursed on a periodic schedule on the basis of the children's attendance, rather than being given one grant for the year. Since you will be working with a large bureaucratic agency, you can generally expect these payments to be late.

Therefore, in order to make such a totally funded program work, you have to have some start-up money on hand both for the planning period and for the first phases of program operation, when the bureaucratic wheels have not yet begun to grind.

As parents complete their training programs, get jobs and leave AFDC, their children are no longer eligible for day care and will probably have to leave the program (unless the parent can afford to pay, which is highly unlikely). Unless families are still eligible for day care under the "former and potential" criteria, they are faced with the bizarre situation of having a substantial new expense of child care as soon as they go off welfare.

In terms of your program, this means that you can expect a high rate of turnover of the children in your center and will have to be recruiting new children fairly continually. This has demoralizing effects on the staff and is very disruptive for the children in the classroom.

If you do not want to fund an entire program in this way, you can fund part of it. Because you will be reimbursed on a per child basis, you can reserve a certain number of places in your center for children who are eligible for federal payments. Other sources of funds can then be used to fund the program for the remaining children.

National School Lunch Act.　Under the National School Lunch Act, any nonprofit center which caters to an area with a high concentration of working mothers or with poor economic conditions can be reimbursed for food costs (at a standard per child per day rate) and for up to 75 percent of the cost of kitchen equipment and the cost of its installation. Under the Child Nutrition Act, a program can get free milk for children. A center cannot take advantage of both federal programs. If you are serving meals to the children, then, almost the entire cost, except for staff, can be paid for. On the local level, the program is administered by state departments of education. Often the department will provide you with free consultation on planning and equipping the kitchen if you are going to take advantage of the reimbursement plan.

Headstart and ESEA.　The Headstart Program and Titles I and III of the Elementary and Secondary Education Act (ESEA) are well-known funding sources for enrichment day care programs for children of low-income families. We do not consider these to be realistic options for most new centers, however, both because of a shortage of appropriated funds, and because the administering agencies (Community Action Agencies and local departments of education) usually operate the service program themselves.

There are no other federal sources of funds for direct day care services. If you want to provide day care for the children of working parents who are either poor but not on welfare, or who are middle class, there are no funds available, except for food.

Funding for Day Care: *Research*
If you have an innovative idea for a child care program which would be a model demonstration for other programs throughout the country, if you have a research plan for studying child growth and development and if you are, or are associated with, a professional researcher, you might be able to receive research funds for your program. Funds are extremely limited, however, and competition is stiff, so that, in general, research as a "back door" to service is not very promising. If all of the above do apply to your program, however, you may want to apply for funding from the various federal research programs which are available. (See the booklet previously mentioned, or get in touch with your federal regional Office of Child Development in the Department of Health, Education and Welfare.)

Funding for Day Care: *Training*
There are many federal training programs within the Department of Labor which are designed to provide unskilled and unemployed people with job training opportunities. Preschool teaching is eligible under several of these programs as a job title for which people can be trained, and day care centers can be appropriate sites for job training.

Two such programs which we have seen day care centers use successfully are the WIN program and the New Careers program. The significance of these programs for the operation of your center is that through contractual agreement with the administering agency, you can agree to provide job training for preschool teachers, and in exchange the agency pays for the teacher-trainees' salaries at your center until the completion of training.

The New Careers program will provide for up to 100 percent of salaries during the first year of training, and up to 50 percent for the second year. At the end of the training period, subject to successful completion of the training program, a trainee would be guaranteed employment at your center. You would have to make this commitment for future employment, would have to provide for a career ladder (such as trainee-teacher to head teacher), and would have to develop a substantial training program which would include on-the-job training and job-related educational training. Salaries would have to be in line with the "prevailing wage" for such jobs in your area. The operation of New Careers programs does vary somewhat throughout the country; we have given a general description of the program.

The WIN program does not provide salaries for the trainees; rather, they continue to receive AFDC payments while they are in training, and in addition receive a small incentive stipend to cover attendant costs, such as travel. Also, as we have discussed, their children's day care is paid for. WIN can also pay for training costs.

If you plan to recruit your assistant teachers from one of these programs, you must have a very good supervisory staff and a well-organized in-depth training program. The teacher-trainees would work in the classroom and at the same time be receiving supervision and on-the-job training from the head teacher. They would also receive extensive out-of-the-classroom training. *(See the chapter on training.)* Because your assistant teachers would be trainees participating in many nonteaching educational activities, you would have to recruit about twice as many trainees as assistant teacher positions. This would enable the trainees to spend half their time in the classroom and half their time in other training activities. If the total number of trainees comes to more than ten, then you would have to have an educational or training supervisor in addition to the head teachers and the director. This would be a hidden cost to using teacher-trainees.

Private Funding

Foundations
Your public library will have a book containing the various

foundations in your state and another of listings throughout the country. There are hundreds of foundations which do make grants to educational and child welfare programs. Many restrict their grants or give preference to programs in their immediate area, so that these are probably your best initial sources. The process involves quite a bit of time and energy and no guarantee of success. You must write a proposal explaining what you plan to do, send it to all likely candidates, and then wait.

Parent Fees

A standard means of acquiring some financial support for your day care center is to charge parents a fee based on a sliding scale, according to their income. Such fees are actually quite nominal for the services they buy in comparison to the usual baby-sitting fees. Charging a fee must be carefully considered, however; it may very well be that parents in your center cannot afford to pay anything. If you decide to institute a sliding fee scale, the usual range at most centers is five to thirty-five dollars a week per child for full day care, and five to fifteen dollars per week for half day care.

We know of no center which prorates the fee on the basis of children's attendance, although parents may request this. You are charging parents in order to provide full day care every day of the week, and must pay staff salaries and other operating costs. The luxury of having a stable program costs money just as the most obvious individualized care does. Parents have to pay for both: the program and the daily care of their children. If parents really do send their children to the center so rarely that the weekly fee is obviously unfair, they should be encouraged to get a baby-sitter instead.

Local Institutions

You can simply make the rounds of enterprises in your community and ask them to contribute something toward the support of your center. This can be in the form of money or of donations in kind. Many large companies do have special funds for community programs, and since day care is a major priority today, receiving a good deal of publicity, you have a good chance of getting the funds for which you are eligible.

Don't overlook the possibility of in kind donations. A toy store might contribute thousands of dollars worth of equipment; a furniture store might provide office furniture; a local college or university might provide free consulting personnel or student teachers. Sometimes leaving a large carton with a list of needed materials at strategic locations (a university cafeteria for example) leads to substantial donations.

It often helps your effort to advertise what you are doing in advance so that when you ask for donations your purpose and needs will be understood.

Fund Raising

Fund raising is not a good way to try to find thousands and thousands of dollars, but a considerable sum can often be raised fairly easily if you have a dedicated staff. There are schools which are free to parents and which are run solely on the proceeds from such fund-raising activities as benefit performances at theaters, cake sales, rummage or white elephant sales, dances, raffles, car washes, flower sales, children's art sales in the form of pictures, note cards, stationery.

These are some of the funding possibilities which are open to you; probably we have not thought of them all. In summary, we would like to say that it *is* possible to fund a center in spite of the high costs involved and that since the prospect of more comprehensive federal funding is a very real one, you should not feel that funding a center will always be a difficult operation. Below is a sample budget which shows where the funds for one center could come from. It is based on our sample low-budget program, for which the budget came to $152,136. We will not repeat that entire budget, but show only where the funding will come from.

Sample Funding Schedule for the First Year of Operation for a Low Budget Day Care Center for Sixty Children

Source of Grant or Donation	Budget Item Covered	Money rec'd or Saved
1. Natl. School Lunch Act	Food	$ 9,360.
2. Natl. School Lunch Act	75% of kitchen-equipment costs	4,500.
3. WIN (provides 12 trainees and training funds for an educational supervisor)	Assistant teachers: 6 at $6,000	36,000.
4. College or university* (provides student teachers)	Assistant teachers: 2 at $6,000	12,000.
Total		$ 61,860.

*The sample program as you remember requires 14 teachers. We think it is advisable to have one full-time paid assistant teacher in each classroom in addition to the head teacher. Therefore, we have allowed for 14 minus 6 or 8 trainees and volunteers.

In order to charge parents and the federal government for fees per child, you need to know the actual cost which must be paid for after all of the grants and donations are subtracted. The new actual budget then, is $157,674 minus $61,860 or $95,814.

5. Social Security Act (pays for children of eligible parents on AFDC)	General grant on fee per child basis. 30 children at $1,597 per yr.	$ 47,910.
6. Parents fees (paid by parents not included in #5)	General grant on fee per child basis. 30 children at an average of $20 per week or $1,040 per yr.	31,200.
7. Private grants from business and foundations	General grant for all budget items for children not covered by #5	16,000.
8. Fund raising activities	" "	704.

Total moneys received: $157,674.
Total moneys budgeted: $157,674.

APPENDICES

Day Care Licensing By State

State	Department of Welfare	Department of Health	Department of Education
Alabama	X		
Alaska	X		
Arizona		X	
Arkansas	X		
California	X		
Colorado	X		
Connecticut		X	
Delaware	X		
District of Columbia		X	
Florida	X		
Georgia	X		
Hawaii	X		
Idaho	X		
Illinois	X		
Indiana	X		
Iowa	X		
Kansas		X	
Kentucky	X		
Louisiana	X		

State	Department of Welfare	Department of Health	Department of Education
Maine	X		
Maryland		X	
Massachusetts		X	
Michigan	X		
Minnesota	X		
Mississippi	X		
Missouri	X		
Montana	X		
Nebraska	X		
Nevada	X		
New Hampshire	X		
New Jersey			X
New Mexico		X	
New York	X		
North Carolina	X		
North Dakota	X		
Ohio	X		
Oklahoma	X		
Oregon	X		
Pennsylvania	X		
Puerto Rico	X		
Rhode Island	X		
South Carolina	X		
South Dakota	X		
Tennessee	X		
Texas	X		
Utah	X		
Vermont	X		
Virginia	X		
Washington	X		
West Virginia	X		
Wisconsin	X		
Wyoming	X		
Virgin Islands	X		

COLLEGES AND UNIVERSITIES OFFERING
EARLY-CHILDHOOD EDUCATION PROGRAMS

ALASKA
Alaska Methodist University

ARKANSAS
University of Arkansas, Fayetteville

CALIFORNIA
California State College, Hayward
San Francisco State College
San Jose State College
University of California, Berkeley
University of California, Los Angeles
Pacific Oaks

CONNECTICUT
University of Connecticut, Storrs

DELAWARE
University of Delaware, Newark

DISTRICT OF COLUMBIA
The George Washington University

FLORIDA
Florida State University
University of Florida

ILLINOIS
Eastern Illinois University, Charleston
Loyola University, Chicago
National College of Education, Evanston
Northwestern University, Evanston
Southern Illinois University, Carbondale
University of Chicago

INDIANA
Indiana State University, Terre Haute
Indiana University, Bloomington
Purdue University, Lafayette

IOWA
Iowa State University, Ames
Morningside College, Sioux City
Northwestern College, Orange City
Parsons College, Fairfield

LOUISIANA
Louisiana State University, Baton Rouge
Tulane University

MAINE
University of Maine, Orono

MASSACHUSETTS
Garland College
Lesley College
Massachusetts Bay Community College
State College at Bridgewater
State College at Springfield
State College at Worcester
Tufts University
Wheelock College

MICHIGAN
Alma College
Central Michigan University, Mt. Pleasant
Eastern Michigan University, Ypsilanti
University of Michigan, Ann Arbor

MINNESOTA
>Bemidji State College
>College of St. Catherine, St. Paul
>Gustavus Adolphus College, St. Peter
>University of Minnesota, Duluth
>University of Minnesota, Minneapolis

MONTANA
>Montana State University, Bozeman
>Nothern Montana College, Havre
>University of Montana, Missoula

NEVADA
>University of Nevada, Reno

NEW JERSEY
>Jersey City State College
>Newark State College

NEW YORK
>Adelphi University, Garden City, Long Island
>Bank Street College of Education
>Briarcliff College, Briarcliff Manor
>Brooklyn College
>College of Mount Saint Vincent, Riverdale
>Finch College, New York City
>Fordham University, Bronx
>Hunter College
>New York University, Washington Square
>Queens College, Flushing
>Sarah Lawrence College, Bronxville
>State University of New York, Brockport
>State University of New York, Canton
>State University of New York, Potsdam
>Wagner College, Staten Island
>Mills College of Education
>Teacher's College of Columbia University

NORTH DAKOTA
    State Teachers College, Ellendale
    University of North Dakota, Grand Forks
    Valley City State College

OHIO
    Kent State University
    Otterbein College, Westerville
    University of Cincinnati
    University of Toledo

OKLAHOMA
    Oklahoma State University, Stillwater
    University of Oklahoma, Norman

OREGON
    Oregon State University, Corvallis

PENNSYLVANIA
    East Stroudsburg State College
    Pennsylvania State University, University Park
    University of Pittsburgh
    Kutztown State College

RHODE ISLAND
    Rhode Island College, Providence

SOUTH DAKOTA
    Yankton College

TEXAS
    University of Houston
    University of Texas, Austin

UTAH
    Utah State University, Logan

VERMONT
　　University of Vermont, Burlington

VIRGINIA
　　Virginia State College, Petersburg

WASHINGTON
　　Central Washington State College, Ellensburg
　　Pacific Lutheran University, Tacoma
　　Seattle Pacific College
　　Seattle University
　　University of Washington, Seattle
　　Washington State University, Pullman
　　Western Washington State College, Bellingham

WISCONSIN
　　University of Wisconsin, Madison
　　Wisconsin State University, Eau Claire
　　Wisconsin State University, La Crosse
　　Wisconsin State University, Superior
　　Wisconsin State University, Whitewater

EVALUATION SHEET

Head Teacher

Name _____

School _____

Class _____

Date _____

I.   Classroom Management;
    A.   Exercises responsible judgment involving decisions related to child care.

    B.   Provides a safe, warm, stimulating classroom environment for children.

    C.   Submits reports and keeps accurate records, forms, and observations.

II. Teaching Skills:
    A.   Displays the ability to perceive the group as a whole while demonstrating skill in working with small groups and individual children.

    B.   Exhibits thoughtful daily planning based on long range goals and individual child needs.

C. Displays skill in presenting curriculum materials appropriate to the needs and interests of children in the classroom.

D. Maintains standards of conduct so optimum learning can transpire.

III. Rapport:
A. Displays a warm, friendly approach to children; an understanding, accepting manner.

B. Displays ability to relate to and work with not only children, but also other staff members and student teachers.

IV. Evaluation:
A. Responds positively to suggestions and constructive criticism.

B. Displays an active desire for learning, self-evaluation, and improvement.

FIRST SEMESTER TRAINING SCHEDULE

Friday

Observation
|----- Group A ----|

Student Teaching
|------- Group B -------| |- First Aid -|

Thursday

Child
Growth   Curric-
& Develop-   ulum   Student Teaching
|- ment -| |Group B| |---- Group B ----|

Wednesday

Observation
|---- Group B ----|

|- Children's Art -|

Student Teaching
|------ Group A ------|

Tuesday

Child
Growth   Curric-
& Develop-   ulum   Student Teaching
|- ment -| |Group A| |---- Group A ----|

Monday

Child   Group A&B
Growth   Preschool
& Develop-   Curric-   Lunch   Creative
|- ment -| |- ulum -| |- Movement -|

8:00 8:30 9:00 9:30 10:00 10:30 11:00 11:30 12:00 12:30 1:00 1:30 2:00 2:30 3:00 3:30 4:00 4:30 5:00

SECOND SEMESTER TRAINING SCHEDULE

Time	Monday Group A	Monday Group B	Tuesday Group A	Tuesday Group B	Wednesday Group A	Wednesday Group B	Thursday Group A	Thursday Group B	Friday Group A	Friday Group B
9:00	Student Teaching	Children's Lit.	Student Teaching	Marriage, Adolescence, and the Family	Student Teaching	Children's Lit.	Student Teaching	Marriage, Adolescence, and the Family	Student Teaching	Student Teaching
9:30										
10:00										
10:30		New Math.				New Math.				
11:00										
11:30										
12:00										
12:30										
1:00	Lunch	Lunch	Lunch	Lunch	Lunch	Lunch	Lunch	Lunch	Lunch	Lunch
1:30	Children's Lit.	Student Teaching	Marriage, Adolescence, and the Family	Student Teaching	Children's Lit.	Student Teaching	Marriage, Adolescence, and the Family	Student Teaching		
2:00										
2:30										
3:00										
3:30	New Math.				New Math.					
4:00										
4:30										
5:00										

NOTE: In order to have all students be exposed to both morning and afternoon teaching, Group A and Group B exchange schedules mid-semester.

TRAINING PROGRAM MODELS

Type of Training Program	Nonprofessionals		Professionals	
	No Previous College Education	*Some Previous College Education*	*Other Related Fields*	*Early Childhood Education*
Basic training program				
Staff meetings	X	X	X	X
Supervision	X	X	X	X
Workshops	X	X	X	X
In-service training	X	X	X	
On-the-job training	X	X		
Training program with college credit and/or release time for courses	X	X		

COURSE OUTLINE: FORMATIVE YEARS

Date	*Content*	*Suggested Readings*

	Introduction:
	    Female Reproductive
	    System
	    Male Reproductive
	    System
	Handout:
	    Agents Which
	    Influence Behavior
		Elise Fitzpatrick and
		Nicholson Eastman.
		Maternity Nursing.
		Philadelphia: J.P.
		Lippincott Co., 1966,
		Chap. 2

	Ovulation and Menstruation	*Maternity Nursing.* Chap. 3

	Genetic Factors in Development
	Film:
	    *Heredity and Prenatal
	    Development*
		Paul Mussen, John
		Couger, and Jerome
		Kagen. *Child
		Development and
		Personality.* New York:
		Harper and Row, 1963,
		Chap. 2

	Fertilization and Changes Following Fertilization	*Maternity Nursing,* pp. 65-81

	Prenatal Development
	Handout:
	    Prenatal Environmental
	    Influences
	Film:
	    *Biography of the
	    Unborn*
		Geraldine Flanagan.
		*The First Nine Months
		of Life.* New York:
		Pocket Books, 1966.
		
		*Child Development and
		Personality,* pp. 67-77

	Labor and Delivery Handouts: Summary of Mechanism of Labor	*Maternity Nursing.* Chap. 10

Date	*Content*	*Suggested Readings*
	Film: *A Normal Birth*	*Child Development and Personality*, pp. 77-80
	Midterm: Prenatal Development	
	Characteristics of the Newborn Infant Film: *Growth of Infant Behavior — Early Stages*	*Child Development and Personality*, pp. 87-106
	Development During First Quarter of Infancy Handout: Erikson's Eight Stages of Man	Arnold Gesell and Catherine Amatruda. *Developmental Diagnosis.* New York: Harper and Row, 1964, pp. 27-34
		Arnold Gesell, et al. *The First Five Years of Life.* New York: Harper & Row, 1940, pp. 18-20
		Erik Erikson. *Childhood and Society.* New York: W.W. Norton and Company, 1963, pp. 247-251
	Development During Second Quarter of Infancy Film: *Early Social Behavior*	*Developmental Diagnosis*, pp. 43-50 *The First Five Years of Life*, pp. 20-22
	Summary of Development During the First Year Handouts: Achievements of the First Year	Selma Fraiberg. *The Magic Years.* New York: Charles Scribner's Sons. 1959, pp. 3-102

Date	*Content*	*Suggested Readings*

	Films:
	    Posture and Locomotion
	    From Creeping to
	    Walking	

	Fundamentals of Child Care
	During First Year
	Handout:
	    Fundamentals of Child
	    Care	

	Later Infancy, 15-24
	Months
	Handout:
	    Piaget's Stages of Intel-
	    lectual Development
	Film:
	    Intellectual Develop-
	    ment of Babies
		Magic Years, pp. 107-176

	The Two-Year-Old Child
	Film:
	    The Terrible Two's
	    and Trusting Three's
		Child Development and Personality, pp. 183-225

	Characteristics of the
	Toddler and Two's
	Handouts:
	    The Teacher's Role
	    The Two-Year-Old in
	    Day Care
	    Socialization
	    Toilet Training
		Childhood and Society, pp. 251-254
		
		Joesph L. Stone and Joesph Church. *Childhood and Adolescence.* New York: Random House, 1968, pp. 105-138

	The Preschool Child
	Handout:
	    Goals for the Early
	    Years
		Childhood and Adolescence, pp. 141-172

Date	Content	Suggested Readings
	Film: *Children of Change*	*Child Development and Personality*
	The Four-Year-Old Child Film: *Frustrating Four's and Fascinating Five's*	*Child Development and Personality*, pp. 302-323
	The Five-Year-Old Child Film: *Understanding Children's Play*	*Child Development and Personality*, pp. 325-349 *Childhood and Adolescence*, pp. 175-200 *Childhood and Society*, pp. 252-264
	Building Feelings of Security and Adequacy Handouts: 　Summary: 　　Security and Adequacy Film: *Fears of Children*	Katherine Read. *The Nursery School.* Philadelphia: W. B. Saunders Co., pp. 167-195
	Handling Feelings of Hostility and Agression Handout: 　Summary: 　　Hostility and Aggression Film: *Personality and Emotions*	*The Nursery School*, pp. 196-221

Date	Content	Suggested Readings
	Helping Children Adjust to New Experiences Handout: Steps in Entering Nursery School	*The Nursery School*, pp. 107-136
	Defining and Maintaining Limits for Behavior Handout: Setting Acceptable Limits Film: *Guiding Behavior*	*The Nursery School*, pp. 222-247
	Working with Parents Handout: Goals for Working With Parents	*The Nursery School*, pp. 339-359

Final Exam: Formative Years

COURSE OUTLINE: LEARNING AND BEHAVIOR PROBLEMS

Date	*Course*	*Suggested Readings*
	Introduction: The Psychology of Exceptional Children Handouts: Teacher's Role Film: *Individual Differences — Introduction*	Karl Garrison and Dewey Force. *The Psychology of Exceptional Children.* New York: The Ronald Press Company, 1965, pp. 5-52 James Magary and John Eichorn. *The Exceptional Child.* New York: Holt, Rinehart and Winston, 1962, pp. 1-42
	Intellectual Deviations: Gifted Handouts: Types of Programs for Gifted Children Advantages of Acceleration Disadvantages of Acceleration Teacher's Role Program Provisions Study Results Film: *The Gifted Ones*	*Psychology of Exceptional Children,* pp. 123-182 *The Exceptional Child,* pp. 490-529
	Intellectual Deviations: Mentally Retarded Handouts: Levels of Mental Retardation	*Psychology of Exceptional Children,* pp. 53-122 *The Exceptional Child,* pp. 286-337

Date	*Course*	*Suggested Readings*
	Parent Counseling Etiological Factors Program Goals for Educable Retarded Children Program Goals for Trainable Retarded Children Aims of Educational Provisions for Mentally Retarded Special Class Programs	Pearl Buck. *The Child Who Never Grew.* New York: John Day Company, 1950.
	Film: *Care of the Young Retarded Child*	
	Intellectual Deviations: Mentally Retarded-Continued Handouts: Vocational Counseling for the Mentally Retarded Summary Study Results	
	Film: *Eternal Children*	
	Physical Disabilities: Speech and Hearing Handouts: Classification of Speech and Language Disabilities Relative Ages for Articulation of Difficult Sounds	*The Psychology of Exceptional Children*, pp. 183-214 *The Exceptional Child*, pp. 311-329

Date	*Course*	*Suggested Readings*
	Causes of Lisping Therapy for Stut- terers Teachers Role	

	Physical Disabilities:
	    Deafness
	Handouts:
	    Causes of Deafness
	    Check List of Symp-
	    toms Characteristic
	    of Hard-of-Hearing
	    Children
	    Program Goals for
	    Deaf and Hard-of-
	    Hearing Children
	Film:
	    *The Auditorially
	    Handicapped Child —
	    The Deaf*
		*Psychology of Ex-
		ceptional Children*, pp.
		183-266
		
		*The Exceptional
		Child*, pp. 286-337

	Physical Disabilities:
	    Partially Sighted
	Handouts:
	    Types of Defective
	    Vision
	    Symptoms of Visual
	    Difficulty
	Film:
	    *The Visually Handi-
	    capped Child — The
	    Partially Sighted*
		*Psychology of Ex-
		ceptional Children*,
		pp. 267-314
		
		*The Exceptional
		Child*, pp. 233-
		287

Date	Course	Suggested Readings
	Physical Disabilities: Blindness Handouts: Known Causes of Blindness Incidence of Blindness Methods for Teaching the Blind Summary Study Results Films: *The Visually Handicapped Child — The Blind*	
	Physical Disabilities: Crippled Children Handout: Classification of Crippling Conditions Film: *The Crippled Child*	*Psychology of Exceptional Children*, pp. 315-342 *The Exceptional Child*, pp. 161-232
	Neurological Impairment: Brain-Damaged Children Handouts: Causes of Brain Injury Characteristics and Problems of the Brain-Damaged Child Symptoms of Neurophrenia Strauss Syndrome	*Psychology of Exceptional Children*, pp. 343-359 *The Exceptional Child*, pp. 125-144

Date	*Course*	*Suggested Readings*

Neurological Impairment:
　Cerebral Palsies

Handouts:
　　Causes of Cerebral
　　Palsy
　　Classification of
　　Cerebral Palsies
　　Neurological Impair-
　　ment:
　　　Cerebral Palsies
　　Incidence of Defects
　　Associated with Cere-
　　bral Palsy
　　Learning Difficulties
　　Often Associated
　　with Cerebral Palsy
　　Goals for Rehabilita-
　　tion

Film:
　　*The Cerebral Palsied
　　Child*

*Psychology of Ex-
ceptional Children*,
pp. 360-384

*The Exceptional
Child*, pp. 151-155

Marie Killilea. *Karen.*
New York: Dell Pub-
lishing Company, Inc.,
1969

Emotional and Social Mal-
adjustment

Handouts:
　　Symptoms of Malad-
　　justment
　　Behavioral Character-
　　istics of Emotional
　　Disturbance
　　Teacher's Role
　　Principles for Working
　　with the Emotionally
　　Disturbed Child

*Psychology of Ex-
ceptional Children*,
pp. 427-485; 518-
537

*The Exceptional
Child*, pp. 338-380

Virginia Axline. *Dibs
in Search of Self.* New
York: Ballantine Books,
1964.

Date	*Course*	*Suggested Readings*

Program Principles
Technical Implications
of Educational Goals
for Normal and Emo-
tionally Disturbed
Children

Film:
*The Socially Mal-
adjusted Child*

COURSE OUTLINE: PRESCHOOL CURRICULUM

Readings.   For the most part, the readings for the curriculum course are suggested rather than required. The realm of curriculum is so broad, and the needs of teachers are so varied, that no one syllabus would be appropriate for all people in the group. However, you are expected to read whatever literature most addresses your needs and interests.

1.	Everybody	Film:	*Jenny is a Good Thing*
		Topic:	Nature and Objectives of Preschool Curriculum
2.	Small Groups	Topic:	The First Few Days of School
		Assignment:	Developing Self-Concepts
3.	Everybody	Film:	*Organizing Free Play*
		Topic:	Free Play
4.	Small Groups	Topic:	Water and Sand Play
5.	Everybody	Film:	*Learning in the Kindergarten*
6.	Small Groups	Topic:	Daily and Long-Range Scheduling
7.	Small Groups	Topic:	Activity Periods and Group Assemblies
8.	Everybody	Topic:	Understanding Children's Art Guest Workshop Leader

9. Small Groups   Topic: Walks and Field Trips
                             Assignment: Developing an Effective Classroom Environment

10. Everybody   Topic: Plants and Animals Guest Workshop Leader

11. Small Groups   Field Trip: Science Museum

12. Everybody   Topic: Plants and Animals Guest Workshop Leader

13. Small Groups   Topic: Children's Math

14. Everybody   Topic: Music Guest Workshop Leader

15. Small Groups   Topic: Children's Math

16. Everybody   Topic: Music Guest Workshop Leader

17. Small Groups   Topic: Language Development

18. Everybody   Films: When Should Grown-ups Help? When Should Grown-ups Stop Fights?
                             Topic: Developing Your Role as Teacher

19. Small Groups   Topic: Discipline in the Classroom

20. Everybody   Film: Discipline and Self-Control
                             Topic: Discipline in the Classroom

21.	Everybody	Film:	Room to Learn
		Topic:	Classroom Environment Setting up
22.	Small Groups	Topic:	Classroom Environment Stimulation
23.	Everybody	Topic:	Developing Good Self-Concepts Be Prepared to Discuss Both Assignments
24.	Small Groups	Topic:	Effective Integration of Social Studies
25.	Everybody	Open Discussion	
26.	Small Groups	Open Discussion	

APPLICATION FORM

FAMILY HEALTH SERVICES — DAY CARE PROJECT

Castle Square Center
436 Tremont Street, Boston, Massachusetts

Hawthorne Center
c/o Highland Park Free School
Hawthorne Street, Roxbury, Massachusetts

Identifying Data:

Date ——————

Name of Child_____ Sex_____
          Last   First   Middle
Birthplace _____ Birth Date _____
           City   State   Mo.   Day   Yr.
Home Address _____ Telephone _____

Family Data:

Father or Guardian's Name _____

  Address _____ Telephone _____

  Business Address _____

  Hours of Work _____ Business Phone _____

Mother or Guardian's Name _____

  Address _____ Telephone _____

  Business Address _____

  Hours of Work _____ Business Phone _____

Caseworker's Name _____ Center _____ Phone _____

Whom should we contact in case of emergency?
  Name _____ Relationship _____

  Address _____ Telephone _____

What is the name of your doctor or clinic? _____

  Address _____

We are interested in your conception of day care. What do you expect this day care program to do for your child? Have you had any previous experience with day care? Do you have any complaints about, or suggestions for this program? Any questions? Ideas?

_____

_____

_____

_____

_____

_____

_____

_____

Child's Behavior Patterns and Habits:

Please briefly describe an ordinary day in the life of your child, from
his rising in the morning to going to bed. _____

_____

_____

_____

What is your child's favorite toy? _____ Book? _____

 Pet? _____ Person? _____

Does your child have any particular habits or mannerisms, such as
thumb sucking, nail biting? Please describe. _____

Does your child have any particular fears, such as of dogs, or sirens; does
he have nightmares? Please describe. _____

_____

Does your child use any peculiar words or expressions (such as "wee-
wee" for urine) that may not be understood by an outsider? Please describe. _____

_____

In general, how does your child react to anxiety or a stressful situation?
Does he cry, withdraw, throw tantrums? _____

_____

Has your child had any previous school or play-group experience? Please
describe. _____

Does your child relate well to other children? Does he seek friendships; or is he a "loner"? _____

_____

How does your child relate to adults?_____

_____

Has your child had the experience of being cared for by adults other than members of your family? Please describe. _____

_____

What is your accustomed mode of reassuring and rewarding your child?

_____

What is your accustomed mode of disciplining your child? What is your "philosophy" of discipline? _____

_____

Does your child speak English? _____Any other languages? _____

Is he talkative, quiet, average? _____

To the best of your knowledge, does your child have any language problems, or learning disabilities? _____

Does your child have any emotional disturbances, or physical handicaps?

_____

How well do you anticipate your child will adjust to this day care program? _____

Are there additional circumstances regarding your child's physical or emotional status that you would like us to be aware of? _____

_____

Family Background:

Father or Guardian's Age _____ Educational Level _____

Occupation _____ Place of Birth _____

Year of Arrival in the United States _____

Languages Spoken _____

Please briefly describe the quality of the father's or guardian's relationship with your child. _____

Mother or Guardian's Age _____ Educational Level _____

Occupation _____ Place of Birth _____

Year of Arrival in the United States _____

Languages Spoken _____

Please briefly describe the quality of the mother or guardian's relationship with your child. _____

Please list the names, relationship, and ages of all brothers, sisters, and
other members of your child's usual household. _____

_____

_____

How would you describe your child's role in your family? Is the child
the "good little sister," "the black sheep," etc. _____

_____

Please describe any alliances and frictions in the family that you think
we should be aware of. _____

_____

Have there been any major changes in the family constellation such as
divorce, or death? _____

Have there been any difficulties or crises in your family — such as, accidents, problems with the law, medical problems — that may have
affected the emotional well-being of your child? _____

_____

What is the language predominantly spoken in your home? _____

Developmental History:

Were there any complications during the pregnancy of this child? _____

_____

Were there any birth difficulties? _____

_____

At approximately what age did your child sit up by himself? _____

    walk unsupported? _____ talk in short phrases? _____

Does your child eat by himself? _____ Does your child en-

    joy eating? _____ If your child is on formula or baby food,

    please mention the type of diet and describe the pattern of eating in

    the course of one day _____

    _____

What are your child's food likes and dislikes? _____

How frequently does your child have between meal snacks? _____

Does your child have any allergies? _____

Do you have any particular concerns about your child's eating habits?

_____

Is your child toilet-trained for urine? _____ for bowels? _____

If so, at approximately what age did your child become toilet-trained

for urine? _____ for bowels? _____

How frequently does he move his bowels? _____

How frequently do accidents occur? _____ Do you have any

particular concerns about your child's toilet habits? _____

_____

Does your child sleep well? _____ Does he usually nap? _____

    How long? _____ When? _____

Do you have any particular concerns about your child's sleeping habits?

Is there anything else in your child's developmental history that you

think we should be aware of? _____

_____

If your child has any physical or emotional disability, would you please

describe to the best of your ability the nature of that disability, its

causation, prognosis, and treatment? _____

_____

_____

(This form must be filled out by a physician and returned to the day care center before school begins.)

DAY CARE PROJECT
DIVISION OF FAMILY HEALTH SERVICES
MEDICAL RECORD

Child's Name _____

Doctor's Name or Clinic Attended _____

Medicaid Number _____ Clinic Number _____

Past History:

Allergies —
Immunizations (date and reaction) —
    Diphtheria
    Tetanus
    Whooping Cough
    Measles
    Poliomyelitis
    Smallpox
    Typhoid
    Typhus
    Influenza
    Other

Acute Infections —

    Measles _____ Rubella _____ Chickenpox _____

    Mumps _____ Whooping Cough _____ Scarlet Fever ____

    Diphtheria _____ Poliomyelitis _____ Other _____

Surgery: Record in chronological order all surgical procedures, noting
for each: the date, type of surgery, results, the surgeon, and
the hospital at which it was performed.

_____

_____

_____

_____

_____

_____

Injuries: Record type, date, and sequelae of injuries.

_____

_____

_____

_____

_____

Summary of admissions to hospitals.

_____

_____

_____

_____

Previously noted problems — please describe briefly.

Head:

Headaches _____ Eyes _____ Ears _____

Nose _____ Teeth _____ Throat _____

Respiratory System:

Cardiac System:

Gastro-Intestinal System:
Genito—Urinary System:
Neuro-Muscular System:

Family History:

T.B. _____ Rheumatism _____ Bright's Disease _____

Heart Trouble _____ Gout _____ Diabetes _____

Cancer _____ Nervousness or Insanity _____ Obesity _____

Asthma _____ Migraine _____

Physical Examination:

General Appearance: (Stature, gross deformities, etc.)
Height
Weight
Eyes and Vision
Ears and Hearing

Nose
Mouth and Teeth
Throat
Neck
Lymph Glands
Spine
Thorax
Lungs
Heart
Pulse
Abdomen
Genitalia
Extremities
Reflexes
Rectal

Summary of findings and recommendations:

_____

_____

_____

_____

_____

Physical exam recommended monthly? Every 3 months? Every 6 months? Once yearly?

Is there any physical disability that may interfere with the Child's learning ability? Please describe?

_____

_____

_____

Date _____ Doctor's Signature _____

O.E.O. Day Care Budget

STANDARDS AND COSTS OF DAY CARE FOR A FULL DAY IN A CENTER

Levels of Quality

Program Element	Acceptable Description	Annual Cost Per Child	Desirable Description	Annual Cost Per Child
1. Food: meals and snacks	Two meals and snacks	$210.	Two meals and snacks	$210.
2. Transportation	Provided by center	60.	Provided by center	60.
3. Medical and dental services	Examinations and referral service	20.	Examinations treatment when not otherwise available and health education	60.
4. Work with parents	General parent activities plus limited counseling services	30.	Parent education, family-type activities, full counseling services	70.
5. Facilities and utilities (rental)	Same	90.	Space providing more generous room for child activities	110.

Levels of Quality

Program Element	Acceptable		Desirable	
	Description	Annual Cost Per Child	Description	Annual Cost Per Child
6. Clothing and other emergency needs	As necessary	20.	plus room for work with parents As necessary	20.
7. Supplies and materials	General developmental program	50.	Individualized developmental program	75.
8. Equipment (annual replacement costs)	General developmental program	12.	Individualized developmental program	15.
9. Staff				
a. Classroom professional at $6,600	One per 15 children	405.	One per 15 children	405.
b. Classroom non-professional at $4,400	Two per 15 children	420.	Three per 15 children	640.
c. Social service professional at $6,600	One per 100 children	65.	One per 100 children	65.

d. Community, social service, parent or health Aides at $4,400	One per 100 children	20.	Two per 100 children	45.
e. Business and maintenance at $4,000	Three per 100 children	120.	Three per 100 children	120.
f. Special resource personnel (psychology, music, art consultants, etc.) at $6,600	One per 100 children	60.	Two per 100 children	120.
g. Supervision at $8,000	Two per 100 children	160.	Two per 100 children	160.
10. Training	Approximately 10% of Salary Costs	120.	Approximately 10% of Salary Costs	145.
Total per child		$1,862.		$2,320.

Note: This analysis is based on centers providing service ten to twelve hours a day, five days a week.

RELEVANT READINGS IN DAY CARE

Aaron, David, and Bonnie P. Winawer. *Child's Play: A Creative Approach to Play Spaces for Today's Children.* New York: Harper and Row, 1968.

Adair, Thelma, and Esther Eckstein. *Parents and the Day Care Center.* New York: Federation of Protestant Welfare Agencies, Inc. 281 Park Ave. South, 10010.

Allen, Marjorie. *Planning for Play.* Cambridge: M.I.T. Press, 1969.

Alschler, Rose H. *Children's Centers.* New York: William Morrow Co., 1942.

American Joint Distribution Committee. *Joint Distribution Committee Guide for Day Care Centers: Handbook To Aid Communities in Developing Day Care Programs for Preschool Children.* Geneva: 1967.

Andrews, Gladys. *Creative Rhythmic Movement for Children.* New York: Prentice Hall, Inc., 1954.

Arbuthnot, May Hill. *Children and Books.* Chicago: Scott, Foresman and Co., 1957.

Ashton-Warner, Sylvia. *Teacher.* New York: Simon and Schuster, 1963.

Association for Childhood Education International (ACEI), 3615 Wisconsin Avenue, Washington, D.C.

ACEI has an extensive number of publications which are directly relevant to the theory, curriculum, and methods of implementing early-childhood programs. Write to them for a list of their books and booklets. Many are free; all are relatively inexpensive and to the point.

Axline, Virginia. *Dibs in Search of Self.* New York: Ballantine Books, 1964.

Baldwin, Alfred. *Theories of Child Development.* New York: John Wiley and Sons, Inc., 1968.

Bank Street College of Education Publications, 69 Bank Street, New York, New York.

Send for a list of their publications. They are directly relevant to all aspects of early-childhood education.

Baruch, Dorothy. *One Little Boy.* New York: Dell Publishing Co. Inc., 1964.

Beer, Ethel S. *Working Mothers and the Day Nursery.* New York: William Morrow Co., 1957.

Bland, Jane Cooper. *Art of the Young Child.* New York: The Museum of Modern Art, 1958.

Boguslawski, Dorothy Beers. *Guide for Establishing and Operating Day Care Centers for Young Children.* New York: Child Welfare League of America, Inc., 1968.

Brearly, Molly, ed. *The Teaching of Young Children — Some Applications of Piaget's Theory.* New York: Schocken Books, 1970.

Brearly, Molly, and Elizabeth Hitchfield. *A Teacher's Guide to Reading Piaget.* London: Routledge and Kegan Paul, 1966.

Bruner, Jerome S. "The Course of Cognitive Growth." *American Psychologist* 19(1954): 1- 15.

Bruner, Jerome S. *Processes of Cognitive Growth: Infancy.* Worcester: Clark University Press with Barre Publishers, 1968.

Bruner, Jerome S. *Towards a Theory of Instruction.* Cambridge: Belknap Press of Harvard University Press, 1967.

Caldwell, Bettye M. "What is the Optimal Learning Environment for the Young Child?" *American Journal of Orthopsychiatry*, 37 no. 1 (1961) pp. 18- 21.

Caldwell, Bettye M. "Programmed Day Care for the Very Young Child — A Preliminary Report." *Journal of Marriage and the Family* 26: 481- 488.

Caldwell, Bettye M., and J. B. Richmond. *Standards for Day Care Services.* New York: Child Welfare League of America, 44 East 23rd Street, 1960.

Canner, Norma. *And a Time to Dance.* Boston: Beacon Press, 1968.

Care of Children in Day Centers. Geneva: World Health Organization, Public Health Papers #24, 1964.

Children in Day Care with Focus on Health. U.S. Department of Health, Education, and Welfare. Social and Rehabilitation Services, Children's Bureau, 1967.

Cohen, Dorothy H., and Virginia Stern. *Observing and Recording the Behavior of Young Children.* New York: Teacher's College Press, Columbia University, 1969.

Cole, Natalie R. *The Arts in the Classroom.* New York: The John Day Co., 1940.

Cole, Natalie R. *Children's Art from Deep Down Inside.* New York: The John Day Co., 1966.

Comstock, N., and E. Spenser. *McCall's Just for Fun.* New York: McCall Corp., 1963.

Costain, Lela B. "New Directions in the Licensing of Child Care Facilities." *Child Welfare.* 49 (1970).

Day Care and Child Development in Your Community. Washington, D.C.: Day Care and Child Development Council of America, Inc., 1969.

Day Care Services. U.S. Department of Health, Education, and Welfare. Children's Bureau, 1964.

Dawson, Mildred A., and Frieda H. Dingee. *Children Learn the Language Arts.* Minneapolis: Burgess Publishing Co., 1959.

Department of Elementary, Kindergarten, Nursery Education (DKNE), National Education Association (NEA), 1201 16th Street, N.W., Washington, D.C. 20036.

Write for a list of their publications

Deutsch, Martin., et al. *Memorandum on Facilities for Early Childhood Education.* Education Facilities Laboratories, Inc., 477 Madison Ave., New York 10022.

Dinkmeyer, Don, and Rudolph Dreikurs. *Encouraging Children to Learn: The Encouragement Process.* Englewood Cliffs, New Jersey: Prentice-Hall, Inc., 1963.

Dittmann, Laura. *Early Child Care.* New York: Atherton Press, 1968.

Education Development Center, 55 Chapel Street, Newton, Massachusetts (EDC).

EDC has numerous invaluable publications ranging from a seemingly unlimited number of really useful things you can make with free or very inexpensive materials to detailed curriculum guides in all areas of curriculum. Write for a list of their publications and treat yourself to many of them.

Elkind, D. "Giant in the Nursery — Jean Piaget." *Contemporary Readings in Psychology* by J. Foley, R. Lockhart, and D. Messick. New York: Harper and Row, 1970.

Erikson, Erik. *Childhood and Society.* New York: W. W. Norton and Co., 1963.

Fitzpatrick, Elsie, Nicholas Eastmen, and Sharon Reeder. *Maternity Nursing.* Philadelphia: J. B. Lippincott Co., 1966.

Flanagan, Geraldine. *The First Nine Months of Life.* New York: Pocket Books, 1966.

Flavell, J. *The Developmental Psychology of Jean Piaget.* Princeton, New Jersey: Van Nostrand, Co., 1963.

Fleming, Robert S. *Curriculum for Today's Boys and Girls.* Columbus, Ohio: Charles E. Merrill Books, Inc., 1963.

Foster and Headley. *Education in the Kindergarten.* New York: American Book Company, 1966.

Fraiberg, Selma, H. *The Magic Years.* New York: Charles Scribner's Sons, 1959.

Frost, Joe L., ed. *Early Childhood Education Rediscovered.* New York: Holt, Rinehart, and Winston, Inc., 1968.

Gaitskell, Charles, and Al Hurwitz. *Children and Their Art.* New York: Harcourt, Brace, and World, 1970.

Gans, Roma. *Common Sense in Teaching Reading — A Practical Guide.* Indianapolis: Bobbs, Merrill Co., Inc., 1963.

Garrison, Karl, and Dewey Force. *The Psychology of Exceptional Children.* New York: The Ronald Press Co., 1965.

Gesell, Arnold, and Catherine Amatruda. *Developmental Diagnosis.* New York: Harper and Row, 1964.

Gesell, Arnold, et al. *The First Five Years of Life.* New York: Harper and Row, 1940.

Good References on Day Care. Department of Health, Education, and Welfare, Social and Rehabilitation Service. Children's Bureau, July, 1968.

Goutard, Madeleine. *Math For Children.* Education Explorers, Ltd., 1964.

Gross, Ronald, and Judith Murphy. *Educational Changes and Architectural Consequences.* Education Facilities Laboratories, Inc., 477 Madison Ave., New York 10022.

Guide Specifications for Positions in Day Care Centers. U.S. Department of Health, Education, and Welfare. Children's Bureau, 1967.

Hasse, Ronald W. *Designing the Child Development Center.* Office of Economic Opportunity, 1200 9th St., N.W.: Washington, D.C., 1968.

Hammond, Sarah Lou, Rule Dales, and Dora Skipper. *Good Schools for Young Children.* New York: The MacMillan Co., 1963.

Hartley, Ruth, Lawrence Frank, and Robert Goldenson. *Understanding Children's Play.* New York: Columbia University Press, 1952.

Harris, Theodore L., and Wilson E. Schwahn. *The Learning Process.* New York: Oxford University Press, 1961.

Hebb, D. O. *The Organization of Behavior.* New York: John Wiley and Sons, Inc., 1964.

Hechinger, Fred, ed. *Pre-School Education Today.* New York: Doubleday and Company, Inc., 1964.

Hess, Robert D., and Roberta Bear, eds. *Early Education.* Chicago: Aldine Publishing Co., 1968.

Hille, Helen. *Food for Groups of Young Children Cared for During the Day.* U.S. Department of Health, Education, and Welfare. Children's Bureau Publication #386, 1960.

Holt, John. *How Children Fail.* New York: Pitman Publishing Co., 1964.

Holt, John. *How Children Learn.* New York: Pitman Publishing Co., 1967.

Hymes, James L., Jr. *Before the Child Reads.* White Plains, New York: Harper & Row & Peterson Co., 1958.

Hymes, James L., Jr. *Teaching the Child Under Six.* Columbus, Ohio: Charles E. Merrill Co., 1968.

Hunt, J. Mc Vicker. *Intelligence and Experience.* New York: Ronald Press, 1961.

Isaacs, Susan. *Intellectual Growth in Young Children.* London: Routledge and Kegan Paul, Ltd., 1963.

Jefferson, Blanche. *Teaching Art to Children.* Boston: Allyn and Bacon, 1963.

Kami, Constance, and Norma L. Radin. "A Framework for a Pre-School Curriculum Based on Piaget's Theory." Upsilanti, Michigan, Public Schools.

Kohn, Sherwood. *The Early Learning Center: Profiles in Significant Schools,* Education Facilities Laboratories, Inc., 477 Madison Ave., New York 10022.

Lederman, Alfred, and Alfred Trachecl. *Creative Playgrounds and Recreation Centers.* New York: Fredrick A. Praeger, Inc., 1967.

Leeper, Sarah, et al. *Good Schools for Young Children: A Guide for Working with 3, 4 and 5 year Olds.* New York: The MacMillan Co., 1968.

Leonard, George B. *Education and Ecstacy.* New York: A Delta Book, 1968.

Lindstrom, Miriam. *Children's Art.* Berkeley, California: University of California Press, 1969.

Lowenfield, Victor. *Your Child and His Art.* New York: The MacMillan Co., 1954.

Maier, Henry W. *Three Theories of Child Development.* New York: Harper and Row, 1965.

Margary, James, and John Eichorn. *The Exceptional Child.* New York: Holt, Rinehart, and Winston, 1962.

Matterson, E. M. *Play and Playthings for the Pre-School Child.* Baltimore: Penguin Books, 1967.

Mayer, Greta, Alaine Krim, and Catherine Papell. *Contributions of Staff Development in Understanding the Needs of Children and Their Families.* New York: Child Study Association of America, 1963.

Moffett, Mary W. *Woodworking for Children.* Early Childhood Education Council of New York, 32 Washington Place, New York.

Mussen, Paul, John Conger, and Jerome Kagen. *Child Development and Personality.* New York: Harper and Row, 1963.

Murphy, Lois Barclay. *The Widening World of Childhood.* New York: Basic Books, 1962.

National Association for the Education of Young Children (NAEYC), 1834 Connecticut Ave. N.W., Washington, D.C. 20009.

Write for a list of their publications and perhaps for a sample of their monthly journal. As their name indicates, they are directly concerned with early-childhood education.

Neill, A. S. *Summerhill — A Radical Approach to Child Rearing.* New York: Hart Publishing Company, 1960.

Nilsson, Lennart, Axil Ingelman-Sundberg, and Claes Wirsen. *The Everyday Miracle.* London: Allen Lan, the Penguin Press, 1967.

Office of Economic Opportunity, 1200 9th Street, N.W. Washington, D.C.

> *Concept of a Child Development Center — Relationship to Pre-School and Day Care.* March 18, 1965.
> *Parent and Child Centers.*

> *Staff for a Child Development Center.* 1967.

Phillips, John L. *The Origins of Intellect: Piaget's Theory.* San Francisco: W.H. Freeman and Co., 1969.

Pines, Maya. *Revolution in Learning: The Years From Birth to Six.* New York: Harper and Row, 1966.

Pitcher, E. G., and Louise Ames. *The Guidance Nursery School.* New York: Harper and Row, 1964.

Pitcher, E. G., Lasher, Feinberg, Hammond, et al. *Helping Young Children Learn.* Columbus, Ohio: Merrill Co., 1966.

Provence, Sally, and R. Lipton. *Infants in Institutions.* New York: International Universities Press, 1962.

Read, Katherine. *The Nursery School — A Human Relations Laboratory.* Philadelphia: W.B. Saunders Co., 1966.

Roeper, Anne Marie. *Preliminary Outline of Life in the Domes.* Bloomfield Hills, Michigan: Roeper City & County School, Inc., August, 1969.

Rudeman, Florence. *Child Care and Working Mothers.* New York: Child Welfare League of America, Inc., 1960.

Russell, David H. *Children's Thinking.* New York: Blaisdell Publishing Company, 1965.

Schneider, Earl, ed. *The Pet Library.* New York: 1969.

Sheehy, Emma. *Children Discover Music and Dance.* New York: Henry Holt, 1959.

Sheehy, Emma. *There's Music in Children.* New York: Henry Holt, 1946.

Sigel, Irvin, and Frank H. Hooper, eds. *Logical Thinking in Children: Research Based on Piaget's Theory.* New York: Holt, Rinehart, and Winston, Inc., 1968.

Spotlight on Day Care. National Conference on Day Care Services. U.S. Department of Health, Education, and Welfare. Children's Bureau, 1965.

Sprinthall, R., and N. Sprinthall, eds. *Educational Psychology: Selected Readings.* New York: Van Nostrand, 1969.

Stendler, D., ed. *Readings in Child Behavior and Development.* New York: Harcourt, Brace, and World, 1964.

Stone, L. Joseph, and Joseph Church. *Childhood and Adolescence.* New York: Random House, 1968.

Tarnay, Elizabeth Doak. *The Why and How of Parent Participation.* CSAS Project Head Start. Washington, D.C.

Taylor, Harold. *Art and the Intellect.* Garden City, New York: distributed by Doubleday and Company for Museum of Modern Art, 1960.

Taylor, Jeanne. *Child's Book of Carpentry.* New York: Greenburg Publishers, 1948.

Vygotsky, L. S. *Thought and Language.* Cambridge: M.I.T. Press, 1966.

Wann, Kenneth D., Miriam Selchen Dorn, and Elizabeth Ann Liddle. *Fostering Intellectual Development in Young Children.* New York: Teachers College Press, Columbia University, 1962.

Warner, Diane, and Jeanne Quill. *Beautiful Junk.* Washington, D.C.: Project Head Start. Office of Economic Opportunity, 1967.

Witmer, Helen, ed. *On Rearing Infants and Young Children in Institutions.* U.S. Department of Health, Education and Welfare. Children's Bureau Research Report #1, 1967.

INDEX